# Environment, Technology and
# Economic Growth

# Environment, Technology and Economic Growth

## The Challenge to Sustainable Development

*Edited by*

## Andrew Tylecote
*University of Sheffield, UK*

*and*

## Jan van der Straaten
*European Centre for Nature Conservation,*
*The Netherlands*

**Edward Elgar**
Cheltenham, UK • Northampton, MA, USA

Published by
Edward Elgar Publishing Limited
8 Lansdown Place
Cheltenham
Glos GL50 2HU
UK

Edward Elgar Publishing, Inc.
6 Market Street
Northampton
Massachusetts 01060
USA

A catalogue record for this book
is available from the British Library

**Library of Congress Cataloguing-in-Publication Data**
Environment, technology and economic growth : the challenge to
   sustainable development / edited by Andrew Tylecote and Jan van der
   Straaten.
      Includes bibliographical references.
      1. Sustainable development.  2. Environmental economics.
   3. Technology—Economic aspects.  I. Tylecote, Andrew.
   II. Straaten, Jan van der.
   HC79.E5E5746  1997
   333.7—dc21

97-24836
CIP

ISBN 1 85898 214 6
Printed and bound in Great Britain by MPG Books Ltd, Bodmin, Cornwall

# Contents

# Figures

# Tables

# Contributors

**Frank J. Dietz** is a Lecturer in Environmental Economics at the Department of Public Administration, Erasmus University, Rotterdam, Netherlands.

**Edeltraud Egger** is Associate Professor at the Department of Computer Supported Cooperative Work, The University of Technology, Vienna, Austria.

**Chris Freeman** is Emeritus Professor at the Science Policy Research Unit, University of Sussex, UK.

**Gerhard Hanappi** is Associate Professor at the Department of Socioeconomics of the Austrian Academy of Sciences, Vienna, Austria.

**Friedrich Hinterberger** is Senior Researcher at the Wuppertal Institute for Climate, Environment and Energy in Wuppertal, Germany.

**Björn Johnson** is Associate Professor and Reader in Economics at the Department of Business Studies, Aalborg University, Denmark.

**Klaus Lindegaard** is Assistant Professor at the Centre for Environment and Development, Aalborg University, Denmark.

**Alain Lipietz** is a Research Director of CNRS at CEPREMAP in Paris, France.

**Joan Martinez Alier** is Professor at the Universidad Autonoma, Barcelona, Spain.

**Markku Ollikainen** is an Associate Professor at the Department of Economics, University of Helsinki, Finland.

**Inge Røpke** is Associate Professor at the Technical University of Denmark in Lyngby.

**Eberhard K. Seifert** is Senior Researcher at the Wuppertal Institute for Climate, Environment and Energy in Wuppertal, Germany.

**Jan van der Straaten** is Senior Researcher at the European Centre for Nature Conservation and Associate Professor at the Department of Leisure Studies, Tilburg University, Netherlands.

**Andrew Tylecote** is Professor of the Economics and Management of Technological Change at Sheffield University Management School, UK.

# Preface

There is a 'romantic tendency' among environmentalists which regards technological change with deep suspicion and even hostility. For such, the title of this book may perhaps have the same unpleasant tension as *The Temperance Movement, Bacchanalian Orgies and the Enjoyment of Moderate Drinking* would have for a campaigner for total abstinence from alcohol. This volume arises from a quite contrary conviction on the part of the editors, encouraged by the Scientific Committee which organized the 1993 EAEPE[1] conference in Barcelona: that technological change has accelerated and will accelerate further, and what is at issue is not its continuation, or even its speed, but its direction.

The world's population will inevitably grow considerably before it levels off, and will demand at least a modicum of material comfort. The only hope of avoiding the devastation of the planet – and with it the frustration of those demands – is an unprecedented burst of technical and organizational creativity, to bring about environmentally-friendly technological change. Such a swerve of the technological juggernaut will not only make development sustainable in the long term, but (we believe) will turn out to be a key element in the solution of the current unemployment crisis in the advanced and developing countries.

Not all the contributors to this book would necessarily agree with all of the above, but their chapters were selected, ordered, and (with their consent) edited so that the book as a whole makes the case – and makes it, we believe, with unusual coherence. You will see that it was a long process. A few of the chapters are much as they were presented at the Conference. Most have been extensively rewritten to suit our purposes. Some – including our own – have been virtually written from scratch since the Conference. We are grateful to all the contributors for their tolerance of our importunate demands, to Pat Sleath at

[1] The European Association for Evolutionary Political Economy

Sheffield for her help with organization and producing camera-ready copy, and to Dymphna Evans and her colleagues at Edward Elgar for not losing faith and patience. We are grateful too to numerous referees and advisers, who for reasons of space will remain nameless – all except one, Simon Ball of Sheffield University. Simon made a crucial contribution to this volume, in time he could ill spare – one expression among many of his deep commitment to the environment. We mourn his sudden death last November, and salute his memory.

Andrew Tylecote
Jan van der Straaten
Sheffield and Tilburg

# 1. Introduction: Ecology, Technology and Institutions

## Andrew Tylecote and Jan van der Straaten

Until recently concern about environmental problems, and concern over poor economic performance, tended to alternate. Thus while industrialized European countries were rebuilding their industries after the destruction of the Second World War, they were not inclined to give environmental problems a high priority. In the course of the 1960s, when industrial success was increasingly taken for granted, environmental problems began seriously to threaten living conditions in many industrialized regions, and the balance shifted. Then the recession of the 1970s and the first half of the 1980s made economic performance – now, above all, unemployment – again the main issue.

In the second half of the 1980s, when the economic depression lifted for a while, Western societies became more conscious again of the declining environmental situation, and for the first time began to perceive that to give it priority might not necessarily be at the expense of economic performance. They certainly recognised that to neglect it might jeopardise *future* economic performance. This had long been clear in principle so far as natural resources like fossil fuels were concerned: these *sources of inputs* were exhaustible – more now meant less later. It was now becoming apparent that the same might hold for pollution – *sinks for outputs* might be exhaustible too in ways which would have major economic effects. The most alarming, though highly uncertain, case in point was the greenhouse effect. These problems moreover were global: the more one country used or emitted, now the worse it would be in future for the whole world. In 1987, the World Commission on Environment and Development published a study entitled *Our Common Future* (the 'Brundtland Report') in which it was argued that the only solution was 'sustainable development'; which was defined as a situation in which current production and consumption took the economic necessities of future generations into consideration. Production growth in the Northern countries could only increase at a moderate rate to make room for production growth in Southern countries. The concept of sustainable development quickly gained wide acceptance. In the environmental policy plans of most European countries, and of the European Commission, it is now invoked as a guiding principle for the formulation of policy goals.

At the same time there was a resurgence of interest in environmental matters among mainstream economists. They had two relevant conceptual frameworks to hand. The older, and more general, was the Pigovian concept of external costs: if these could be measured, for the emission of a pollutant or the use of a resource, then they could be reflected in a tax or charge levied by government which would solve the problem by *internalizing the externality,* and leaving the rest to the market mechanism. This elegant solution had, however, one obvious flaw, so far as the mainstream was concerned: it gave too important a role to government. Accordingly it was decidedly unpopular in the United States, where an alternative approach gained ground: assign property rights. So long as there was individual ownership – of the right to use a field, say, or enjoy clean water – then the individual could charge for use, or sue for infringement, and again, the externality would disappear. (As authority for this view, Garret Hardin's 'Tragedy of the Commons' (1968) was much cited. Hardin, a biologist, had attracted much attention among scientists with this article, whose central message was that human population could be expected to increase to exceed the availability of resources. He explained this by analogy with the use of a common pasture by herdsmen: each herdsman ignores the negative effects of his animals' grazing on the other herdsmen, so that more than the optimum number of sheep are put on the land.  Neither Hardin nor his original audience was particularly interested in whether in fact historical evidence showed what his example implied: that agricultural backwardness had been associated with the lack of individual ownership of land, and that assigning property rights had been the springboard to the agricultural revolution in Europe and North America.) The prospect that assigning property rights to sinks for pollution could be a nightmare for everyone but lawyers, was strangely not seen as a decisive objection – in the United States.

The contributors to this volume all take a very different view. They belong to a broad school of thought which may be described as evolutionary, or institutional, political economy. So far as ecological or environmental economics is concerned this implies a *contingent* view of both government and markets. Governments are neither a *deus ex machina* to wave an internalizing wand, nor a monstrous interference with the market mechanism, but institutions of most variable character. Markets are embedded within institutional frameworks, which affect the way they work. If governments are in some way to impose respect for the environment on the market, this will involve a long evolutionary process of institutional learning - as to what environmental costs are, and how to respond to them.

## PART ONE: THE ECOLOGICAL AGENDA FOR SUSTAINABLE DEVELOPMENT

**Joan Martinez Alier**, in Chapter 2, addresses the first issue, of environmental costs. Is it possible to assign monetary values to the use of environmental resources and services, as is said in the introductory chapter of many environmental economics textbooks? He is not opposed to the use of economic instruments such as emission permits, carbon taxes, or refundable deposits to reduce consumption or to change production processes in such a way that nature and the environment suffer less harm. However, the implementation of these economic instruments does not mean that we really know how high the environmental costs of present and future consumption and production are. There are too many uncertainties regarding the reactions of economic agents as well as the functioning of the ecosystem. This implies that the internalization of environmental costs cannot be separated from political and ethical judgements. This judgment is reinforced when we consider the thorny issues of distribution, within and among countries, which arise whenever any ecological policy measure is mooted. Martinez Alier comes to the conclusion that economics, and thus environmental economics as well, is embedded in politics. The valuation of nature and the environment, the calculation of environmental costs and, in particular, the resolution of environmental distributional conflicts, can only be achieved by politics. He rests his case with two examples of how his proposals could be applied, to European agricultural policy and tourism in Catalonia.

Martinez Alier points out that the *diachronic* environmental issues – where an action now affects the situation later – are the most difficult. Unfortunately the whole concept of sustainable economic development revolves around such issues.

In Chapter 3, **Markku Ollikainen** shows that the interpretation of sustainable development – what rate of use of sources and sinks is sustainable – depends on the values society has with regard to nature, future generations and the meeting of needs. Different ethical positions imply different rates of use. Ollikainen chooses to demonstrate these points by evaluating two proposals for sustainable development in terms of their ethical underpinnings and their rules for conservation and preservation. The first is Daly's (1991) programme of steady-state economy, which is contrasted with a neoclassical programme of sustainable growth economy proposed by Pearce and Turner. Anthropocentric and biocentric ethics are used as a means of evaluation. The programme of sustainable growth economy has the features of weak anthropocentrism, and that of steady-state economy shares a considerable number of features with biocentric ethics. The rules for conservation and preservation in both programmes, however, turn out to be partly inconsistent with their ethical basis. Both viewpoints have shortcomings. The point of sustainable development is to solve environmental and social problems at the same time. What, then, is the correct balance between fighting poverty, starvation and unemployment, and saving the environment? And how is it affected when long-term effects and regional differences in the use of the endowments of the earth are taken into account?

**Inge Røpke** starts Chapter 4 by insisting, as did Martinez Alier in Chapter 2, that there is undoubtedly some degree of tension between economic growth, as it is normally understood, and the environment. While optimists like the Brundtland Report and the World Bank can point to some environmental successes which seem to be associated with a high level of development, most of these relate to more-or-less local pollution. It is very hard to avoid an increase in depletion of exhaustible resources, or in contribution to the greenhouse effect, as an economy grows. (Moreover the cleaning-up of production processes in developed countries may achieved partly by buying in 'dirty' products from less developed ones.) Since economic growth is an aim of government and a measure of success to be brandished at the voters, this is dangerous for the environment. But what exactly is economic growth, growth *of*? Gross domestic (or national) product (GDP) – a statistical concept, which was hurriedly botched together by Keynesian economists in the Second World War, for the needs of that time. It is also called national income, and as such, following Hicks' (1946) definition of income, should measure the value of what we can afford to consume over a period without depleting our overall capital stocks. This of course GDP as currently measured does not do – among other flaws, it ignores the depletion of natural capital, does not count non-market production, and does count as consumption to be valued, many activities which are actually costs to be incurred. Røpke acknowledges the value of the work in progress to construct more meaningful measures of 'national income', but she shows, through critical analysis of work by Herman Daly, that it is ultimately impossible to construct a measure which can, so to speak, be handed over to technicians to maximize. There is, and will remain, no alternative to value judgment and political processes at all levels.

Without disagreeing with Røpke's conclusion, in Chapter 5, **Friedrich Hinterberger** and **Eberhard Seifert** insist, and focus, on the positive possibilities of measurement. They begin by reviewing the requirements for 'sustainability' both of resource use and 'sink' (for pollution) use, and the uncertainties attached. They argue that both resource use and sink use can be usefully proxied by 'the sum of man-induced material flows from eco-sphere to techno-sphere', measured in kilograms. Economic activities can be usefully compared for environmental impact, in terms of their materials intensity per unit of service (MIPS). This leads to a target of a reduction of material flows, within the next 40–50 years, by 50 percent globally *and by 90 per cent in the northern hemisphere*. They then consider the compatibility of the MI (materials intensity) approach with current work towards the 'greening' of GDP measures – their adjustment to reflect environmental impacts. They see particular scope for convergence with the 'avoidance costs' approach of Hueting *et al.* at the Netherlands Central Bureau of Statistics. However, 'income', even 'greened income', can only be taken as an element of 'well-being'. The Human Development Index (HDI) has been developed as a broad measure of socio-economic progress – or well-being – but it does not yet reflect environmental factors. The authors argue that the most practicable way of doing so is to integrate materials input indicators into a new Sustainable HDI. Likewise it may be possible to integrate MI indicators into the UN Commission for Sustainable Development's core set of 'sustainability indicators'. They conclude by distinguishing between efficiency and sufficiency: in striving to raise efficiency by reducing MIPS, material input per unit of service, we must not overlook the scope to reduce our aspirations in terms of total services. We need to rethink our ideas of 'eu zen', the 'good life', and we need to do it publicly in the knowledge of what is at stake ecologically.

## PART TWO: THE INSTITUTIONAL AGENDA FOR SUSTAINABLE DEVELOPMENT

The first four chapters thus set out a formidable ecological agenda, and set the scene for the second part of the book, which focuses on the institutional means – in the broadest sense – by which development may be made sustainable. In Chapter 6, **Björn Johnson** in a sense picks up where Hinterberger and Seifert leave off: why do capitalist economies have such a need for economic growth? He discusses the institutional dynamics driving growth forward; and then the institutional limits, or constraints, to growth. They have combined with ecological problems to create a situation in which growth is difficult. Yet what makes it possible in principle to make enormous reductions in MIPs (to use Hinterberger and Seifert's term) is the existence of knowledge as a factor of production which can be substituted for materials inputs. Knowledge is not exhaustible, and indeed the more it is used, the more it grows. What is required are changes in institutions and routines which will improve and speed up all the relevant kinds of learning, so that existing knowledge is more fully used, and more quickly extended in the required directions. Can the learning process within a new technological paradigm based on information and communication technology (see Freeman in Chapter 9 below) provide the answers required? Johnson stresses that even the development of the required technologies, let alone their optimum use, will require major institutional reforms. Drawing on the work of Kjærgaard (1991) he gives a fascinating historical example of how technological and institutional changes can work together to solve ecological problems while relaunching growth – the case of Denmark, 1500–1800. Denmark – after some false starts which *inter alia* showed the limitations of Hardin's 'Tragedy of the Commons' argument – finally developed and displayed an impressive 'social capability for technical and institutional change'. That is what is required now to shape the new techno-economic paradigm; and Johnson concludes by delineating the forms and purposes of national and institutional learning.

Among Johnson's institutional desiderata are modifications to the cost and price regime which will 'lead technical development into environmentally safer directions'. The remaining chapters in Part Two are concerned with how this may be done.

In Chapter 7, **Frank Dietz** and **Jan van der Straaten** discuss the 'Pigovian solution' of using economic instruments – eco-taxes, in particular - to internalise environmental costs. As means to an agreed end – of achieving an $x$% reduction in $CO_2$ emissions, say – they agree that such instruments can be extremely useful. However the theoretical rationale implies that an eco-tax can be set at the measured level of the external marginal cost, and the pollution then allowed to find its own 'optimum' level. Should we be so lucky! Dietz and Van der Straaten show that the estimation of this external marginal cost faces fundamental problems. First, according to the mainstream approach, it must be based on the sum of the individual preferences of the population for, say, clean air. However the valuation of individual preferences, and their aggregation, in the absence of a market, are fraught with difficulties partly arising from distributional issues. These problems are greatly compounded by the diachronic nature of most environmental decisions: A's fumes do not merely get up B's nose now, they will affect her comfort, safety, and prosperity later; and A's; and their children's and grandchildren's. Not only does this cause problems of valuation, it introduces enormous uncertainties: even if the current direct effect of, for example, a pollutant, is well understood – if! – its long-term effects are much less certain due to delays, thresholds and synergies. Accordingly, they argue that governments must come at the problem from another direction. On the basis of the best available understanding of eco-cycles, and with caution in the face of uncertainty, critical loads, emission standards and extraction quotas have to be formulated; only at that point can the traditional optimization criteria take over as means of achieving the targets set.

**Klaus Lindegaard** in Chapter 8 discusses the use of legal remedies for environmental problems. He starts from the besetting problem of uncertainty in this area as to causes and effects, which makes it very difficult to operate a system of cost-internalization through taxes and charges. (For example, if government wishes to control sulphur dioxide emissions through 'eco-taxation', it needs first to know what damage each unit of $SO_2$ does, so that it knows how much to charge per unit, and then to measure each firm's emissions, so that it knows how much to charge for.) Polluters have a strong incentive to maintain and even increase this uncertainty, and to exploit it to maintain the present regime, dominated by undemanding command-and-control regulations supplemented by voluntary agreements. There is, however, the alternative of cost internalization by litigation for damages. This in its nature is retrospective; so the common problem that the polluter knows more than the public authorities or any victim, at the time, about his actions, their environmental consequences, and how they might be mitigated, can be turned to advantage, as long as that information comes out – or might come out – in the end. The possibility of such litigation has long been generally available, but in practice has been largely nullified by rules such as the need to show negligence, and the burden of proof being on the prosecution. The United States, however, has led the way in establishing liability which is *strict* (that is there is no need to show negligence). Discussion of the *ex post* effects of this change and its Danish counterpart – including a serious blockage of land markets – has obscured the very promising possibilities for *ex ante* cost internalization through this route: that is, polluters will in future be able to estimate in advance what liabilities their actions would or might expose them to and will have a strong incentive to minimize them. They will also have a strong incentive to learn as much as possible about the effects of their actions since ignorance will be no defence. This leads to a discussion of the long-term effects of a strict, joint and several liability regime on innovation. These will be all the better if the regime can be 'tilted' in favour of an open culture within firms, in which employees are encouraged to find out and reveal as much as possible about the firm's environmental impacts and how they can be reduced – notably, by environmental audits. The chapter concludes with a discussion of the political possibilities for the development of such a regime, nationally and internationally.

PART THREE:   ECOLOGY, TECHNOLOGY AND LONG
              FLUCTUATIONS IN ECONOMIC GROWTH

Part Three stands, on the face of it, quite aside from the rest of the book. Here are five authors and four papers for whom the problematic appears to be not the threat to the ecosystem and the human species, but 'long wave' fluctuations in Røpke's dinosaur, the GNP. As will appear, there is method in this juxtaposition; but let us begin by picking out the patterns among the four. **Chris Freeman** in Chapter 9 and **Andrew Tylecote** in Chapter 12 both base their analysis on the *technological long wave*: the idea proposed by Perez (1983) that technological and economic history is moulded by the succession of dominant 'technological styles' which follow one another at intervals of (very roughly) half a century. A technological style is an 'ideal type' of production organization, which becomes the common sense of management and design and charts a course for present production and future innovation; it is based on the appearance of one or more inputs which show clearly perceived low and rapidly falling relative cost, almost unlimited availability of supply over the long term, and clear potential for use or incorporation in many products and processes throughout the economic system. A new style clearly has the potential to bring about a long period of relatively fast technological change and economic growth, but this potential can only be released within a well-matched 'socio-institutional framework'. At the time the new style 'crystallizes', the existing framework is to some extent mismatched with it everywhere, and in most countries acutely so; the result is at least some *decline* in growth rates, and a period of economic, social and political crisis, ending in radical reform, a rematch of framework and style, and a long, strong upswing.

As to the present situation, it seems reasonable to see it as one of crisis, and to claim that a new style has recently appeared which has information and communications technology (ICT) at the heart of it. Freeman, having surveyed recent developments in the world economy and traced the development of economic analysis of fluctuations, focuses on ICT and its differences from its predecessor, the 'Fordist' style. He delineates the current path of technological change and the structural changes to which it is giving rise, and also the various 'socio-institutional' changes (in the organization of firms as well as national and international economic institutions) which he argues are required to release the new style's full potential.

On the face of it, **Gerhard Hanappi** and **Edeltraud Egger** in Chapter 10 take a very different view. While for Freeman (and Tylecote) it is the technological long wave which is historically established, back to the early 19th century, and the corresponding economic fluctuations which are contingent and arguable, for Hanappi and Egger the economic long wave is historically established, and conditions technological change much more than the other way about. For Freeman (and Tylecote) the world economy has been, since about the early 1970s, in a 'depression crisis', which continues; for Hanappi and Egger a new long wave upswing probably began in about the early 1980s. But the differences are more apparent than real. If it turned out, on looking back, that a long upswing, in terms of economic growth rates, had begun in the early 1980s, that would be little skin off Freeman and Tylecote's noses: their main point is that the old 'framework' continues to block much of the new style's potential, as witness high unemployment and socio-political crisis. Nor would they deny Hanappi and Egger's basic point of departure, that at this point of the 'wave' – whether we call it late downswing or early upswing – economic and technological developments are by no means fully determined: these are interesting times, when much hangs on social and political developments which could go in different directions. Hanappi and Egger focus, like Freeman, on ICT, but their concern is with its impact on culture and lifestyles in the very broadest sense. They argue that the present tendency is to ever-greater concentration of control over culture, accompanied by its commercialization and 'privatization' in the sense of consumption by atomised individuals. The result is the impoverishment of culture, and growing inequality of access which tends to reinforce other social inequalities. They argue that a quite different path of development is conceivable and even feasible, given the political will, which will equalize access and bring out ICT's potential for interaction, cultural enrichment, and empowering communities.

Like Hanappi and Egger, **Alain Lipietz** (Chapter 11) does not use the term 'technological style' or 'socio-institutional framework'. As a 'regulationist' of the school of Aglietta (1979) and Boyer (1986) he sees 'models of development', which are composed of three elements: an 'industrial paradigm' – the general principles of the organisation of work; a 'regime of accumulation' or macroeconomic structure; and a 'mode of regulation' or rules of the game at the broadest social level; which must all be mutually compatible. As Freeman talks of a Fordist style, so for Lipietz there is (was) a Fordist paradigm, regime and mode: together, Fordism, as a model of development. Certainly something of 'technological style' is implicit within the idea of 'industrial paradigm', along with a 'social compromise' on what one might call 'micro-institutions'. When explaining the crisis in which we now find ourselves, there is much less discussion of technology, and more stress than Freeman lays on the development of internal contradictions within Fordism. But a crisis we now have, and the challenge for Lipietz, as for Freeman, Tylecote, and Hanappi and Egger, is to make appropriate changes in our institutions at various levels. Lipietz is concerned here principally with production, not consumption institutions, and his main focus is on the choice – or range of choices – to be made between 'liberal flexibility' and 'negotiated involvement' in industrial relations. Nonetheless, while arguing for the latter, he shows how it can be combined with changes in the directions of greater equality, democracy, decentralization – and sustainability – to make up a coherent new 'post-Fordist' model of development.

Andrew Tylecote's Chapter 12, which concludes the book, has been rewritten *as* a conclusion. Having begun by reviewing his many points of agreement with the preceding authors in Part Three, it goes further in three directions. First, it relates the current crisis to other cycles besides the Kondratieff. It shows how fluctuations of the shorter, Kuznets cycle can explain the upswing of the middle to late 1980s and the relapse into deeper crisis since then. It shows also how a very long historical perspective can help us to understand the differences between our current crisis and that of the 1930s: the whole 1914–45 period can be understood as a period of international 'anarchy', after the collapse of British, and before the establishment of US, *hegemony*. This explains why the crisis has never become as deep as that of the 1930s (and 1940s); on the other hand we cannot look forward to anything as fresh and new and tailormade as the socio-institutional frameworks of the Pax Americana of the 1950s, for as time passes a hegemon gradually loses both the strength and the inclination to push through reforms. Second, it broadens the focus from the advanced countries to the whole world economy, and shows how the relationship of rich North and poor South follows the long wave, and how the South experiences the crisis. Third, and crucially, it discusses the interrelation between the economic crisis and the ecological crisis, as set out in earlier chapters. It shows how the acceleration of Fordist growth in part of the South has exacerbated ecological problems, and how both the developing eco-crisis and the limp government responses to it have exacerbated economic problems.

Johnson is right: while the ICT style is not, as it stands, the answer to all our ecological prayers, it has the potential to be far more sustainable than Fordism, once it is set within the appropriate socio-institutional frameworks. One key change will be a shift from taxation mostly on labour to a system bearing mostly on resource depletion and pollution. Another will be the acceleration and guidance of the development of biotechnology. A third will be the development of decentralized institutions for resource allocation. All these reforms will be valuable for the South – the more so because with the more fragile tropical ecology, and the greater dependence of poor countries on natural resources, the eco-crisis is a greater threat to Southern welfare and Southern GNP. But one further reform will be needed, directed at the South's special problem, that whatever technology is developed for the North is inappropriate to the Southern 'factor endowment' - short of skills and capital, but abundant in low-skilled labour. Much effort needs to be put into developing variants of the ICT (plus biotechnology) style *appropriate* to the needs of the South. In combination, these reforms may finally meet the challenge to sustainable development: to allow some acceleration of income growth and a great acceleration of growth in employment, while diminishing the threat to the ecology of the planet.

## References

Aglietta, Michel (1979), *A theory of capitalist regulation*. London: New Left Books.

Boyer, Robert (1986), *La theorie de la régulation: une analyse critique*. Paris: La Découverte.

Daly, H.E. (1991), *Steady-State Economics, Second Edition with New Essays*, Washington, DC: Island Press.

Hardin, Garret (1968), 'The Tragedy of the Commons', *Science*, 162, 1243–8.

Hicks, John (1946), *Value and Capital*, Oxford: Oxford University Press.

Kjaergaard, Thorkild (1991), *Den Danske Revolution 1500–1800. En oekohistorisk tolkning*, Aalborg: Gyldendal.

Perez, Carlota (1983), 'Microelectronics, Long Waves and World Structural Change: New Perspectives for Developing Countries', *World Development* **13** (3), 441–63.

World Commission on Environment and Development (Brundtland Report) (1987), *Our Common Future*. Cambridge: Cambridge University Press.

PART ONE


# The Ecological Agenda for Sustainable Development

# 2.   Ecological Economics and Environmental Policy: A Southern European View[1]

**Joan Martinez Alier**

## Introduction

We shall begin with some familiar doubts on the ability of conventional economics to give money-values to the use of environmental resources and services. One main point is that market instruments such as emission permits, refundable deposits or a carbon and energy tax, are an incentive to reduce consumption and/or change technologies, but the use of market instruments does not mean that we know how to correct market prices in order to have ecologically-correct, present-day values that internalize the relevant, future, uncertain externalities. Which indicators of environmental impact are chosen? Which limits are set for each indicator? These questions cannot be solved by cost–benefit analysis or other forms of economic valuation. Environmental policy cannot be based on pure economic rationality. The economy is therefore embedded in politics. How are environmental policies actually established? How are ecological distribution conflicts solved? As an answer to these questions, we shall discuss some environmental indicators and targets, some international environmental issues, and some 'bottom-up' environmental policies.

## 1. Two Views of the Economy (Neoclassical and Ecological)

From the point of view of ecological economics, the economy is seen as a system necessarily open to the entry of energy and materials, and which produces residues which are not entirely recycled. The Earth itself is open to the entry of solar energy. The metaphysical vision of the economy as a carousel between producers and consumers which turns around (*Figure 2.1*), a *perpetuum mobile* lubricated by money and pushed by the desire to maximize utility (in consumers) or profits (in firms), is not shared by the ecological economists who insist on the distinction traced by Aristotle in *Politics* between *oikonomia* (as the study of the material and energy provisioning of the oikos, and in general of human society), and *chrematistics* (as the study of price formation in markets). Although we do not share Aristotle's motivation – to keep merchants in their social subordinate place, since he disliked the threat to the social order which freedom of trade could produce – we still argue as ecological economists that human livelihood should not be guided by the price system, because the price system is unable to give convincing evaluation to the inflows of energy and materials, to the outflows of waste, and in general to the environmental conditions for life and production, including biodiversity. There is a parallel here with debates on the value of domestic work, essential for the well-being of the population, and usually done by women at a low or zero price because of their social subjection and segmented labour markets. The analogy is not far-fetched, since the debates within the feminist movement were connected with the same root economic cause, the failure of the market to measure services essential to the human economy, in the sense of *oikonomia*. In the case of environmental externalities, there are two further issues: damages to future human generations, and damages to other forms of life. The schemes in *Figure 2.1* reflect this conflict of visions between neoclassical economics and ecological economics. Externalities are not minor cases of market failure. Rather, the market economy should be seen as a small rocking boat in an ocean of uncertain, incommensurable externalities.[2]

*Distributional issues*

The pattern of prices in the neoclassical economy depends on the distribution of income. The functioning of the neoclassical economic circuit may be disrupted by distributional conflicts. For instance, firms are individually inclined not to pay high wages, and therefore there might be a lack of effective demand from households in the aggregate to buy all the goods and services which would be available with production running at full capacity utilization. This is a well known internal contradiction of capitalism. Or, for instance, in a period of full employment, wages might increase more than productivity, and if there were strong internal or international competition among firms, it would be difficult to translate such pressure into higher prices, and there might occur a 'profit squeeze', and a crisis from the 'supply side'. Similarly, *if* natural resources and

*Figure 2.1: Two visions of the economy*

*(a) The neoclassical economy*

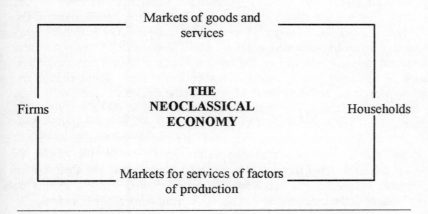

*(b) The ecological economy*

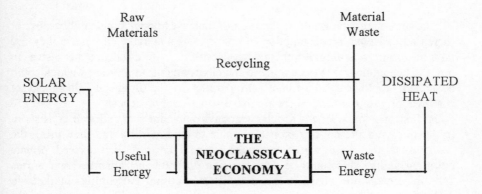

environmental services became more scarce, and *if* such scarcity were reflected in costs (a big 'if'), then there might also occur a 'profit squeeze'. James O'Connor (1988) referred to this as the 'second contradiction' of capitalism.

Since, in ecological economics, we see the market economy as embedded in a physical–chemical–biological system, the question immediately arises of the value of such natural resources and environmental services for the economy. Is it possible to translate such environmental values into money values? This will be considered below, under the rubric of 'incommensurability'. Here some asymmetries as regards distributional conflicts will be pointed out. In the ecological economy, future human generations, and the existence values attributed to other species, play a role, precisely because the time horizon of the ecological economy is much longer, as we take into account slow biogeochemical cycles, and irreversible thermodynamics. Also, many natural resources and environmental services are not in the market, because they have no owner; attribution of 'property rights' and inclusion in the market, would change the distribution of income, and the pattern of prices in the market economy embedded in the ecological economy. For instance, are there owners of the ability of the Earth to recycle a good part of the $CO_2$ pumped into the atmosphere? Are there markets for such property? Are there owners of wild and agricultural biodiversity? What is the role of environmental movements acting *outside* the market in pushing up prices which firms (or governments) have to pay for their use of environmental resources and services? The distributional aspects should be integrated into both the neoclassical and the ecological views of the economy.

## 2. Indicators, Limits and Instruments

The larger our economies grow (because of increased populations, and because of increased exosomatic consumption of energy and materials), the more they use natural resources and environmental services. Externalities become pervasive. In order to accommodate the economy to the environment, in a process which could be called 'ecological adjustment' (in parallel to the financial adjustment of stabilization programmes), there are two distinctive approaches.

The first one characterizes neoclassical environmental economics. It consists in trying to give a present-day monetary value to externalities, and then bring the economy to the point where marginal external costs do not exceed private marginal gains. This could be done through different instruments: legal norms and fines, economic charges, levies or taxes, Coasian bargaining, markets in pollution permits ... (If we take case by case, in a partial equilibrium analysis –see section 3 – we shall miss the general consequences for quantities transacted and for prices that the internalization of externalities would have. These could only be captured through a general equilibrium analysis. As prices change in one market because of internalization of externalities, all prices will change to a greater or lesser extent. This is an interesting and well known point, but not relevant in the sense that the argument here is that there is no way of exactly internalizing externalities even in the simple cases of partial equilibrium analysis.)

The second approach is that of ecological economics which argues that it is not merely technically difficult but actually impossible to give present-day monetary values to the myriad externalities, many of which are unknown, many of which will have irreversible, uncertain, future effects. When politicians are advised to use phrases such as 'Getting the prices *right*', or 'We must include the *full* social environmental costs', this is impracticable advice. For instance, a calculation of the marginal external costs of nuclear power would require estimates, at present-day value, of the costs (or benefits) of radioactive waste for tens of thousands of years. At which rate of discount? A Coasian solution in terms of attribution of 'property rights' and subsequent market negotiations over radioactive waste and pollution, would not really cope with today's uncertainties or solve the intergenerational question. Ecological economists have argued that elements of an economy with pervasive uncertain future externalities are *incommensurable*. However, this does not rule out of court an environmental policy which makes use of economic instruments.

The argument of ecological economics is that environmental *limits* (or targets, standards or norms) to the economy cannot in general be set through a process of comparison of private profits and social, external costs, but rather they must be set, and *are* set in practice, through a process of 'social evaluation' (how else?) after scientific–political debates.[3] Once such limits are set (for instance, in the Fifth Environmental Action Programme of the European Union, translated into a set of concrete indicators and quantitative norms, or the Dutch Environmental Policy Plan), then the conventional economists can come back on to the stage, with special competence in discussing *instruments* (for example, for a reduction of $SO_2$ emissions of $x$ percent, would a tax or levy be more cost-effective than a market in emission permits, or vice versa?).

There have been proposals of *monetary indicators* on the state of the environment, such as a 'green' GDP. Also, 'weak sustainability' has been proposed, that is net investment should be at least equal to the depreciation of 'natural capital'. Pearce and Turner's (1990) concept of 'weak sustainability' is a synthetic *monetary* indicator. However, to assert that the economy would be 'weakly' sustainable if net investment exceeds the sum of depreciation of renewable and non-renewable environmental resources, implies faith in the substitutability of capital for environmental resources, and faith in the possibility of measuring the depreciation of environmental resources in the same units as capital. 'Weak sustainability' assumes we know how to value in money terms the services of non-appropriated, non-marketable natural resources and life support systems (Victor, Hanna and Kubursi 1994). (See Ollikainen, Chapter 3 below.)

Techniques of economic valuation are unable to give convincing updated value estimates to the use of natural resources, or to future, uncertain externalities. Therefore, monetary indicators are only believable for captive audiences of professional environmental and resource economists. They are useless for policies.

We are then left with *physical indicators* (or, equivalently, with 'satellite' accounts of variations in 'natural patrimony', not integrated in money terms within national income accounting). Behind a list of indicators such as the one shown in *Table 2.1* (adapted from work in progress at DGXI) there would always be a history of scientific research and political controversy. Notice, however, that a list of indicators is far from being a list of *targets* for indicators and, moreover, that the list is always incomplete. For instance, one could add loss of agricultural land (through desertification, urbanization, and so on) as one important indicator. Or availability of water, comparing rainfall and extraction. Or, for instance, there is a new European proposal on the preservation of agricultural biodiversity (COM 93-337), but as far as I know there is no indicator of 'genetic erosion', that is the loss of agricultural biodiversity in European regions.[4] Once an indicator was constructed, and a target was set, then the instruments in order to reach such objective could be discussed. Of course, we must decide on policies before knowing all facts and before an economic quantification of such facts.

One indicator of loss of natural biodiversity would be human appropriation of the annual biomass net production. There is the well known figure of 40 percent for the whole (terrestrial) world, which comes from the sum of direct human use (4 percent), indirect use (26 percent), and losses (10 percent), and which clearly indicates how the space for other species is narrowing down (Vitousek *et al.*, 1986). This would be an interesting indicator for different European regions, some of which are using more biomass than they themselves produce. Now, however, how much biomass and space do other species need for conservation and future evolution? Are we going to be guided by present use values and (discounted) option values, or also by intrinsic values which arise from the belief that other species have a right to exist?

How could such indicators be aggregated? Often, some indicators improve while others deteriorate. The Wuppertal Institute is trying to develop one synthetic physical indicator, MIPS (material input per unit service), in the expectation that the economy is moving towards 'dematerialization'. (See Hinterberger and Seifert in Chapter 5.) In general, there have been inconclusive attempts to decide on whether economic growth is bad (or good) for the environment, and in the wake of the Brundtland Report of 1987, the fashion was to argue that poverty was the main enemy of the environment. True, the amount of energy used for cooking might go down with economic growth (as kerosene or LPG cookers are substituted for open fires burning woodfuels or dried dung), but in general economic growth goes together with environmental degradation, although selected indicators follow different trends (*Figure 2.2*).

*Table 2.1: Issues and indicators*

| Environmental Issue | Environmental Indicator |
| --- | --- |
| Acidification | acid emissions calculated from:<br>$- SO_2$<br>$- NO_x$<br>$- NH_3$ |
| Tropospheric ozone | precursor VOCs |
| Global warming | $CO_2$ equivalent emissions from:<br>$- CO_2$<br>$- CH_4$ |
| Toxic/persistent pollutants in the environment | total emissions/discharges to environment of:<br>– dioxins<br>– heavy metals<br>– organics |
| Water quality | total nutrients discharges:<br>– nitrates<br>– phosphates<br>– pesticides<br>total de-oxygenation potential:<br>– BOD + COD |
| Coastal zones | total hydrocarbons into the marine environment |
| Waste reduction | total municipal waste generated<br>total hazardous waste generated |
| Resource conservation | % recycled materials<br>energy consumption<br>water consumption<br>– total annual demand<br>– seasonal demand |

There is then no single, synthetic criterion by which to judge the impact of the economy on the environment. Usually, in practice, some sort of consensus is reached on a list of indicators and on the targets for each indicator by diffuse processes of 'social evaluation', the study of which would be essential for the research on environmental policy-making. Conventional environmental economics is irrelevant to such processes of 'social evaluation', as will be shown.

*Figure 2.2: Selected environmental indicators and income levels*

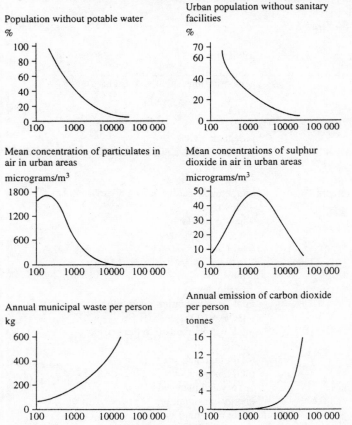

*Source*: Shafik and Bandyopadhyay, for the World Bank (taken from *Nueva Sociedad*, n.122, Caracas, Nov.–Dec. 1992, p.195).

The horizontal axis measures income per capita in US $ on a log scale.

## 3. Internalization of Externalities in Neoclassical Environmental Economics

One may easily agree with the 'polluter pays' principle, but of course the question is, *how much* will the polluter pay? The orthodox answer is the marginal value of the damage caused. In some cases, instead of trying to sell to politicians and the public the idea of internalization of externalities, it would be intellectually more honest, and possibly politically more useful, to confess that we do not know the present value of future, uncertain externalities. This is not an extremist position, but a well–known argument.

The belief that the value of externalities can be easily estimated by the cost of restoration of the environment is justified in some cases, but not in general because some externalities are irreversible (loss of biodiversity), or there are no known or reliable techniques for neutralization of the effects (radioactive waste), or because the costs of restoration lie in the distant future (for instance, neutralization of increased $CO_2$ through reforestation, or cleaning up waste dumps, or restoring landscapes spoiled by tourist developments), and therefore the present value of such future costs will be greatly affected by the chosen rate of discount.

What is needed is a political decision on the chosen indicators and on the different limits to be set to indicators, and then a separate discussion on the instruments to be used in order to accommodate the economy to such limits.

As explained in textbooks, internalization of externalities requires us to give money values to external effects. Let us assume for instance a power station burning coal or oil, and producing kwh. If prices are regulated, and marginal private costs increase, we could draw the point of maximum private profit (OA), as shown in *Figure 2.3*. However, this power station also produces sulphur dioxide, and also $CO_2$, $NO_x$, and so on. (To simplify the discussion, we focus only on $SO_2$). Therefore, in *Figure 2.4* we draw a line of marginal private profit (taken from *Figure 2.3*, so that OA indicates the same point in both figures), and we also draw a line of marginal *external* cost, translating into present money values the damage caused (now and in future) by $SO_2$. The analysis requires the identification and quantification of physical damages, and the 'transmutation' of such physical damages into money values. In the case of a nuclear power station we would have to give money values to radioactive waste – and let us remember that the radioactive half-life of plutonium is about 24,000 years. Is plutonium a positive or a negative externality? Believers in fast reactors, or in some forms of military security, have in fact considered plutonium a positive externality produced by some forms of civil nuclear power production (such as the Magnox reactors in Britain). At which rate of discount should future negative impacts be discounted, in order to obtain present values? Therefore, the orthodox analysis of externalities is not convincing.

*Figure 2.3:  The depiction of externalities in neoclassical environmental economics*

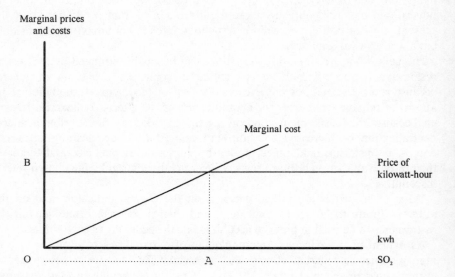

## 4. Incommensurability. Are there 'environmentally–correct' prices?

Cost–benefit analysis, or impossible attempts at Coasian bargaining over future externalities, or contingent valuation: all such techniques of valuation replace the 'social evaluations' reached through scientific–political–democratic debate by arbitrary numbers or at best by surrogate market mechanisms which are supposed to mimic the workings of ideal markets. Lay people are more aware of this than economists, as is reflected in the many refusals to answer in contingent valuation experiments. As analysed by Sagoff in *The Economy of the Earth*, such refusals show the conflict between people as money-spending consumers, and as democratic citizens.[5]

The issue of incommensurability should be squarely faced (O'Neill 1993). For instance, one kwh from fossil fuels is not commensurable in money terms with one kwh of nuclear energy, once externalities are internalized, because we do not know which money values to give to such externalities. Much will depend on the time horizon and discount rate, and on the uncertainties of future technical change. Thus, in the years ahead the cost of decommissioning nuclear plants will loom larger and larger. Of course, adjourning the decision makes nuclear energy appear cheaper just by virtue of the discount rate. But we are then compromising the ability of future generations to meet their own needs. The money values given to externalities appear therefore as a consequence of political decisions (which are themselves based on spurious economic arguments) (Thomas *et al.*, 1994).

*Figure 2.4: The internalization of externalities in neoclassical environmental economics*

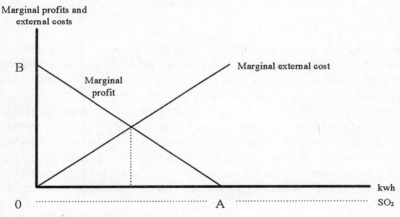

*Note* opt = 'social optimum'

These are two different questions which need to be addressed separately. First, how to set environmental limits to the economy, that is the issue of sustainability. The European limit of emissions of $CO_2$ equal to 1990 emissions (instead of 1890, or 1790, before the Industrial Revolution), comes straight from politics, and properly so. (Unfortunately there is no similar European limit on production of radioactive waste.) Thus, the question of limits to the economy is approached in different terms according to the problem. For instance:

- for $SO_2$, the 'critical loads' of the RAINS model, based on detailed scientific information (but nevertheless open to challenge). Using the model, it is possible to calculate which emissions could be reduced at lowest cost, or it is possible to find out which emissions are most relevant to reduce deposits in certain places. During negotiations on the reduction of $SO_2$ emissions some of these possibilities have been used. A flat percentage reduction of emissions (30 per cent, in the first instance) was agreed upon, but negotiations later became more flexible.
- for $CO_2$, the politically-chosen, post-Rio, *ad-hoc* modest European limit at 1990 levels, which leaves open distributional issues both inside Europe and internationally, and which unless the eco-tax is implemented, will perhaps not be achieved.
- for production of radioactive waste in Europe, no limit (I believe), apart from national policies on nuclear energy.
- for car traffic, limits on $NO_x$, no quantitative limits on other externalities (for instance, casualties).

Secondly, once limits are determined there is the question of how to enforce such limits through policy measures that may include market instruments. Such market instruments are usually more cost-effective as a means of reaching a given reduction goal than legal instruments. In other words, there are no 'ecologically correct' prices, in the sense that they convincingly internalize all the future, uncertain externalities, but there might be 'ecologically corrected' prices. The goals for each indicator (and the indicators themselves) come from *outside* economic analysis, if economic analysis is defined as the study of phenomena which fall under the 'measuring rod of money' (although perhaps economics, as a general science of choice, is relevant after all to the choice of indicators and goals).

Incommensurability means that there is no common unit of measurement, but it does *not* mean that we cannot compare alternative decisions on a rational basis, on *different* scales of value, as in multi-criteria evaluation. For instance, in the case of fossil fuel energy versus nuclear energy, we could rank both sources on different criteria (see *Table 2.2*).

Rather than reducing these and other factors to a common unit expressed in present-value terms, we could try to reach a rational decision by verbal discussion (or perhaps through *fuzzy* numbers), giving implicit weights to such criteria (Munda 1993).

*Table 2.2: Comparisons between nuclear energy and fossil fuel energy*

|  | Nuclear energy | Fossil fuel energy |
| --- | --- | --- |
| CO$_2$ production | – | X |
| N0$_x$ production | – | X |
| SO$_2$ production | – | X |
| Chrematistic cost | $/kwh | $/kwh |
| Radioactive waste | X | – |
| Decommissioning problems | XX | X |
| Danger to human life | XX | X |
| Fear to population | X | – |
| Cogeneration facilities | – | X |
| Technocratic control | XX | X |
| National independence | X? | – |
| Military links | X | – |

Incommensurability is in the tradition of ecological economics since Otto Neurath and William Kapp. As Kapp wrote:

To place a monetary value on and apply a discount rate (which?) to future utilities or disutilities in order to express their present capitalised value may give us a precise monetary calculation, but it does not get us out of the dilemma of a choice and the fact that we take a risk with human health and survival. For this reason, I am inclined to consider the attempt at measuring social costs and social benefits simply in terms of monetary or market values as doomed to failure. Social costs and social benefits have to be considered as extra-market phenomena; they are borne and accrue to society as a whole; they are heterogeneous and cannot be compared quantitatively among themselves and with each other, not even in principle. (Kapp 1970, p. 49)

Otto Neurath had written in 1919:

The question might arise, should one protect coal mines or put greater strain on men? The answer depends for example on whether one thinks that hydroelectric power may be sufficiently developed or that solar heat might come to be better used, and so on. If one believes the latter, one may 'spend' coal more freely and will hardly waste human effort where coal can be used. If however one is afraid that when one generation uses too much coal thousands will freeze to death in the future, one might use more human power and save coal. Such and many other non–technical matters determine the choice of a technically calculable plan ... we can see no possibility of reducing the production plan to some kind of unit and then to compare the various plans in terms of such units. (Neurath 1973, p. 263)

Neurath could already have included in his discussion the increased greenhouse effect, and nuclear energy. His example shows that comparability need not presuppose commensurability. We can rationally discuss sources of energy, transport systems, agricultural policies, patterns of industrialization, taking into account both monetary costs and socio-environmental (present and future) 'costs', without an appeal to a common chrematistic unit of measurement.

## 5. Sustainable Development or an Ecological Economy?

The economy, from an ecological point of view, does not have a common standard of measurement. Economists are left without a theory of value. Valuations of diachronic externalities such as the exhaustion of non-renewable resources, loss of biodiversity, global warming, or radioactive pollution are so arbitrary that they cannot act as the basis for rational environmental policies. On the other hand, policies cannot be based only on pure ecological rationality in terms of carrying capacity norms or 'sustainability'. These are inescapable conclusions reached some time ago in *Ecological Economics* (1991) which I co-authored with Klaus Schluepmann and which John O'Neill (1993) has analysed and developed most competently.

Which indicators should be chosen? How to establish their limits? Sometimes such problems are *rhetorically* solved by appeals to a synthetic, unique criterion such as 'sustainable development', or 'sustainability', or 'carrying capacity'. Indeed, the intellectual origin of the notion of 'sustainable development' (popularized by the Brundtland Report (1987), but born a few years before in IUCN), is the link of the biological concept of *carrying capacity* (that is the maximum number of population of a species which a given territory can sustain without degradation of the resource base), with the concept of economic development or growth. Here we take economic growth and economic development as equivalent ways of indicating growth of GDP, despite the well-meaning attempt by Herman Daly to use 'development' for a change in the structure of the economy without growth of GDP. This is contrary to common usage in the economic literature. Witness the Nobel prizes awarded to Robert Solow for theories of economic growth, and to Arthur Lewis for theories of economic development: different theories, certainly, with different types of economies in mind, but nevertheless a common belief in growth in GDP.

As explicitly stated by Jeffrey A. McNeely (1988, p.2), 'sustainable development' united the ecological concept of carrying capacity with the economic concepts of growth and development. However, unless levels of exosomatic consumption of energy and materials, patterns of urbanization and transport, types of food intake, and objectives for preservation of other species are determined, unless currents of energy and materials across borders are specified, the notion of the ecological sustainability of a given group of humans on a given territory cannot be applied. Futhermore, territories are not given, but rather politically shaped; and also obstruct migrations.

Because of the specificities of human ecology (mainly, but not only, the lack of genetic instructions on exosomatic consumption of energy and materials, which depends on culture, economy and politics, and the enormous volume of horizontal transport of energy and materials, which makes limiting factors disappear in the importing territories), there is no way of applying directly the notion of carrying capacity to the human species, as a whole, or to any contemporary nation. Thus, the relation between the economy and ecosystems cannot be simply ascertained by appealing to 'carrying capacity' (or its close relative, 'sustainability', let alone 'sustainable development' or 'sustainable growth'). We should instead choose a battery of concrete indicators on a practical, *ad-hoc* basis – for instance, $CO_2$ emissions – and then see whether the economy is becoming less or more sustainable in terms of such indicators. Often, some indicators improve ($SO_2$ goes down) while others deteriorate (loss of biodiversity). Political evaluations are then required. Human ecology is also embedded in politics.

The Maastricht Treaty, art. 2, states that one of the goals of the European Union is 'sustainable growth'. Some reasons have been given why sustainable development and sustainable growth are suspect notions. There is an alternative approach to the discussion of the relations between the ecology and the economy which is less controversial. An 'ecological economy' would fulfil the following three criteria.[6] The use of renewable resources would be at a rate not greater than the growth of resources. Secondly, the use of exhaustible resources (for example, fossil fuels) would not exceed the rate at which they are substituted by renewable resources (photovoltaics for example – as an application of this rule, an ecological economy would preserve biodiversity. And thirdly, an ecological economy would produce waste only at the rate at which it could be assimilated by the biosphere.

However, such criteria are *not* operational. They would require that we know the stock (and the reproduction rates) of exhaustible and renewable resources, and that we decide on the thresholds of pollution which can be tolerated over given time spans. It could be argued nevertheless that, as a general concept, an ecological economy is to be preferred to sustainability, or sustainable growth or sustainable development because it is less charged with biological reductionism, and because it does not presuppose that the economy can grow or develop without damage to the environment. But this concept of an ecological economy cannot directly provide either one single synthetic indicator or a set of indicators, with their limits.


## 6. International Aspects

We are still moving away from an ecological economy (as regards $CO_2$, radioactive waste, and so on), and because of this, ecological distribution conflicts will increase. The ecological debt is piling up, and there are the international difficulties associated with the eco-tax (on top of the internal European lack of enthusiasm for it).

What does *ecological distribution* mean? This refers (following suggestions from Frank Beckenbach and Martin O'Connor) to the social, spatial, and temporal asymmetries or inequalities in the use of environmental resources and services, that is in the depletion of natural resources (including land degradation, and the loss of biodiversity), and in the burdens of pollution. Three examples:

1.  the distribution of per capita exosomatic energy consumption would be an instance of unequal social ecological distribution;
2.  the territorial asymmetries between $SO_2$ emissions and the burdens of acid rain (as shown in the RAINS model), of spatial ecological distribution;
3.  the intergenerational inequalities between the enjoyment of nuclear energy (or emissions of $CO_2$), and the burdens of radioactive waste (or global warming), of temporal ecological distribution.

Some of these asymmetries are beginning to have names. For instance, 'environmental racism' in the US means the siting of polluting industries or toxic waste disposal installations in areas of Black or Hispanic or Indian population. Again, there is increasing discussion on 'ecologically unequal exchange' and on the 'ecological debt' (with both spatial and temporal aspects). Another example is the work which has been done in the Netherlands on the 'environmental space' really occupied by her economy (both for procuring resources and for disposal of emissions).

Let us look again at $CO_2$ emissions. 'Sustainability' would mean the level of zero *net* emissions, which would be much lower than the commitment to the 1990 level. In the case of Spain (whose emissions of $CO_2$ per capita are above the world average and much above the world median), official policy has been an *increase* of $CO_2$ emissions (because that increase would put Spain still under the European average for 1990). Clearly, these are *ad-hoc* decisions, the stuff of real politics which cannot be explained either by the strict logic of cost–benefit analysis, or by a purely ecological logic in terms of carrying capacity or sustainability. In the European Union it is possible (partly because of the role played by the nuclear industry, in itself a polemical point) that $CO_2$ emissions could be kept almost within the limit set after Rio 1992, that is equal to those of 1990. This is not sustainable, in the sense that such emissions *exceed* per capita the amount that, if extended to the world population, would still be absorbed by new vegetation and the oceans. Therefore, European $CO_2$ emissions at the 1990 level would still increase the *ecological debt* which Europe owes future generations in Europe and the rest of the world (Azar and Holmberg 1994). The ecological debt arises from this invasion of the 'environmental space' belonging to other people, and also from two other sources: primary products (such as oil) have been paid at prices which possibly undervalue future demand; and such prices have not included any allowance for externalities (such as oil pollution at the point of extraction).

Moreover, the proposed European carbon and energy tax would have clear international effects, in the sense that it would curb demand for fossil fuels (which is its intended purpose), and therefore it would probably diminish revenues (directly and indirectly) of oil- and gas-exporting countries. Why should not these countries themselves charge the eco-tax? Or, alternatively, should eco-tax revenues collected in Europe be sent back to poor oil- and gas-exporting countries? At least we should be aware of such international issues.

*Trade Policy*

There exists something which could be called an ecological balance of payments between the European Union and the rest of the world, or different sections of the world, but we do not know really how to count the different items. Europe (and most countries in Europe) are net importers of energy, for instance; we have probably profited from an 'ecologically unequal exchange'. GATT rules pay no attention to the ways in which products are manufactured (with exceptions such as prison labour). Inside Europe, apart from such ridiculous cases as exports of tomatoes 2000 kilometres from the Netherlands to Southern Spain (only possible because of lax environmental standards in tomato production in the Netherlands, and lack of allowance for the environmental cost of the transport), there is the controversial issue of French exports of nuclear energy. Does the price of one kwh of nuclear energy include the environmental costs? We do not know how to count in money terms the present value of future negative (or perhaps positive) externalities from nuclear power. The issue is rather whether freedom of trade should take precedence over environmental objectives politically established.

There is at present a debate on whether environmental objectives should be pursued by means of 'green' tariffs or levies (Daly 1993). The assumption that environmental standards are higher in wealthier countries than in poor countries does not always apply; consider $CO_2$ emissions, or the production of radioactive waste. Also, 'modern' agriculture is environmentally inferior (as regards energy use, biodiversity, pesticides or water pollution with nitrates) to 'traditional' agriculture. Therefore, compensatory 'green' levies would work rather against exports from the 'North' than from the 'South'. For instance, US exports of maize could be subject to a 'green' levy in Mexico. If we assume, on the contrary, that wealth correlates positively with environmental standards, then Europe and the US could choose between imposing levies on imports from polluting producers located in the poorer world countries or instead play a significant role in enforcing internal high environmental standards all across the world. By focusing on cases such as Mexican dolphin-unfriendly tuna fishing, and by assuming that the most polluting production processes are in poorer countries – true for $SO_2$, untrue for $CO_2$ and radioactive waste – the debate on trade and environment makes the US and Europe appear 'generous' by playing according to GATT rules and not trying to levy compensatory 'green' tariffs. The background to this is the common and questionable assumption that growth is good for the environment, that is that richer countries are environmentally more advanced. If this assumption is questioned, then there arise awkward questions on ecological dumping from North to South, and from South to North. Thus, in the South of the planet there are two different positions in the context of the Uruguay Round. Some complain about long-standing barriers to trade in the North, and against the novel use of environmental norms in order to prevent imports (for instance, barriers against bananas from Costa Rica or Ecuador, to protect 'European' bananas from the Canary Islands, Martinique or Guadeloupe). There are also those who are against exports of primary products (because of deteriorating terms of trade, because they are produced by ill-paid labour, and also because of the new awareness of the local environmental impacts), while favouring a self-reliant policy of food security against imports of surplus food from Europe and the US.

## 7. Bottom-up Policies Geared to Consumers' Groups

It has been argued above that we cannot establish environmentally-correct prices, or equivalently, full-social-cost prices, but that this is not an argument against eco-taxes or similar instruments. Now, instead of financing a *general* reduction of charges on labour (including labour employed in the aluminium, cement, car industries?), as proposed in the Delors White Paper of December 1993 (Commission of the European Communities, 1993), the revenues from carbon and energy charges, urban congestion charges, water charges, and so on could go to finance bottom-up policies in favour of a transition to a more ecological economy, and in favour of new employment in ecological activities.

Market instruments and legal norms are top-down instruments. What would be an appropriate mix of top-down and bottom-up policies? Bottom-up policies mean, in the internal European context, supporting already existing groups of cyclists or friends of solar energy, helping them to grow, instead of, for instance, tax policies targeted at the general recalcitrant population. The usual classification of instruments is: a) legal norms and sanctions (fines, and so on); b) economic incentives and penalties (taxes, tradable emissions permits, 'green' levies, refundable deposits, and so on). There is a third category, c) concerted policies. Concerted policies are usually between the administration and producers (or producers' organizations). This is common in the field of toxic waste reduction, and it should become common for 'organic' agriculturists. There could also be a *concerted policy with consumers' groups* which would be cheap to implement because it would rely on already existing groups and interests: for instance, organized cyclists, organized vegetarians, organized friends of solar energy, organized rehabilitators of rural or urban housing. To the extent that groups promoting changes in lifestyles are able to sell something in the market, they could do their own publicity (though clearly a bicycle contains less value-added than a car, and therefore the financing of publicity on equal terms is difficult). When consumers' groups advocate less consumption, then there is no way of financing their publicity in market terms. Exploration is required of the legal and economic bases for public support of consumers' groups which already follow or promote more sustainable lifestyles – an increasing proportion of Europeans.

In the case of taxes on tobacco (also taxes on liquor, or formerly taxes on salt), the expectation from the fiscal authorities is precisely that demand will be inelastic. Tobacco consumption is going down, not because of taxes, but because of increased public awareness and because since the 1950s some scientists in the medical profession have persuaded some governments to finance publicity against tobacco, thereby shifting backwards the demand curve. Why not devote some public finance to counter publicity for cars, advertising the fact that these products are dangerous to human health? This publicity could complement the effects of the eco-tax and the urban congestion tax. The proposal is *not* that the

State should dictate to citizens what they should or should not consume, but rather to give more equal opportunities to the supporters of different lifestyles.

Grassroots social movements against actual or threatened externalities play an important role in environmental policy, because they perform a function at which the market fails, by raising the costs that firms (or governments) have to pay for their use of resources or for polluting the environment. Instead of an arrogant top-down emphasis on 'educating consumers', or on taxing consumers (or even polluters), we need bottom-up environmental policies based on support for the already converted. *Bottom-up* policies rely on environmental social movements, which try to shift demand curves rather than diminish demand along a given demand curve. If there is already a social demand for bicycle lanes which is not felt in the market (or through market publicity) but which is nevertheless expressed as a social movement, then the question is not 'consumers' education' but helping the converted. For instance, it would be easy to find and help consumers' groups interested in solar energy for thermal purposes in Southern Europe, and in general in bioclimatic housing.

Notice that the term 'bottom-up policies' is used here instead of the more managerial *'demand-side' management*. Demand-side management is also useful. It would include, for instance, both urban physical planning measures favourable to cycle lanes, and also a change in the system of regulated prices of public utilities (allowing increases only if they sell less water, or electricity). A system that is in force in some states in America. In a system of *regulated prices* for utilities, prices are allowed to increase only if the utilities show they are selling *less* kwh. (The same could be applied to water use.) The utilities invest in conservation. The essence of the system is the *regionalization of supply and the regulation of prices*. Is this good policy instrument compatible with a free, deregulated market for energy?

## 8. A New European Agricultural Policy as an Example

There is a general agreement in Europe that agriculture and livestock rearing must be de-intensified. At present, a policy of high internal prices has led to intensification. There is disagreement on two issues: whether Europe should open up to agricultural imports; and whether de-intensification should be principally in the regions of most intensive farming, or whether it should affect Europe as a whole, with set-aside policies in areas of marginal farming. The policy outlined here is unfavourable to agricultural imports from the US, and favourable to de-intensification of farming not in marginal areas but on the contrary in areas where the environmental impact is greater, such as the Netherlands, the Po Valley, the Paris basin. Such policies could be based on existing environmental movements.

Sometimes the expression 'bottom-up policies' is used for policies on technology; here it is used for policies based on support for existing environmental movements. For instance, how much would some farmers need to be paid to move towards more 'organic' farming, respectful of biodiversity? Farmers would offer environmental-cum-agricultural products at a price. If the environmental goods to be supplied were defined in a general way (to preserve as much agricultural biodiversity as possible, to decrease as much as possible the input of fossil fuels in agriculture, to raise happy animals, to preserve interesting or beautiful agricultural landscapes), then this would imply, in general, a programme of high prices, extensive agriculture, a large active agricultural population, producing 'organic' agricultural and livestock products. A green dream! Why not? However, this is not politically plausible.

Eco-farming could also be promoted through subsidized agreements with eco-consumers' co-operatives. There is no reason why the State or regional authorities should pay *only* farmers for the supply of environmental goods. What might be needed is a subsidy to consumers who are already ready to buy products from 'organic' farming (in the most general sense: for example, expensive almonds from the mountains of Alicante, which produce beautiful flowers in February, and support the terraces), but who would need an incentive in order to opt for them. In general, we should pay more attention to economic–environmental policies based on and geared to the growing groups of ecological consumers (or non-consumers). Such policies would be most cost-effective.

Through such 'bottom-up' policies geared to eco-farmers and eco-consumers we could be successful in achieving a double objective: to reduce subsidies in the form of high prices for *intensive* agriculture and livestock, and simultaneously achieve an environmentally functional farming system.

Decreasing or eliminating agricultural surpluses and exports from Europe is clearly a win-win policy (good for the economy and the environment), but opening Europe to US exports (as distinct, perhaps, from exports from Uruguay or Argentina) is environmentally unfriendly to the environment, because of the strong environmental impact of US agriculture. The issue would be how to support crops and rotations in European agriculture which substitute imports and are at the same time good for the environment. Decreasing prices means sometimes that the type of farming (including livestock) which was less intensive in resource use and less polluting is abandoned, while regions of very intensive farming and livestock further intensify the abuse of environmental resources to compensate for the low prices. Reallocation of milk quotas away from

Galicia/Asturias/Leon to Northern Europe is unfavourable both to the environment, and to employment. Abandoning cultivation of Mediterranean hills, with almonds, olives and vines, is also an environmental mistake, since the scrub cover which might stop erosion and preserve the terraces, is likely to burn repeatedly – desertification is growing in some European Mediterranean regions. What is really needed is increasing support for specific types of farming, based on Produces and consumers favourable to eco-farming, and on decreasing subsidies for intensive (so-called productive), 'competitive' farming.

## 9. The Example of Tourism

Let me end this chapter with another concrete suggestion, regarding the conflict between tourism and environment which is so well-known in Catalonia. What direction could an environmental policy on tourism take? Which policy instruments could be deployed in this case? The ecological critique of neoclassical environmental economics (as outlined above) should be pushed as much as possible, so that environmental policy does not follow single-track chrematistic priorities based on capricious valuation of environmental resources and services. In specific cases, environmental policies will be established by a judicious mixture of economic and ecological reasoning. Thus, despite my distrust of biological reductionism in *human* ecology, one could agree with the use of the concept of carrying capacity in order to reach concrete objectives on the number of tourists allowed in different areas at different seasons of the year. How the demand would be kept within such bounds, would then require a discussion of instruments. It has been proposed that governments would define 'tourist quotas' according to carrying capacity, and issue tradable permits. Such limits will be extremely important: governments would need good guidance on 'carrying capacities' by region. But, for instance, could Mallorca increase its tourist carrying capacity (as is currently proposed) by importing by tanker water from the Ebro river?

Let us define 'carrying capacity' as the limit of visitor use of an area without degrading its 'environmental quality'. In the visitors' experience? Which types of visitors? Eco-tourists or the usual kind of beach-discothèque tourist? Or in the natives' experience? Or are we to talk of 'environmental quality' in the abstract? In fact, some authors are taking short cuts and defining carrying capacity in *ad hoc* terms for instance, the number of tourist beds compared to the number of natives' beds, or bed-nights (with a maximum ratio of 1 to 2 on any given night?). Arbitrary perhaps, but not more so than 'environmental quality'. Here some conventional environmental economics could be useful. For instance, contingent valuation techniques could elicit how much the loss of landscapes, of access to peaceful beaches, the increase in summer traffic congestion, and so on is valued in money terms by relevant populations (in Italy, Spain). However, those interviewed might not take adequate thought for the future, and therefore their estimation of damage to historical monuments or to the scenery arising from tourism, would not be realistic. Such considerations are self-evident; therefore, there is necessarily an element of practical judgement in the definition of 'tourist carrying capacity quotas', which cannot be reduced to pure economic reason or to pure ecological reason. We are back again to the question of choice of *indicators*, and fixing of *targets* or *limits*, prior to and more important than the question of *instruments*, such as tradable tourist quotas.

## Notes

1.   This paper developed from my speech to the EAEPE conference in Barcelona in October 1993, with stimulus from consulting work for DGXI, EU, and from the Paris Conference on Models of Sustainable Development in March 1994. I acknowledge the support of DGXII, EU, Brussels (Contract EV5V-CT92-0084).
2.   That the 'boat' is itself overcrowded – to use Herman Daly's analogy of the Plimsoll line – is more relevant for some externalities (for example, loss of biodiversity), than for others (ozone layer, radioactive waste, acid rain).
3.   Compare Funtowicz and Ravetz (1991, 1994), with their idea of 'post-normal science' and 'extended peer reviews'.
4.   For a general introduction to this issue see Vellvé (1992). There are attempts to measure loss of agricultural biodiversity in terms of the decrease in the number of varieties. Apart from the non-availability of data for non-commercial varieties, or for reutilization of seed by farmers, there is also the question of the genetic distance between varieties which have different ethnic or commercial names but which genetically might be distant or similar. Therefore, there is yet no agreed indicator of genetic erosion.
5.   In some parts of the world, the generalized market system has deeply influenced culture. Thus, in the US there is a common use of the expression 'the bottom line', in order to give final reasons for any decision, which comes from the last line in a firm's profit and loss account.
6.   The author is rephrasing here ideas by several other authors.

# References

Azar, Ch., and John Holmberg (1994), *Defining the Generational Environmental Debt*, Paris Symposium on Models of Sustainable Development, 16–18 March, also in *Ecological Economics*, **14.**

Commission of the European Communities (1993), *Growth, Competitiveness, Employment* (COM (93) 700 final), Brussels.

Daly, Herman (1993), 'The Perils of Free Trade', *Scientific American*, **269**, 50-57.

Funtowicz, S. and J. Ravetz (1991), 'A New Scientific Methodology for Global Environmental Issues' in R. Costanza (ed.), *Ecological Economics*, N. York: Columbia UP

Funtowicz, S. and J. Ravetz (1994), *Epistemología política: Ciencia con la gente*, Centro Editor América Latina, Buenos Aires.

Kapp, K.W. (1970), *Social Costs, Economic Development, and Environmental Disruption*, J.E. Ullmann (ed.), Lanham, University Press of America, Md. (1983).

Martinez Alier, Joan and Klaus Schluepmann (1991), *Ecological Economics, Energy, Environment & Society*, Blackwell Publishers, UK.

McNeely, Jeffrey A. (1988), *Economics and Biological Diversity: Developing and using economic incentives to conserve biological resources*, IUCN, Gland, Switzerland.

Munda, G. (1993*), Fuzzy Information in Multicriteria Environmental Evaluation Models*, PhD thesis, University of Amsterdam published by Physika Verlag, Heidelberg, 1995.

Neurath, O. (1973), *Empiricism and Sociology*, Dordrecht, Reidel.

O'Connor, James (1988), 'Introduction', *Capitalism, Nature, Socialism*, n.1, Santa Cruz, Calif.

O'Neill, John (1993), *Ecology, Policy and Politics*, London, Routledge.

Thomas, Stephen, Gordon MacKerron and John Surrey (1994), *Sustainability and Nuclear Plant Decommissioning*, Paris Symposium on Models of Sustainable Development, 16–18 March.

Vellvé, Renée (1992), *Saving the Seed. Genetic Diversity and European Agriculture*, London, Earthscan.

Victor, P.A., J.E. Hanna and A. Kubursi (1994), *How Strong is Weak Sustainability*, Paris Symposium on Models of Sustainable Development, 16–18 March, also in *Economie Appliquée, XLVIII* (2).

Vitousek, P., P. Ehrlich, A. Ehrlich and P. Matson (1986), 'Human Appropriation of the Products of Photosynthesis', *Bioscience*, **36** (6), 366–73.

# 3. Sustainable Development from the Viewpoint of Ethics and Economics[1]

## Markku Ollikainen

## Introduction

The term 'sustainable development' was proposed by the World Commission for Environment and Development as the guiding principle behind environmental policy in 1987. Still, as Colin Clark points out, environmental economics lacks a workable definition for sustainable development (Clark 1990). Even though there are different theories that deal with resources, pollution and preservation, there is no consensus on the guiding principles under which they should be subsumed. The number of proposals for the proper interpretation of the concept is large. The reason for this proliferation lies in the fact that the properties of social welfare functions are highly normative.

The normative content of sustainable development is expressed in the requirement to save the environment and the means of sustaining life for future generations. It is by no means clear when we regard the environment as saved. For example, some people may accept the extinction of some species, while others would deny the right of extinction to any species. Many differences in attitudes towards nature can be traced back to the fundamental concern: do we regard nature as an instrument for our purposes or as an inherently worthy entity? This question illustrates the demarcation between anthropocentric and biocentric environmental ethics. Future generations and the satisfaction of needs pose a similar problem: how should they be taken into account? For example, is selfishly increasing our own standard of living in fact the most efficient way of making future generations better off, or should we abstain from the use of some natural resources even though future generations will probably be wealthier than we are? Finally, do we have to satisfy all our needs or just some of them? These questions show that any definition of sustainable development must define values in terms of nature, future generations and the satisfaction of needs. The rules for conservation and preservation must be based on the chosen values.

The need to find a new ethical basis for development is strengthened by the observation that market forces are not capable of achieving sustainability. As trust in the market's ability to produce smooth adjustments to natural resource depletion and pollution has collapsed, the question has been raised of how to organize the economy in a sustainable way. The analysis of the relevant ethical basis for sustainable development thus arises from both practice and theory.

Among the various interpretations of sustainable development are two which move towards making the ethical basis very explicit. The first one is given by Daly, (1990) whose interpretation is based on steady-state thinking and is motivated by a thermodynamic approach. The second, by Pearce and Turner, (1990), is based on neoclassical environmental economics. They enlarge the mainstream approach by imposing the requirement of constant natural capital as a constraint on social welfare maximization.

This chapter analyzes the value commitments and policy prescriptions of these two interpretations. The approach to environmental policy in Daly's theory is from institutional or ecological economics, that in Pearce and Turner's from neoclassical economics, although neither offers the only possible interpretation from their respective standpoints. For convenience, Daly's interpretation of sustainable development will be called *a programme of sustainable steady-state economy*, and the one given by Pearce and Turner labelled *a programme of sustainable growth economy*.

The theories of environmental ethics will be used to study the value commitments and prescriptions of these programmes. The weak anthropocentrism of Norton and the biocentric system of Taylor are chosen for this purpose, because they cover the same issues as the economic programmes under study. Furthermore, both authors are well acquainted with and refer to environmental economic research. These ethical theories are utilized to clarify what sort of ethical attitudes both programmes have towards nature, future generations and the satisfaction of needs. Further, as the basic goal of environmental ethics is to define the moral rules that inevitably lead to the preservation of nature, these rules are used as a yardstick to evaluate the prescriptions (conservation and preservation rules) that the two programmes give. The analysis is organized as follows. Section 1 presents two theories of anthropocentric and biocentric ethics that can be linked to the economic programmes, which are described in detail in Section 2. The correspondence between economic programmes and ethical theories is analysed in Section 3 and in Section 4. The programmes are compared.

## 1. Two Ethical Attitudes towards Nature and Future Generations

Norton (1987) takes seriously the fact that traditional western anthropocentric ethics has led to serious deterioration of the environment. Nevertheless, he does not accept the idea of the inherent worth of nature suggested by biocentrism. He would like to develop a concept that avoids the problems of strong anthropocentrism and guarantees the preservation of nature. He calls this weak anthropocentrism, a collective ethical theory which lacks the individualism of strong anthropocentrism. The collectiveness is based on a fundamental distinction between two sorts of preferences. People have felt and considered preferences. Felt preferences may lead us to harm nature and they can be justified only if they can be given the status of considered preferences. Considered preferences are those felt preferences which are compatible with a world view of environmental protection. Considered preferences can be used against felt preferences when they happen to promote misuse of the environment. Considered preferences are collective, because they are governed by an environmental world view. This world view is articulated by advanced scientific theories which are, of course, vague, but further research will increase our knowledge.

While the relationship between human beings and nature is collective, social behaviour among human beings is governed by the same individualistic rules as in traditional ethics. This forms the basis of the need to take future generations into account. Collectivism and individualism are combined to formulate the moral rule of weak anthropocentrism: it is the duty of every generation to sustain a steady flow of natural and environmental resources over an infinite time horizon because of the need to guarantee the continuity of human life (Norton 1984).

What are the implications of this moral rule for resource conservation? Norton stresses the need to utilize renewable resources according to maximum sustainable yield. Non-renewable resources can be used if substitutes are developed to keep the resource base constant. Preservation should be understood in the context of natural variety, not only of single species, and it is best brought about in large preservation areas. Furthermore, the environment must be compensated for the losses we have brought about. The growth in the world population must be adjusted at a level that is consistent with the resource base. Thus Norton does not restrict the scale of mankind − the levels of population and economic growth can be as large as possible on a sustainable basis.

Taylor rejects the anthropocentric approach and develops a biocentric theory of the Earth's community of life. His ethics concern individuals, and he considers animals and plants individuals as well as humans. He distinguishes between the good of a being and its inherent worth. The good of a being is what can be said to be good for it without any reference to other entities. Every being that has a good of its own is inherently worthy. Thus, human beings are not the only individuals that have inherent worth. The moral community includes all such entities and all have to be treated with respect. This attitude of respect forms the basis of biocentric ethics. Once we accept that animal and plant individuals must be considered from a moral point of view, we arrive at the world view of biocentric ethics, which denies the human being the status of the master of the universe. This insistence on equality classifies Taylor's ethics as egalitarian biocentrism. Biocentric ethics also enlarges the concept of future generations to include future animal and plant individuals. The role of future generations differs, however, from the status they are given in anthropocentrism. Biocentrists do not need future generations as an argument for preservation. Nevertheless, they must be treated equally (Taylor 1983).

Taylor suggests some principles for governing situations in which the interests of humans and non-humans clash. These principles cut across the domain of human and environmental ethics, being consistent with the requirement of species-impartiality. Human beings can protect themselves against dangerous or harmful organisms (the principle of self-defence). The principle of proportionality requires that if our non-basic interests, which are incompatible with respect for nature, conflict with the basic interests of non-humans, priority should be given to the latter.[2] The principle of minimum wrong must be applied when our non-basic interests, which are compatible with respect for nature, conflict with the basic interests of non-humans. According to this, we may pursue non-basic interests only by doing minimum wrong to non-humans. In addition, some compensation must be provided to wild animals and plants for the wrong that has been caused. The principle of distribution dictates that when the interests of the parties are all basic and there exists a natural source of good that can be used for the benefit of any party, each party must be allotted an equal share.

Taylor sets the following norm as the criterion of biocentric ethics: man acts morally correctly when he abstains from unnecessary influence on the environment. This formulation allows the fulfilment of the basic interests of humans, but places strict conditions on pursuing non-basic interests which lead to tight rules for conservation and preservation. Renewable resources must be used as little as possible, and it is preferable to use plants rather than animals. Non-renewable resources should be used wisely and with care. The environment should be polluted as little as possible. The number of areas devoted to preservation both as compensation and due to respect for nature should be increased (Taylor 1989). These rules indicate very clearly the need to restrict the scale of the global economy whenever possible.

## 2. Two Interpretations of Sustainable Development

The programme of sustainable growth economics may be obtained by putting an ecological constraint (constant capital rule) on a neoclassical approach (Pearce and Turner 1990; see also Common and Perrings 1990; Klaassen and Opschoor 1991). Another way is to redefine the social welfare function to ensure sustainability. Sustainable steady-state economics is based on this approach (Daly 1989, 1990; Daly and Cobb 1989). Both ways of defining sustainable development represent a response to the three important values (environmental ethics, future generations and relationship to the satisfaction of needs).

*The programme of sustainable growth economics*

There are, in fact, three different formulations for the constant capital rule of sustainable growth economics. Following the distinction given in Turner (1992) I will start with very weak sustainability.

1.  *Very weak sustainability rule*
    Maximize social welfare so that the sum of man-made, human and natural capital is constant (Victor 1991).

This rule is an extreme neoclassical version of sustainability. It allows man to substitute the man-made capital for the whole of nature, which leads inevitably to the extinction of certain species which do not decrease the sum of all forms of capital. It may even threaten the life-support system if the summing of capital does not reflect the crucial thresholds of nature.[3] The rule is, therefore, an unsatisfactory interpretation of sustainable development. It corresponds with the strong anthropocentric attitude which does not guarantee the preservation of nature and species. Thus the neoclassical approach must be enlarged by some truly ecological rule.

2.  *Weak sustainability rule*
    Maximize social welfare so that the amount of natural capital necessary for the life-supporting system of the earth is non-decreasing, and the sum of man-made and non-critical natural capital is constant (Pearce and Turner 1990).

This definition has a tight rule for the use of critical, non-substitutable natural capital, but it allows some substitution between non-critical natural and man-made capital. The rule does not explicitly limit the scale of the economy but it facilitates the adjustment of economic growth in an ecological direction. How do we know what is necessary for a life-support system (critical capital)? We cannot know for certain. Any judgment has to make use of all available biological information; it has to rely on the environmental preferences of agents; and finally, it has to take environmental uncertainty seriously into account by the use of a safe minimum standard. Therefore, the rule includes both empirical and judgmental elements. It is not normative *a priori*, but *a posteriori*. As things change, the definition of sustainable development changes, too. Nevertheless, the definition helps cost-benefit analysis to account for risks and future generations, since it requires compensation if the use of any resource is increased (Pearce and Turner 1990).

There are, however, some problems with the weak sustainability rule. It relies on the use of the contingent valuation method which is unable to take many uncertainties and irreversibilities in the environment adequately into account (Victor *et al.* 1994, Hanley and Spash 1993). It is also unable to observe the 'ecosystem primary value', that is the prior value of the aggregate ecosystem structure and its life-supporting capacity (Turner 1992). For these reasons Turner proposes a rule for strong sustainability, which he calls – misleadingly – the Ecological Economics Approach.

3.  *Strong sustainability rule*
    Maximize social welfare so that the amount of critical and non-critical natural capital is constant and the amount of man-made capital is non-decreasing (Turner 1992).

According to Turner, this formulation overcomes the problems of rule 2 because it is monitored and measured via physical indicators. His formulation has, however, some logical problems. Even though he makes the distinction between critical and non-critical natural capital, he requires that the non-critical capital, too, must be non-decreasing. Suppose that renewable resources are used in a sustainable way, but very close to the point of extinction. How sustainable is this? Further, assume a previously unused renewable population in its maximum steady-state size. According to the rule, one is not allowed to use it at all. Similar problems can be found with non-renewable resources. In order to allow their use, some substitution must be accepted. Thus, the formulation of strong sustainability fails to be meaningful despite its good intention.

As Turner's analysis shows, the neoclassical approach with an ecological constraint can thus lead to the weak sustainability rule (rule 2) for sustainable growth economy. What are the feasible rules for conservation in this programme? These are often devised by resorting to the familiar basic results of neoclassical resource and environmental economics (Common and Perrings 1992). For renewable resources, there is the Golden Rule of Resource Conservation (fisheries) and the Faustmann Rule (forests). These state that the optimal sustainable use of a resource differs slightly from its maximum sustainable yield under a positive interest rate. If the interest rate is zero and harvesting costs zero, the optimum harvest is the maximum sustainable yield.

Two rules also govern the use of non-renewable resources. The Hotelling Rule gives the conditions for their efficient extraction. The Hartwick Rule suggests how much capital must be accumulated to substitute for non-renewable resources in production. According to these rules, society first uses the best and the richest deposits and accumulates man-made and human capital with the intention of creating favourable conditions for substituting capital for resources and developing better technology (Dasgupta and Heal 1979). Pollution control is based on optimization or cost-efficiency. (Note that this approach may, sometimes, lead to even more stringent control than the critical load would require.) Rules for the preservation of species and biodiversity are based on existence, bequest and option values. These aspects of total economic value have to be taken into account as development costs in every project.

The programme of sustainable economic growth acknowledges that the price mechanism does not reflect the environmental impact of various economic decisions. Environmental impact must therefore be included in the price system, and the goal of this new price mechanism is to promote recycling, substitution and the development of environment-saving technology. The impact of this mechanism relies on the assumption that it is now profitable for consumers and producers to protect the environment.

## The sustainable steady-state economy

The notion of the steady-state society dates back to John Stuart Mill, who stressed keeping the population constant so that people could enjoy their solitude and the amenities of nature. Mill's ideas were seized on much later, in the 1960s, when Boulding and Daly incorporated them into thermodynamics, which was introduced into economics by Georgescu-Roegen (1971). Steady-state thinking stresses that the throughput of materials and energy in society must be minimized. The reason for this lies in thermodynamics, as the law of entropy implies that increasing the use of natural resources leads to exhaustion and pollution problems.[4] Thermodynamic thinking is at the heart of ecological economics, even though there are alternative ways to formulate the theories (Klaassen and Opschoor 1991, Opschoor and Van der Straaten 1993 or Swaney 1988).

4. *The very strong sustainability rule*
   Minimize the materials and energy flow through society for a given welfare and man-made capital.

Society aims at satisfying its basic needs using as few materials and as little energy as possible. This rule is often described as the zero-growth position. That is not, however, an accurate description. According to the definition, requiring ecological production is not enough, we must also consider the scale of the economy. Physical production is not allowed to grow at all, and the influence of man on nature must diminish when we have resource- and pollution-saving technical progress.

Daly formulates the following rules for conservation and preservation (Daly 1990). Renewable resources should be used according to the maximum sustainable yield rule, which simultaneously defines the optimum size of populations independently of prices. Non-renewable resources can be used provided that the resource base is kept constant and that society promotes resource-saving technical progress. Most importantly, the amount of renewable resources must be increased at the rate of decline in non-renewable resources. Pollution must be diminished to the level that corresponds with the critical load that the environment can sustain.

Daly does not explicitly describe how to ensure the preservation of the wilderness and other natural areas. There is, however, a hint in rule four, which could push his thinking forward. If society follows the diminishing scale of its influence on the earth, more and more nature will be left intact. This programme leads to ever-increasing preservation and the decreasing influence of man on nature.

The basic means of promoting the programme of a sustainable society are thermodynamic efficiency and institutional changes that are favourable to the environment (Daly 1990). The price mechanism is not regarded as central, as in the programme of sustainable economic growth. Nevertheless, it may be acceptable if it promotes conservation goals. For example, Ayres and Kneese stress the need for price as a control for pollution (1989), whereas Swaney accepts the use of such pricing only if it constitutes institutionally progressive reform (1988), an opinion which is shared by Opschoor and Van der Straaten (1993).

## 3. Combining Ethics and Economics

The rules of weak and very strong sustainability represent neoclassical and institutional approaches, and are worth further study. What is the relationship between these approaches and theories of environmental ethics? Can we argue that they are economic presentations of weak anthropocentric or biocentric ethics? If so, are the definitions accurate enough to be considered feasible economic programmes for such ethics?

### *Sustainable growth economy as a weak anthropocentrist programme*

The basic features of sustainable growth economy and weak anthropocentrism are given in two columns in *Table 3.1* on page 50. Weak anthropocentrism required the current generation to keep the resource base constant for future generations. The weak sustainability rule does the same through its constraint on economic growth for three reasons. Firstly, it has an anthropocentric basis. Secondly, future generations are taken into account through a constant critical natural capital base. Finally, economic growth is allowed to satisfy needs, which is compatible with Norton's maxim as set out above. Thus, neoclassical sustainable growth economy belongs to the set of possible economic interpretations of weak anthropocentrism.

The question remains whether the programme of sustainable growth economy contains rules for conservation, preservation and pollution control that are compatible with weak anthropocentrism. This is one way of testing whether the economic programme is consistent. A look at *Table 3.1* reveals that there is a difference between rules A and A' for renewable resources. How important is the difference between maximum sustainable yield and some other level? In most cases it is of no importance, but in some rare instances it may be considerably so. For example, what is the solution when the extinction of a renewable resource is socially optimal due to a certain price and growth structure (see Clark 1989, 35)? There is no answer to this in the neoclassical programme, unless the resource happens to belong to critical natural capital. One is, of course, tempted to say that, due to the application of existence and option values, extinction is not allowed in the case of non-critical natural capital, but the interplay of these two approaches has not been thought through in this formulation.

Rules B and B' are similar in spirit, and here the programme of sustainable growth economy offers economic insight to explain how to guarantee the condition. Rules C and C' appear to be different, but are in fact very similar. The economic formulations B' and C' just pick up the optimal solutions from the larger set of sustainable outcomes. The greatest difference between economic and ethical formulations is in preservation. Norton explicitly denies this way of approaching preservation. He argues that those concepts are not operational, they focus on wrong entities (particular species instead of biodiversity), and omit important aspects of preservation. Thus he would not give this rule the status of weak anthropocentrism.

*Sustainable steady-state economy as a biocentric programme*

The programme of steady-state economy as related to Taylor's biocentric theory is illustrated in *Table 3.2* on page 51. The test or criterion for truly biocentric ethics was man's abstaining from influencing the environment whenever it was not absolutely necessary. Man is allowed to influence nature for his basic needs, and in some cases under very stringent conditions for non-basic needs, provided that nature is compensated. The very strong sustainability rule fits very well with the biocentric maxim. It captures brilliantly the spirit of biocentric thinking through decreasing the scale of the economy. Taylor and some other biocentrists have noticed this correspondence, as they mention Daly's ideas as a good application of biocentric ideas in economics (see for example Taylor 1989, 258, and Attfield 1991, 195). Thus, the programme of steady-state economy belongs to the scope of Taylor's definition. Consequently, the very strong sustainability rule automatically satisfies the interests of future generations of human beings and other living organisms.

Let us check whether Daly's formulations for the rules of conservation and preservation correspond coherently with the biocentric outlook. A comparison of formulations E-H and E'-H' reveals some interesting points. There seems to be

*Table 3.1: Ethical and economic programmes for sustainable development: anthropocentrism*

| Moral rule of weak anthropocentrism: | The weak sustainability rule: |
|---|---|
| It is the duty of every generation to sustain a steady flow of natural and environmental resources over an infinite time horizon. | Maximize social welfare so that the amount of natural capital necessary for the life-supporting system of the earth is constant, and the amount of the sum of man-made and natural capital is non-decreasing. |
| A. Renewable resources should be used at the level of maximum sustainable yield. | A' Renewable resources should be used at an economically sustainable level, which differs from maximum sustainable yield under a positive interest rate. |
| B. Non-renewable resources may be used if, by discovering substitutes, we can keep the resource base constant. | B'. Nonrenewable resources should be used efficiently and capital must be accumulated to substitute for nonrenewable resources in production. |
| C. Pollution should not exceed the amount that the natural environment can assimilate. | C'. Pollution should be controlled to the point where its marginal benefits are equal to its marginal damage. |
| D. Preserve natural variety and biodiversity and compensate nature for damages. | D'. In order to ensure preservation, the irreversibility of nature and its existence, bequest and option values have to be taken into account. |

both a considerable similarity and a major difference between Taylor and Daly. The similarity lies in the stress on biological, instead of economic, criteria. This means that conservation and preservation do not depend on human preferences but on nature itself – just as biocentrism requires. The difference arises from the fact that Daly relies on constant biological sustainability criteria, which are not strict enough for biocentric ethics or for the very strong sustainability rule. This becomes clear in formulations E and E'. He defines maximum sustainable yield as the proper guide for the use of renewable resources, whereas Taylor wishes an ever greater proportion of resources to be kept intact. One way of stressing the difference is to say that Daly does not take the need for the ever-diminishing influence of man on earth seriously into account. The same holds for nonrenewable resources and pollution in formulations F' and G'. The rule for preservation is difficult to evaluate, because Daly does not formulate it explicitly. Taylor insists on increasing preservation because of compensation and distributive

*Table 3.2: Ethical and economic programmes for sustainable development: biocentrism*

| Moral rule of biocentric ethics: | Very strong sustainability rule: |
|---|---|
| Man acts morally correctly when he abstains from unnecessary influence on the environment. | Minimize materials and energy flow through society for a given social welfare and man-made capital. |
| E. Use the minimum amount of renewable resources; instead of animals use plants. | E'. Renewable resources should be used according to the maximum sustainable yield rule. |
| F. Use non-renewable resources in diminishing amounts, wisely and with care. | F'. Nonrenewable resources may be used provided that the resource base is kept constant through substitution and that society promotes resource- saving technical progress. |
| G. Pollute the environment as little as possible. | G'. Pollution must be diminished to the level that corresponds with the critical load that the environment can sustain. |
| H. Increase the areas for preservation both as compensation and due to respect for nature. | H'. Preservation – open. |

justice. If one assumes that society will consistently follow the very strong sustainability rule, technical progress allows increasing preservation by diminishing the influence of man on the earth. In its present stage, however, the programme of steady-state economy has been formulated inconsistently with the very strong sustainability rule.

## 4. Comparison of the programmes discussed

The above analysis has revealed an astonishing similarity between the two strands of environmental ethics and environmental economics. Neoclassical and ecological economic approaches to sustainable development seem to rely quite heavily on weak anthropocentric and biocentric ethics. Due to differing values, these approaches end up with differing rules for conservation and preservation. This section advances the analysis further by addressing three questions. First, is ecological economics necessarily biocentric in its values? (It should be obvious, thus far, that the neoclassical approach is anthropocentric.) Second, why do all environmental economists encounter difficulties in their approach to the preservation of species and biodiversity? Third, is one approach to sustainable development superior to the other?

First, we have seen that steady-state thinking, when taken seriously, is very close to biocentric ethics. Even though its rules contain some contradictions with its very strong sustainability requirement, there seems to be no principal obstacle to a more accurate formulation. (I think, however, that the steady-state programme has to be articulated more clearly on this question.) Are all theories of ecological economics biocentric? The answer is, not necessarily, even though we have found one common feature in ecological economics and biocentric ethics: the stress on biological rather than economic rules for conservation. This follows from the consideration of the linkages between ecosystems and economic systems (see Martinez Alier, Chapter 2 above).

There seem, in fact, to be two alternatives for ecological economics. One is to accept the very strong sustainability rule with its implication of diminishing scale and constant material welfare and to adopt the biocentric position fully. This position requires a reformulation of the rules for conservation in the way indicated in the previous section. The other possibility is to reject the very strong sustainability rule and to adopt only the requirement of the constant use of natural resources. Under resources-saving technical progress, this position implies growing material welfare. It brings ecological economics closer to weak anthropocentrism. Klaassen and Opschoor (1991) noticed the existence of this kind of tension between Daly and Norgaard. More serious discussion among ecological economists is needed to clarify this point further.

Looking at the environmental values sheds new light on the old debate on biological versus economic/efficient criteria for conservation. The use of biological criteria in defining sustainable development stems from respect for nature and the need to ensure that conservation is not a function of human preferences. This is also supported in the findings of Common and Perrings (1992), whose study on the neoclassical approach revealed that intertemporal efficient prices are not necessary for sustainability, and that consumer sovereignty is incompatible with sustainability. Thus, neither neglecting the opportunity cost of money held in natural resources nor losing some economic efficiency has been at the heart of the debate. Taking nature seriously has.

Second, ethicists are quite critical towards the way preservation is dealt with in environmental economics, regardless of the approach in question. This is not to deny that preservation always entails economic aspects, but the issue is not dealt with in a satisfactory way. The problems of the neoclassical approach in guaranteeing preservation became clear in the analysis in the previous section. This seriously undermines its intention to follow weak anthropocentrism. Neither has the steady-state approach much to say about preservation. Why is that? One answer could be the problems in combining ethics and economics here. Should we simply admit that – as Mark Sagoff argues – people act in the preservation business as citizens not consumers, and preservation is basically an ethical decision which can be executed with the help of economics (Sagoff 1988)?

Third, are we able to maintain that one programme is superior in content to the other? The problem with comparison, of course, is that both programmes are incommensurable in values. To say more, one has to compare the negative growth position with an environmentally constrained positive growth position. In order to ensure the non-deterioration of the environment, both approaches should guarantee that i) the level of the material cycle between nature and the environment is adjusted to the assimilative and growth capacity of nature, ii) the tendency of markets to overuse resources is changed, and iii) human knowledge and technologies are developed enough to effect the substitution of exhaustible resources.

Because of diminishing scales, the ecological economics approach can achieve sustainability more easily than the positive growth position. However, this is said to be too narrow a view for judgment. The point of sustainable development is to solve environmental and social problems at the same time. What, then, is the correct balance between fighting against poverty, starvation and unemployment, and saving the environment? It is often argued that negative growth necessarily increases social problems and therefore a growth position should be accepted at least in the South – and perhaps to some extent also in the North. Steady-state thinking denies this argument and stresses constant growth as a global economic strategy. The North should thus save the required amounts as the South grows (Goodland and Daly 1993).

## Notes

1. I have benefitted from helpful comments made by the economists Markus Jäntti, Klaus Kultti, Richard Norgaard, Jan van der Straaten, Kerry Turner and Andrew Tylecote; the methodologists Bengt Hamminga, Tony Lawson, Uskali Mäki and Jorma Sappinen; and the ethicist Robin Attfield. Financial support from the Alfred Kordelin Foundation is gratefully acknowledged.
2. Basic interests are what rational, enlightened people value as an essential part of their very existence as persons and include subsistence, security, autonomy and liberty, which are universal values, common to all. Non-basic interests are the particular ends we consider worth seeking and the means we consider best for achieving them, that is what makes our individual value systems.
3. Assume that society sums up the values of man-made and natural capital. Problems may emerge even in the case of exhaustible resources. Anthony Fisher proved that technical progress may decrease extraction costs to the extent that they offset the increase in royalty. The market price may be stable although the resources may actually be near exhaustion.
4. The co-evolutionary approach suggests the following rule: sustain the productivity, stability and resilience of managed and natural ecosystems for a given welfare and man-made capital (Norgaard 1984).

## References

Attfield, R. (1991), *The Ethics of Environmental Concern*. Second Edition. Athens: Georgia University Press and Oxford: Basil Blackwell.

Ayres, R. and Kneese, A. (1989), 'Externalities: Economics and Thermodynamics', in F. Archibugi, and P. Nijkamp, (eds.), *Economy and Ecology: Towards Sustainable Development*, Dordrecht: Kluwer Academic Publishers.

Boulding, K. (1968), 'The economics of the coming spaceship earth', reprinted in H. Daly, (ed.) (1973), *Toward a Steady-State Economy*, San Francisco: W.H. Freeman and Co.

Brundtland, G.H. (1987), *Our Common Future*, Oxford: Oxford University Press

Clark, C. (1990), *Mathematical Bioeconomics*. 2nd ed. New York: John Wiley & Sons.

Common, M. and Perrings C. (1992), 'Towards an ecological economics of sustainability', *Ecological Economics* **6**: 7-34.

Daly, H. (1989), Steady-State and Growth Concepts for the Next Century, in F. Archibugi and P. Nijkamp, *Economy and Ecology: Towards Sustainable Development*. Dordrecht: Kluwer Academic Publishers.

Daly, H. (1990), 'Toward some operational principles of sustainable development', *Ecological Economics* **2**, 1-6.

Daly, H. and Cobb, J. (1989), *For the Common Good: Redirecting the Economy Toward Community, the Environment and a Sustainable Future*, London: Green Print.

Dasgupta, P. and Heal, G. (1979), *Economic Theory and Exhaustible Resources*, Cambridge, UK: Cambridge University Press.

Georgescu-Roegen, N. (1971), *The Entropy Law and Economic Process*, Cambridge MA: Harvard University Press.

Goodland, R. and Daly, H. (1993), 'Why Northern income growth is not the solution to Southern poverty', Ecological Economics **8**, 85-101.

Hanley, N. and Spash, C. (1993), *Cost-benefit Analysis and the Environment*, Aldershot: Edward Elgar.

Klaassen, G. A. and Opschoor, J. B. (1991), 'Economics of sustainability or the sustainability of economics: different paradigms', *Ecological Economics* **4**, 93-115.

Norgaard, R. (1984), 'Coevolutionary Agricultural Development', *Economic Development and Cultural Change* **32**, 525-46.

Norton, B. (1984), 'Environmental Ethics and Weak Anthropocentrism', *Environmental Ethics* **6**, 131-48.

Norton, B. (1987), *Why Preserve Natural Variety?* Princeton: Princeton University Press.

Opschoor, H. and van der Straaten, J. (1993), 'Sustainable development: an institutional approach', *Ecological Economics* **7**, 203-22.

Pearce, D. and Turner, K. (1990), *Economics of Natural Resources and the Environment*, London: Harvester Wheatsheaf.

Sagoff, M. (1988), *The Economy of the Earth*, Cambridge: Cambridge University Press.

Swanye, J. (1988), 'Trading Water: Market Extension, Social Improvement, or What'. *Journal of Economic Issues* **22**, 33-47.

Taylor, P. (1983), 'In Defence of Biocentrism', *Environmental Ethics* **5**, 237-43.

Taylor, P. (1989), *Respect for Nature. A Theory of Environmental Ethics*, Princeton: Princeton University Press.

Turner, K. (1992), 'Speculations on Weak and Strong Sustainability', *CSERGE (Centre for Social and Economic Research on the Global Environment) Working Paper GEC (global environmental change)* no. 92-26.

Victor P. (1991), 'Indicators of sustainable development: some lesson from capital theory', *Ecological Economics* **4**, 191-213.

Victor P., E. Hanna and A. Kubursi (1994), 'How Strong is Weak Sustainability?' *Paper in the Conference on Models of Sustainable Development*, Paris.

# 4.    Economic Growth and the Environment – or the Extinction of the GDP-Dinosaur

**Inge Røpke**

## Introduction

Market economies are fundamentally characterized by economic growth. Growth rates may be higher or lower, but the GDP seldom stagnates or diminishes – and when it does, this is considered a symptom of crisis. During the past few decades environmental problems have caused increasing concern and, as a consequence, it has been questioned whether an ever-increasing GDP is compatible with overall environmental improvement. The prevailing answer is clearly affirmative, and the adherents of this position can refer to very influential sources. First of all, the Brundtland Report from 1987 states that economic growth in industrial countries is necessary both to combat environmental problems and to improve the conditions of life in developing countries. Since then, some of the main international economic organizations have dealt with the question. Examples are the OECD report *The State of the Environment* from 1991, the GATT report *International Trade 90–91* with a special section on trade and environment, and the World Bank's 'World Development Report 1992' focusing on development and the environment. All these organizations defend the position that economic growth in industrial countries is compatible with environmental improvements and the reduction of global inequality.

The present chapter argues that this prevailing position is wrong. However, the contrasting position – that economic growth is necessarily damaging – is also wrong. Consequently, if we seriously want to address environmental problems, we will have to develop different terms and to manoeuvre in the direction of other goals than growth in the GDP. The argument will be set out on two levels.

First, the arguments, especially those of the World Bank, will be considered directly on their own terms. Second, the conventional use of concepts will be questioned on a theoretical level. In the present situation, with an urgent need for reorientation, some very old discussions about the foundations of economic theory regain relevance. This chapter will thus re-examine questions such as: what have we got at our disposal as a result of our economic activity, and what are the costs?

## 1. The Relationship between GDP and the Environment

In conventional reasoning about the relationship between the GDP and the environment, the GDP is often conceived as a 'pie'. Using the pie metaphor implies the idea that the greater the pie, the more we have at our disposal, for instance, for environmental purposes (or for improving the conditions of the poor). However, the environmental effects of the 'GDP-pie' are determined to a large degree in the process of 'baking' it – only some effects can be determined afterwards. The composition of the GDP is crucial for the environmental impact, because different sectors of production have very different impacts on the environment, and because the usefulness of the output in relation to environmental improvements can vary.

Disregarding the possible uses of the GDP, the World Bank (1992) summarizes the relationship between the production of GDP and the quality of the environment in the following formula (p. 39):

| scale | | output | | input- | | environ. | | quality |
|-------|---|-----------|---|------------|---|-----------|---|-------------|
| of the | x | structure | x | output | x | damage | = | of the |
| economy | | | | efficiency | | per unit | | environment |
| | | | | | | of input | | |

The formula demonstrates that the size of the GDP (the scale of the economy) is only one of the factors determining the impact on the environment from production in a given period (to be more precise the last term should have been *change in* the quality of the environment). The output structure is crucial, because for instance production of steel and chemicals put more strain on the environment than child care and education. The importance of the input–output efficiency is dramatically illustrated by the different energy intensities per unit of production in a given sector in Eastern Europe and Western Europe, respectively. Lastly, the importance of the environmental damage per unit of input can be exemplified by the difference between the use of lignite and oil for the same purpose – Eastern Europe again providing a frightening example.[1] From a static point of view, it is thus obvious that a GDP of a given size can entail very different environmental impacts - and that a larger GDP may be less damaging than a smaller one.

A more complicated problem, however, arises when the point of view is dynamic: what will happen to environmental quality when the scale of the economy grows? Will the factors that tend to reduce environmental damage per unit of activity more than compensate for any negative consequences of the overall growth in scale? The World Bank answers the questions rather optimistically: if we develop our economic and environmental policies carefully, we can encourage efficiency in resource use, substitution of scarce resources, development of cleaner technologies reducing emissions and waste, and structural changes that reduce environmental stress. As empirical evidence, the Bank refers to an OECD report (1991) that states 'Industrial countries have achieved substantial improvements in environmental quality along with continued economic growth' (The World Bank 1992, p. 40). The statement is supported by examples: air quality in OECD countries has vastly improved since 1970 because emissions of particulates, lead and sulphur oxides have decreased. Another example is the reduction of persistant pollutants such as DDT, PCB and mercury compounds. This conforms quite well with two observations in Meadows *et al.* (1992): environmental regulation has had its greatest successes with regard to poisonous substances that have been prohibited outright (p. 89), and Western countries have succeeded in keeping some of the more visible problems within reasonable limits (p. 90). This is of course positive and a much better situation than in Eastern Europe, but, unfortunately, this only describes a small part of the situation.

In all fairness, the World Bank mentions that the OECD report 'also identified a large "unfinished agenda" of environmental problems, as well as emerging issues, that remain to be addressed' (The World Bank 1992, p. 40). Examples are increasing municipal waste, human exposure to toxic pollutants, $CO_2$ emissions, groundwater pollution, soil degradation and reduced biodiversity. However, these examples do not affect the World Bank's main conclusion that the link between growth and environmental degradation can be broken. Emphasizing this conclusion seems to be unduly optimistic. Comparing the diminishing problems with the growing ones discloses that we are coping with some of the local and visible problems while some of the growing problems are of a much more global and irreversible character. Furthermore, the stock character of some of the problems has to be considered: even if the yearly emissions of a substance have lessened, the accumulated problem will increase –

if the increase is not offset by technical changes and/or natural forces, which is rarely the case.

The optimism of the World Bank contrasts sharply with the conclusions of Meadows *et al.* (1992). Some of the observations from Meadows *et al.* can illuminate the formula shown above in a more detailed manner than is done by the Bank. Take first of all the output structure. Growth optimists often suggest that industrial countries are being transformed into information and service economies and, consequently, the demand for material resources and the related pollution problems will decrease. However, this is not so certain. Certainly, the relative shares of the GDP are changing, and services are increasing at the expense of industry and agriculture, but industry and agriculture are still increasing in absolute terms (p. 36). Furthermore, services are not only information-intensive: they often depend upon a significant input of material resources. One example is the use of computers, where rapid technological development entails correspondingly rapid scrapping of obsolete equipment. In addition, some service activities such as transport are very energy-intensive. Thus, we cannot be sure that changing output structure will sufficiently offset the negative environmental impact of increasing the scale of the economy.

Related to the problem of output structure, it should be stressed that, from a global point of view, it is no solution that a given country changes its output structure in a less damaging direction, if, simultaneously, it imports environmentally damaging products from other countries – no matter where the damage occurs. It is thus more relevant to focus on the environmental impact of the consumption of a given country rather than its production. This will give a more realistic measure of the damage that this country is responsible for.

The factor 'environmental damage per unit of input' does not offer a very promising perspective either. Meadows *et al.* (1992) present evidence to show that this might change in the wrong direction. For example, the extraction of resources becomes increasingly complicated when more marginal deposits are used: the quality of ores deteriorates (the percentage of metal falls) and so more energy is required to extract resources, and more waste will be produced in the process (pp. 86, 116, 87).

Consequently, much faith has to be put in the last factor, input–output efficiency, to offset the scale problem. Although Meadows *et al.*, are aware of many recent improvements based on cleaning technology or cleaner technologies, they emphasize that these have been overtaken by simultaneously growing quantities of production, transport activities and so on. Better results might be obtained in the future, but technological change is a mixed blessing, and the two factors in the problem, technology and scale, are interdependent. As mentioned above, introduction of more efficient equipment often entails scrapping much technically obsolete equipment, and introduction of new products encourages consumption. Technical change thus stimulates growth, which undermines some of its positive environmental effects. On the other hand, growth may be a prerequisite for technical change, so the relations between technical change and economic growth are complex and cannot be satisfactorily dealt with here. It must suffice to say that it is in no way certain that improving input–output efficiency will offset the scale problem.

The formula introduced by the World Bank is a helpful device in discussing the relations between growth and the environmental impact. It is, however, limited to the flow discussion, while some of the most important environmental problems are stock-based. For example, emissions of CFC not only have to be delinked from economic growth, but have to be abandoned altogether if the ozone hole is to be reduced – otherwise the ozone layer will continue to be destroyed, only more slowly. To elaborate on the relationship between economic growth and the environment would thus presuppose stock-based accounts of the environmental situation, and the environmental effects of the GDP as a whole would have to be included.

Furthermore, the perspective of the World Bank should be broadened to include the output side of the GDP, as environmental effects are not only related to the production of the GDP, but to the use of the output as well. Two considerations are relevant here. The first relates to the environmental effects of products *in use* and when they appear as waste. In principle, these effects could be covered by the World Bank formula, if the term 'environmental damage per unit of input' is given a very broad interpretation including effects produced during the whole lifecycle of the products or services provided. However, this interpretation takes the formula a long way from its focus on production processes, and it seems more reasonable to emphasize the need to supplement this focus with all the other effects from cradle to grave, including such things as private transportation, energy use in households and so on. The second consideration applies a kind of investment perspective by focusing on what the products can be used for: some products are helpful in reducing environmental problems, while others add to the problems. The environmental situation might thus be improved if alternatives to polluting technologies are produced. Fossil fuels could be replaced by renewable energy sources and energy-saving equipment, which means that the GDP would have to include windmills, solar cells, insulating materials and so on. Correspondingly, the production of soil-cleaning services could reduce accumulated problems from the past. On the other hand, the production of energy-consuming devices may entail increasing environmental problems over time.

To illuminate the relationship between economic growth and the environment, the World Bank formula thus has to be qualified in at least three important respects. First of all, the stock problems have to be taken into account, secondly, the output side should be included, and thirdly, when the discussion is on the national level, trade relations are relevant, because the environmental 'balance of payments' might be in surplus or deficit. These considerations – related both to the formula and the supplementary qualifications – add up to a serious question, whether it is at all meaningful to discuss the relationship between growth in GDP and the environment. The only reason for doing this seems to be the idolatry of the GDP. Politicians, economists and statisticians cling to the GDP as a well-defined concept and to the idea that this measure must grow to keep the economy healthy and to raise our standards of living. When environmental concerns enter the agenda, it consequently becomes of paramount importance to show that these two aims can be attained simultaneously. However, the arguments end in a complicated web from which the only means of escape is ideology. If environmental concerns are to be taken seriously, we should stop discussing the growth and environment issue and replace it with the elaboration of more relevant ways of conceiving the problems.

## 2. Critique of the GDP Concept

The GDP is the focal point of much economic and political debate. This focus is based on the idea that the GDP is somehow a measure of what we have at our disposal – as suggested in the pie metaphor. This measure is also seen as an important determinant of our welfare – otherwise it would be of no interest. A theoretical discussion of the GDP comes close to fundamental questions of economic theory, such as:

- What do we have at our disposal?
- What are the costs of providing this?

These two questions will be the main focus of the rest of the paper.

In the environmental debate, the GDP has been heavily criticized for not representing a relevant measure of what we have at our disposal (see for example Hueting 1990, Tinbergen and Hueting 1992). The main problem is confusing ends with means, that is some of the contributions to the GDP should be counted as costs not gains. For example:

- When exhaustible resources are extracted, the sales increase GDP although natural capital is reduced.
- Car driving entails heavy costs such as hospital treatment which are added to the GDP.
- Industrial and agricultural production pollute the environment and impair the conditions for production in future. However, these effects do not enter the accounts, except in the case of restoration, where the activities add to GDP.

In the formal definition of the GDP, only final consumption counts and all costs should be subtracted. As environmental costs cannot be seen as final consumption, current GDP accounting obviously does not even reflect what it is intended to; thus the attempts to 'correct' national income accounting taking place in many countries and in the UN.

Another critical perspective is raised by researchers studying developing countries, who have stressed the importance of all the informal economic activities that are not counted in GDP. An increase in GDP could conceal a deterioration of welfare, if the increase is based on a shift of activities from informal to formal sectors of the economy.

The flaws of the GDP from an environmental point of view are related to the pre-analytic vision of traditional economics (Daly 1991, p. 14ff.). In this basic vision, economic activities take place in a circuit, where households and producers exchange factors of production and products for money, and the natural environment is, in fact, absent. Herman Daly[2] replaces this vision with another describing the economy as an open subsystem of a greater ecological system (the globe) that is materially closed, but exchanges energy with the outside. In this description it is obvious that we are ultimately dependent on natural resources and on the capacity of the environment to absorb our waste. Based on this premise, Daly elaborates some concepts that differ fundamentally from those related to the GDP. Daly's theoretical apparatus is inspired by Irving Fischer's concepts of capital and income: capital

> is the stock of material objects owned by human beings at an instant of time. Income is the flow of service through a period of time that is yielded by capital. Capital includes the inventory of all consumer goods and human bodies, as well as producer goods. Income is ultimately psychic income, subjective satisfactions that come through the want-satisfying services rendered by the human body and all of its material extensions, which together constitute the stock of capital (Daly 1991, p. 32).

Based on this, Daly defines three basic magnitudes (pp. 35ff.):

- The final benefit of economic activity is to provide service. '*Service* is the satisfaction experienced when wants are satisfied' (that is 'psychic income' above). Service is a flux, not a flow, since it cannot be accumulated.
- Service is yielded by the stock. '*Stock* is the total inventory of producers' goods, consumers' goods and human bodies', that is, 'all physical things capable of satisfying human wants and subject to ownership'.
- The stock is maintained and renewed by the *throughput*, which is the physical flow of matter and energy 'from nature's sources, through the human economy, and back to nature's sinks'. Throughput is the ultimate cost of economic activity.

In principle, Daly's concepts give a clear answer to the two questions raised at the beginning of this section. At our disposal we have the services that can be yielded by the existing stock, and the cost is the throughput that is needed to maintain and renew the stock. With these concepts, the critique of the GDP can be expressed more precisely: the concept is too muddled, because

> it adds together three very unlike categories: throughput, additions to capital stock, and services rendered by the capital stock. It makes no sense to add together costs, benefits, and changes in capital stock. It is as if a firm were to add up its receipts, its expenditures, and its change of net worth. What sense should any accountant make of such a sum? (p. 30).

These matters are crucial from an environmental point of view. As the human economy is a subsystem of a materially closed ecosystem, we have to keep the economy within some limits to avoid a breakdown. Daly suggests that we choose levels of stocks (people and artifacts) that are sufficient for a good life and sustainable for a long future. Within this steady-state economy, economic aspirations should concentrate on maximizing the service to be obtained from the given stocks and minimizing the throughput necessary to maintain them. In the formula:

$$\frac{service}{throughput} = \frac{service}{stock} \times \frac{stock}{throughput}$$

$$(1) \qquad\qquad (2) \qquad\qquad (3)$$

this means improving both service efficiency (2) and maintenance efficiency (3).

Summing up, the GDP is not a relevant measure of what we have at our disposal because it mingles ends and means. It is mainly a measure of market activities, supplemented with non-market activities in the public sector. While welfare in the 1930s had some correlation with a growing GDP, this is not the case today in industrial societies, and neither is there a clear relationship between the GDP and the environment. Daly's concepts constitute a theoretical alternative and provide a basis for a systematic critique of the GDP concept. The next obvious question is whether Daly's concepts can be operationalized and provide a relevant substitute for the GDP measure.

## 3. The Concept of Service

The final benefit, service, cannot be directly measured, as there is no unit for measuring service. However, Daly suggests that the concept can be operationalized along the same lines as are used in the calculation of the GDP. First, the 'psychic income' must be split up into two components: an empirical concrete service component (the service of the apple lies in the eating, the service of the house lies in living there) and a valuation component.[3] It is obviously impossible to provide a quantity measure by adding together the service components that are not things, but rather 'activities'. Valuation must be used to aggregate the 'activities'. Daly suggests that a measure of the aggregate valuation of the different quantities can be obtained by the use of market prices and by practices corresponding to those used in current GDP accounting. The services of stock that lasts less than one year (for example, food) could be valued at the market prices of the items, while the services rendered by assets lasting longer could be valued at an imputed rental value (like the treatment of owner-occupied houses) (p. 30). All the problems related to the provision of such a statistical measure of Daly's service concept could probably be solved just as satisfactorily (or unsatisfactorily) as they are solved in GDP accounting. However, for several reasons, prices are not a good measure of values and thus not a suitable tool for solving the aggregation problem.

First, prices depend on a host of factors: technologies, income distribution, level of income, preferences formed by the social and physical structures, market structures, externalities and so on. Market valuation is a social product of history: had social and technological development taken a different path, prices would have been different. In other words, a great element of chance is reflected in prices. Second, prices reflect a valuation at the margin. Consequently, to multiply price and quantity in no way reflects the total value of the units produced, which is obviously unsatisfactory when the aim is to achieve an aggregate measure. Third, market valuation is based on individual valuations and decisions. There is no reason to believe that these are more relevant than social decision-making based on discussions of priorities.

Are any alternatives available to provide an aggregate measure of what we have at our disposal? Historically, it has been suggested that objective values should be used instead of prices. This is based on the idea that we can distinguish between an objective value and a subjective or social valuation. The former is determined from the cost side and reflects the use of an ultimate factor or a limiting factor of production, while the latter can either be an individual or a social expression of an item's value. The relative objective values of two products can easily differ from the relative subjective values, as they are seen from two different points of view. Even if a successful method of measuring objective values could be found (see the next section), it would not provide a satisfactory way of measuring service. It obscures Daly's clear distinction between final benefit and ultimate cost: Daly aims at a valuation of 'satisfaction experienced' which in principle would involve only the subjective valuation and not the cost side at all.[4]

To sum up the discussion of Daly's concept of service, it captures something intuitively relevant. However, the concept can only be made operational if 'satisfaction experienced' – the purely subjective (or human) valuation – can be defined. Prices are no solution as a measure of something that is not really defined. The concept is thus metaphysical in Joan Robinson's sense – just as is the concept of utility (Robinson 1962).[5]

## 4. The Concept of Stock

If service cannot be measured in a reasonable way, could we then proceed to measure the stock instead – to get some idea of what we have at our disposal? Of course, this is an indirect method, and the measure of service efficiency ((2) in the formula above) is lost, when it is assumed that service is directly correlated with stock. However, lacking a direct measure we may suppose that the greater the stock, the more service we can get.

In relation to stock it becomes more relevant to imagine measures in physical terms, because the stock consists of people and artifacts and not of 'activities' such as those implied in the service concept. Furthermore, it seems more relevant to use the concept of objective values, because focus is no longer on a valuation of 'satisfaction experienced'. These considerations open up two different strategies for obtaining a stock measure: one is to find a physical unit to measure the stock quantitatively, and the other is to aggregate by the use of objective values.

Trying first the physical strategy, it seems obvious just to count the stock of people in numbers, but how can the stock of artifacts be measured in a physical sense? Energy accounting has been suggested as a method suitable for this purpose. For a unit to be relevant as a quantity measure, it must be possible to relate this unit to a property of the artifacts themselves. It should not only be possible to measure the 'embodied input' of something in the artifact, but to measure the contents of something independent of the input side. In relation to energy accounting this condition is fulfilled, because it is possible to separate the measurement of output from that of input in a meaningful way. In agricultural production it is relevant to measure output in energy terms, for example, the number of calories in a grain harvest. Correspondingly, the input of seeds, fertilizers, manpower and so on can be measured in energy terms – leaving out the direct input from the sun, as this is not a cost, but rather a present that we get by setting the process into motion.[6] Energy accounting provides a good measure of efficiency, as output and input are comparable, and as they are empirically observable. However, the relevance of this output measure as a measure of what we have at our disposal is questionable. First, if our aggregate production is to be measured as a quantity, this quantity must have some kind of relevance. Therefore, no one has suggested measuring it in weight, for example. Energy content seems to be relevant especially for agricultural products, and in some industrial production a corresponding relevance could be argued (for example, the energy saved by clothing and houses). However, for many products the energy content is meaningless, as it is not the energy service of the product that is of interest. Second, energy accounting does not distinguish renewable energy sources from non-renewable ones (for example, the energy content of manure and chemical fertilizers can be the same), which is obviously problematic from an environmental point of view.

As it is difficult to suggest a reasonable physical measure of the stock of artifacts, the alternative strategy of aggregation by the use of objective values can be tried. One way to do this is to use the labour theory of value, which is based on the idea that labour is the ultimate production factor.[7] The labour theory of value has been conceived (and heavily criticized) as a theory of prices, that is labour time as the fundamental explanation of relative prices. This price theory is not relevant here, where the theory is used as a suggestion for a measure of objective values based on abstract labour time. What we have at our disposal would then be the aggregate embodied labour time. There is, however, an obvious objection to this solution: it implies that the greater the costs, the more we have at our disposal. For example, if we collect the fruits of an abundant natural environment with little effort of labour, these fruits would be worth less than fruits grown under less favourable conditions. Valuing the output of production from the cost side implies that we cannot separate the question of what we have at our disposal from the question of the costs of providing this, losing an important measure of efficiency. Furthermore, abstract labour time is just as random a measure of value as prices.

Energy accounting was discussed as a possible suggestion for measuring aggregate quantities. Another approach could be to see energy accounting as analogous to the labour theory of value, thus suggesting that energy could be a measure of objective values – based on the view that energy is the limiting factor of production. Counting the input of energy could be relevant for all production, and in this case the solar energy captured by photosynthesis should also be included. However, the same objections related to the resulting measure could be raised as those in relation to labour values. For example, a ton of iron will be worth more, the more energy it requires for its extraction, and again the efficiency measure is lost, that is how well the energy input is used in the provision of output. Both Daly (1991) and Joan Martinez Alier (1990) warn against an energy theory of value. Among other things, they object to the idea of objective values. Even if the purpose here is not to estimate 'satisfaction experienced', an indirect relationship is suggested: the whole operation is only meaningful under the assumption that service is positively correlated with stock.

Summing up, neither of the two strategies is very successful in relation to measuring the stock. Daly's concepts are well suited for criticizing the GDP thoroughly on the basis of intuitively relevant and correct considerations. However, the concepts provide the answer to the question of what is at our disposal only at an abstract level (the question of costs will be dealt with below). The conclusion of the discussion is that we have no good proposal for a measure of what we have at our disposal, neither at the service level nor at the stock level, and neither as a kind of aggregated quantity nor as an aggregate valuation of a sum of different quantities. This is close to the conclusion of Martinez Alier (1990) who summarizes the main point of his book in the statement that, from an ecological point of view, economists are left without a theory of value, and consequently, the economy is inseparable from politics.

## 5. Costs

The lack of good answers does not imply that the questions are irrelevant. For the moment, however, we will let the question of what we have at our disposal rest, accept the lack of a precise concept and turn to the question of costs. The basic point is that some scarcities are absolute (Daly 1991, p. 39) and not just relative as in neoclassical theory. What we have at our disposal is a result partly of the appropriation of nature's resources and partly of the use of human labour. From a physical point of view we are not creating anything, only transforming nature's resources. Therefore, Daly suggests that only matter and energy (the throughput) should be considered the ultimate cost of providing service. Labour is only a kind of intermediate cost that is not visible in Daly's theoretical apparatus. In relation to the presentation of Fischer's concepts, Daly mentions that Fischer takes labour costs into account by subtracting the disservice of labour from the amount of service (p. 32). It is not clear whether Daly does this too, but obviously labour costs are treated as secondary.

Even if we are not creating anything in a physical sense, it does not seem satisfactory to ignore labour costs in this way. Firstly, nature's resources cannot be appropriated without working. Secondly, besides the necessity of labour in the appropriation of resources, we also add to the value of products: from a human point of view labour also has a creative part. For example, wood can be appropriated from nature to make a chair, but the same quantity of wood can be transformed into a simple or a more refined chair according to the skill and the amount of labour spent in the process. Treating matter and energy as the only ultimate costs of service implies an underestimation of the importance of labour.

Presumably, this underestimation is related to the present historical situation, where nature is considered to be a seriously limiting factor. From a historical point of view it is interesting to note that the limiting factor is not always the same. The labour necessary to appropriate nature's resources differs enormously according to the natural conditions in different areas and over time. Ester Boserup has explained that slash-and-burn is a rational agricultural method in an abundant nature, as a small effort of labour is required. If the population increases, it can be necessary to exploit the resources of nature more efficiently, and then agricultural methods become more labour-intensive (Hoffmeyer 1982, pp. 94ff). Thorkild Kjærgaard (1992) described the increasing effort of labour needed as an ecological crisis developed in Denmark in the seventeenth and eighteenth centuries. This crisis was overcome when the exploitation of fossil fuels started: nature then seemed to be abundant and labour became the scarce factor.

Kjærgaard suggests that this might soon change if the present ecological crisis deepens.

Historical experience demonstrates a trade-off between nature and labour: in an abundant nature we can provide necessities with little effort, and in a sparse nature much labour is required (possibly in an indirect form such as tools, requiring investment instead of consumption). To characterize a given historical situation well, labour must be visible as a cost, and it will be relevant to supplement Daly's formulation with the question: how much labour do we use to maintain and renew the stock? The answer to this question reflects two circumstances: first, the natural conditions, that is the abundance of nature in relation to the population pressure; second, the efficiency of the social system in relation to the appropriation of resources from a given nature. Just as more or less energy can be used for making a given product (compare Daly's maintenance efficiency), more or less labour can be used.

This last kind of efficiency is interesting to discuss in a contemporary perspective. Apparently, we have low labour-intensity in the manufacturing of most products. Outside material production we have, however, several labour-intensive activities that are indirectly necessary for material production in a system with an extended division of labour. At the aggregate level this system should ensure that less labour is used than in a system with a less developed division of labour, if production is optimized at all levels. This result assumes that all costs are paid, but this is not the case: for example, education, medical care, administration, infrastructure, and research are costs which are only partly included in the optimization processes at the micro level. Thus, in principle, our labour-saving system might demand much labour at the aggregate level. To study whether this in fact occurs would require a kind of labour accounting.

In Section 4 concerning the concept of stock, it is concluded that neither energy nor labour constitutes a good foundation for objective values and thus for measuring what we have at our disposal. The discussion of costs in this section points to another use: like labour accounting, energy accounting can be a very valuable tool for critical assessment of the results produced by the 'price accounting' actually occurring.

The critical assessment can be deepened even further, if it is taken into account that some of the output usually considered to be at our disposal is, in fact, a means rather than an end. Daly's formulation seems to have solved the problem, as the stock is a means, and service the final benefit. This is, however, misleading, because part of the service is a means rather than an end. In a society with an extended division of labour, transport, for example, is often a means – even part of private transport is a cost rather than a service adding to 'satisfaction experienced'. Intuitively, it seems relevant to distinguish between 'core service' (or real final use) and 'means service'. Then only the 'core service' should be seen as a relevant measure of what we get out of the throughput of natural resources and the effort of labour. Daly suggests that the present situation might be characterized by a falling service per unit of stock. Maybe it is even worse, if the 'core service' is reduced relative to total service? As these intuitive suggestions can never be operationalized, we are left here with political discussions. When we use so many natural resources and work so much today, do we then get a rich and refined service out of this, or do we have a very inefficient system for providing service? Or both?

To sum up very briefly the discussion of costs, it is argued that ultimate costs include not only matter and energy, but also labour. Furthermore, a concept of intermediate costs is relevant, as only part of service is real final benefit.

## 6. The Extinction of the GDP-dinosaur

The first section of the paper demonstrated that even a rigorous discussion of the relationship between GDP and the environment cannot result in a reasonable answer to the question of whether or not a growing GDP will improve the environmental situation. The second section explains that the concept of GDP is highly problematic, as it adds together costs and benefits. Therefore, the discussion of growth and environment is even more absurd than shown in the first section. The obvious conclusion is that the GDP-dinosaur is one of the few species that deserve extinction.

The third and fourth sections discuss whether we can develop an alternative concept describing what we have at our disposal. The predominance of the market system has given us the illusion that products can be added in a meaningful way. Prices are, however, not very suitable for the purpose, and unfortunately, other ways of solving the problem are no better. We are consequently left in a situation where our intuitive understanding that we have 'something' at our disposal cannot be operationalized at an aggregate level. This implies that the extinction of the GDP-dinosaur should not be followed by new theoretical constructions of dinosaurian dimensions – it is a condition that we cannot define an aggregate pie.

This conclusion is substantiated in the fifth section, where the costs of providing the undefined pie are discussed. It is especially a problem if parts of the expected pie turn out to be costs.

The conclusion that the GDP-dinosaur deserves extinction and that it should not be followed by related theoretical constructions is obviously far from political reality (see for example, Opschoor and Van der Straaten 1993). In the short run, it is necessary to accept the task of improving GDP accounting and to supplement it with satellite accounts and so on in ways that will inform politics better than the present accounting. It is, however, beyond the scope of this paper to discuss the different suggestions that have been made.

What should be emphasized here is the request that these different exercises to provide more relevant measures should not be used as ways of escaping complicated political questions concerning the scale of the economy, distributional issues and social priorities. Economics should not be used to divert attention from politics, and we have to find ways to discuss questions such as:

- How much can be used of different natural resources? They cannot be treated as an aggregate, so we have to discuss different kinds of matter and energy.
- Which ends should have a high priority? We cannot rely on the price system to take all the decisions here.
- How can the different efficiencies be improved? For example, energy accounting and labour accounting can provide us with useful tools for modifying the results of the price system.

The need for dinosaur concepts is related to large scale economies, integrated via the extended division of labour. If we are going to discuss the use of natural resources, priorities and so on democratically, we might in the long run have to reorganize our economies in a more decentralized manner. The short-term improvements of measures should thus be supplemented with long-term considerations regarding structural change.

## Notes

1. The World Bank includes only two aspects of technology: input–output efficiency and environmental damage per unit of input. In fact, the importance of technology is somewhat broader. For instance, environmental consequences are not only determined by the effectiveness in the use of a given input, but by the use and quality of cleaning technology as well – it matters whether a poisonous substance is spread widely or deposited. Of course, prevention is better than cure, and clean technology better than end-of-line solutions, but cleaning is better than nothing. This can be illustrated by the lignite–oil example above: lignite is used not only in Eastern

Europe, but also in Nordrhein-Westfalen, where the related pollution is much more effectively reduced by cleaning technologies.
2. This part of the paper concentrates mainly on presenting and commenting on the work of Herman Daly. His work is a very important contribution to a renewal of economic theory, and the critical comments in this paper should be understood as suggestions for more elaboration.
3. Daly does not mention this split but, as far as I can see, the following operation is not meaningful without it.
4. Interestingly, this could be used as an argument against the use of prices as well: they reflect more than the subjective valuations, as they are also influenced by costs.
5. The discussion of the service concept has much in common with the old discussion of the utility concept as part of neoclassical welfare theory. Besides Robinson (1962), see Sen (1987).
6. Difficulties in carrying out energy accounting in practice are dealt with in Martinez Alier (1990). See especially Chapter 2 on agriculture.
7. This idea obviously differs from Daly's idea about ultimate costs. This question will be dealt with in the next section on costs.

# References

Daly, H.E. and Cobb, J.B. (1989), *For the Common Good*, Boston: Beacon Press.
Daly, H.E. (1991), *Steady-State Economics, Second Edition with New Essays*, Washington, DC: Island Press.
Ekins, P. (1993), "Limits to growth' and 'sustainable development': grappling with ecological realities', *Ecological Economics*, **3**, 269–88.
GATT (1992), *International Trade 90–91*, Vol.1: including Special Topic: Trade and the Environment, Geneva.
Hoffmeyer, J. (1982), *Samfundets naturhistorie*, Copenhagen: Rosinante.
Hueting, R. (1990), 'The Brundtland Report: A Matter of Conflicting Goals', *Ecological Economics*, **2**, 109–17.
Kjærgaard, T. (1992), Den danske revolution 1500–1800, en økohistorisk tolkning, Copenhagen: Gyldendal.
Martinez Alier, J. (1991), *Ecological Economics, Energy, Environment and Society*, Oxford: Basil Blackwell.
Meadows, D.H., D.L. Meadows and J. Randers, (1992), *Beyond the Limits*, London: Earthscan Publications Ltd.
OECD (1991), *The State of the Environment*, Paris.
Opschoor, J.B. and J. Van der Straaten, (1993), 'Sustainable development: an institutional approach', *Ecological Economics*, **7**, 203–22.
Robinson, J. (1962), *Economic Philosophy*, London: C.A. Watts & Co.
Sen, A. (1987), *On Ethics and Economics*, Oxford: Basil Blackwell.

Tinbergen, J. and R Hueting, (1992), 'GNP and Market Prices: Wrong Signals for Sustainable Economic Success That Mask Environmental Destruction' in R. Goodland, H.E. Daly and S.E. Serafy (eds): *Population, Technology, and Lifestyle. The Transition to Sustainability*, Washington, DC: Island Press.

The World Bank (1992). 'World Development Report', *Development and the Environment*, Oxford: Oxford University Press.

World Commission on Environment and Development (1987), *Our Common Future*, Oxford: Oxford University Press.

PART TWO

# The Institutional Agenda for Sustainable Development

# 5. Reducing Material Throughput: A Contribution to the Measurement of Dematerialization and Sustainable Human Development[1]

## Friedrich Hinterberger and Eberhard K. Seifert

### 1. Sustainability – From Vision to Concept

The term 'sustainable development' has become *the* focus in the debates on environmental policy in recent years. The most well-known and often cited definition with a growing consensus is probably that of the Brundtland Report (WCED 1987): development should meet the needs of the present generation without compromising the ability of future generations to meet their own needs.

Goodland and Daly (1992) discussed the Brundtland perception of sustainability and found that it contains two ambivalent meanings: one still based on conventional economic growth which can be empirically measured in terms of GDP, the other directed to a new understanding of 'real' qualitative development: They summarise: '...one is to revert to a definition of sustainable development as 'growth as usual', although at a slower rate. The other reaction is to define sustainable development as *'development without growth in throughput'* beyond environmental carrying capacity' (1992, p. 37, emphasis added).

In a more detailed discussion of the implicit goals of the sustainability concept (Tisdell 1991), at least the following objectives can be distinguished:

1.  sustaining intergenerational economic welfare of humans,
2.  ensuring survival of the human species for as long as possible,
3.  seeking resilience in production and economic systems and/or stability of their attributes (their ability to recover when subjected to shocks),
4.  ensuring sustainability of community,
5.  maintaining biodiversity,
6.  stabilising the biosphere.

These various meanings of sustainable development lead to different priorities and policies ranging from traditional economic growth to environmental protection at a zero or even negative growth of the physical output of the economy (Daly 1991, 1992). But neither the structure of modern economies (whether market, planned or mixed economies) nor economic rationality *per se* guarantees a long-term compatibility between the economy/society and the environment/nature. Therefore, the visions and priorities need to be specified and operationalized.

An economic conceptualization of sustainability traces the discussion back to Hicks's (1946) definition of income as the maximum flow of money that can be spent for consumption without diminishing real future consumption per period. This means that we have to subtract the resources needed to restore the stock of capital from the revenues:

> The purpose of income calculations in practical affairs is to give people an indication of the amount which they can consume without impoverishing themselves. Following out this idea, it would seem that we ought to define man's income as the maximum value which he can consume during a week, and still expect to be as well off at the end of the week as he was at the beginning. Thus when a person saves he plans to be better off in the future; when he lives beyond his income he plans to be worse off. (Hicks 1946)

If the stock of capital cannot be sustained, future opportunities to earn income will be diminished. Although such a view can be criticized for economic as well as ecological arguments as regards its operationalization (Nordhaus 1994, Hinterberger *et al.* 1995) it provides a better understanding of the economic problems related to sustainability than the somewhat vague Brundtland definition.

In this context the differentiation between 'man-made capital' and 'natural capital' is important. Including natural capital in addition to man-made as *the* limiting factor for further development, one finds a starting point for a workable definition of *sustainable income*.[2] This means that income is the flow of monetary resources after restoring the stock of man-made capital *and* natural capital. But what *is* natural capital? While produced capital can be expressed in monetary terms and is thus comparable on a single scale, this is not so easy with natural capital, which is a heterogeneous concept: it includes renewable resources, such as plants and solar energy, non-renewables, such as fossil fuels, and non-material 'goods' such as the aesthetic value of nature (Sachs 1994).

If mankind irreversibly consumes the rest of the entire patrimony, which was 'produced' over millions of years, within only the next one or two generations, then not only are political and social turbulences (such as the second Gulf War) foreseeable but the survival of humankind is in danger.

A further distinction can be made between *weak* and *strong* sustainability (Pearce and Turner 1990, Turner *et al* 1994). *Strong sustainability* means keeping natural capital intact over (infinite) time, where natural capital includes energy and natural assets as well as ecosystem functions.

*Weak sustainability* claims that there are possibilities for substituting between natural and man-made capital and it is assumed that it is possible to keep constant or even increase mineral and energy assets economically, even if they are being used at some positive rate.

Summarizing the intensive literature and arguments on intergenerational equity/fairness and resource substitutability (Toman *et al*, 1994)[3] – some categorical conditions can be extracted, which form a theoretical (or hypothetical) 'existence-theorem' for sustainability (Pearce and Turner 1990) recognizing the double nature of natural capital as differentiated between renewable and exhaustible resources:

## 1. Renewable resources/assimilative capacity:

a. Use renewable resources at rates less or equal to the natural rate at which they can regenerate.
b. Keep waste flows to the environment at or below the assimilative capacity of the environment.

## 2. Exhaustible (non-renewable) resources:

c. Ensure that as exhaustible resources are depleted, their reduced stock is compensated for by increases in renewable resources.
d. Allow for the fact that a given standard of living can be secured from a reduced stock of resources.

## 3. Population growth:

e.   A given standard of living may be supported with less resource inputs over
     time, but if population grows rapidly the effect of the increased demand for
     resources can 'swamp' such efficiency gains.

Whereas the first two of these hypothetical conditions (a and b) look quite
plausible at least from a purely theoretical point of view, the second two are
much more problematic and difficult, even in theory – let alone in practice.[4]
Concerning condition c substitution is the implicit and doubtful condition,
whereas in d rising efficiency is afforded. Although the real population
development – verifying the 200-year-old Malthusian thesis of a geometric
growth tendency (a doubling every 25 years) – lies beyond the present
discussion, the following paragraphs concentrate on the issues of throughput and
its measurement (see Seifert 1993).

## 2. Material Throughput, the Ecological Impact of Human Activities and a New Safety Factor of Dematerialization.

In trying to measure natural capital, we face two related problems for the
maintenance of natural resources, renewable as well as non-renewable: the
availability of resources for economic use, and (crucially) the endangered
buffering capacity of the ecosphere. If non-renewables are used they dissipate
into the environment and natural capital decreases as long as it is not
compensated by a growing stock of renewable resources. Empirical data show an
explosive consumption of virtually all non-renewable raw materials (see Brown
1992). This illustrates the absolute necessity of both efficiency increases
(resource productivity) and substitution by renewables and man-made capital.
But all these efforts will and must come to an end some day. The various
compartments of capital are substitutable - but only to a certain extent. This raises
the fundamental ethical question of our real responsibility and the time horizon
(100, 500, 1000, 5000 years or more?) of 'sustainability'. Given the very
optimistic assumption that we are willing and still able to manage the
stabilization of the population, of renewable resources, and the more urgent
problem of the overused sink functions of the environment – which is only the
flipside of our extensive consumption of energy and all anthropogenic material
flows – even then we must face our permanent *conditio humana* in the future:[5]

- the limits of perpetual substitution, inherent in the promises of everlasting technological progress, indicating real physical (entropic) limits to growth, and
- the long-run energetic dependence of humankind on ecologically viable (in)direct solar technologies

The issue of greatest immediate concern is nature's capacity to buffer man-induced disturbances. As Goodland and Daly recently stated, 'Earlier studies of environmental limits to growth  emphasized the source limits (depletion of petroleum, copper, and so on). Experience has shown, however, that the sink constraints (greenhouse, ozone depletion, local air and water pollution,  and so on) are the more stringent.' (1992, p. 37).  Concern in the 1990s has shifted away from resource scarcity as discussed in the 1970s to the impact of rising throughputs.

Schmidt-Bleek (1993, p.308) has identified the sum of man-induced material flows from eco-sphere to techno-sphere as a good indicator for assessing these disturbances: 'The massive man-induced shifts of materials are the fundamental cause of the present incompatibility between human business and the ecosphere'. This is why a group at the Wuppertal Institut is working on a method to consistently calculate the life-cycle-wide material input of well specified services delivered by economic products in order to screen the anthropogenic impact on nature. This is the core of the MIPS concept. 'MIPS' stands for Material Intensity Per Service Unit (see Schmidt-Bleek 1994, Liedtke *et al.* 1994 and Schmidt-Bleek 1993).

As a necessary precondition for all measures of economic policy, and a guide for every environmentally-conscious consumer or entrepreneur, there is obviously a need for a comprehensive base of information on the life-cycle-wide material intensity of services. What consumers and producers need to know in order to behave environmentally 'correctly' and what the government needs to know in order to set the 'right' incentives where markets function insufficiently, is the sum of all materials needed to produce, operate, maintain and correctly dispose of a good. To use material input (in kg) as a measure of anthropogenic impairments of nature has the advantage of being universally applicable. In that sense, material input (MI) can be regarded as a proxy measure of the human use of natural capital. As we cannot be sure about the complex ecological and economic interrelations and effects of material throughputs, we need a safety factor to make sure that nature's buffering capacity can be sustained. A reduction of human-induced material flows by 50% on a global scale within the next 40 to 50 years is seen as necessary in order to ensure nature's assimilative or buffering capacity. Given the economic dynamics in the less industrialized countries and that 80% of the material flows are currently induced by the highly industrialized part of the world, a reduction of material flows is necessary by a factor of 10 for the Northern hemisphere (see The Factor 10 Club 1995).

What has to be considered goes beyond the conception of (renewable and non-renewable) resources as discussed above, which

> excludes very large quantities of material which are translocated by mankind for the purpose of creating material wealth: erosion due to plowing or timber harvesting, overburden; mine spoils, earth movements for road, tunnel or dam constructions, water pumped off to allow mining and drilling operations, rainwater diverted by sealed surfaces, diverted rivers, dredged sludge and so on. (Schmidt-Bleek 1993 p. 409).

These *translocations* (see Bringezu 1993) have to be considered in addition to renewable and non-renewable resources in order to measure the environmental impact of economic activities. In other words, material input reflects the total *throughput* of economic activities (in pure quantitative but not qualitative terms), that is extracted resources *and* translocations. If this is true, a *de-materialization* – or increase in material productivity – of our economies would be an essential condition for approaching sustainability.

As a first screening of the environmental impact potential, this approach avoids weighting different kinds of materials differently. In principle, any other weighting scheme can be introduced but at this stage of the argument it is important to stress that we should get *all* activities into the picture. Recall, for example, that twenty years ago, $CO_2$ emissions were not regarded as ecologically harmful. The material intensity approach would include both all carbons extracted and all oxygen burned, which on the output side of the system leads to $CO_2$ emissions.

We shall now consider some other conceptualizations of measuring sustainability and investigations of their compatibility with the material input/dematerialization approach as presented in this chapter. The main aim is to exemplify their differences as well as their (possible) compatibilities with the MI-approach for measuring sustainability.[6]

## 3. Greening GDP: Toward a Sustainable National Income?

Taking the Hicksian income definition as providing a starting point for conceptualizing sustainability, progress towards sustainability could be measured by adjusting domestic income by the decrease or increase in natural capital. GDP is a misleading indicator of 'real income' and therefore needs to be corrected. Today GDP growth rates work as a 'speedometer' – not indicating whether we are speeding in the right direction or into some catastrophe. What is needed today therefore is an environmentally adjusted income, an indicator of 'sustainable' income as the essential step towards an 'eco-domestic product'. In the last decade, some new approaches and new international efforts in this field have got under way, also supported by the United Nations' proposal of the 'SEEA-Handbook' (1993), a new System of integrated Environmental and Economic Accounting.

According to the '*defensive cost*' approach within the welfare tradition (Kapp 1950/71), one could first adjust the actual expenditures for restoring environmental (and other) damage caused by economic growth, so-called '*defensive expenditures*', to conventional GDP figures. According to moderate calculations by Leipert (1989) for Germany, these costs of economic progress in 1989 were about DM269 billion., that is about 12% of the is GDP (DM1189 billion) – and rising. This is more than the GDP of the Philippines, Egypt and Argentina together. Whatever the outcome of the current debate on including these real (already spent) costs in the depreciation procedure towards an 'environmentally adjusted national income', and whatever the practical problems of a valid and harmonized statistical system in this field (Eurostat 1994), it is already clear that these defensive expenditures cover only a small part of the entire 'costs' of the environmental impact of the total material throughput induced by economic activities.

Let us now return to a more comprehensive approach by referring again to the Hicksian concept of income: GDP is to be adjusted first by capital depreciation to get Net Domestic Product (NDP). By analogy we must correct NDP by a further category – the *depreciation of natural capital* – to come to an environmentally adjusted income and an appropriate (national) accounting procedure (see Stahmer and Seifert 1994, Welfens 1993). There are several approaches to sound accounting and 'depreciation' of natural capital or resources, but there is still much to do (see for example Franz and Stahmer 1993 – the proceedings of the IARIW Conference on Environmental Accounting in Baden/Vienna 1991). A most promising conceptual framework is the '*avoidance costs*' approach, initially developed by Roefie Hueting and colleagues at the Netherlands Central Bureau of Statistics (1992) and proposed also in the UN Handbook.

This approach is an indirect or hypothetical way to measure real depreciation; it is the amount of money needed to avoid environmental deterioration (degradation, depletion). The avoidance of deterioration depends on an assumption regarding preferences for the environment, and one has to determine environmental standards, the so-called 'sustainability standards'. Then, avoidance costs will show how far a country is from sustainability. So far, this approach is not really operationalized, but an on-going EU research project[7] attempts to take some essential further steps towards a calculation of such figures; therefore the debate is still conceptual, not yet data-based. Nevertheless, the linking of physical targets for sustainability with the difficult additional monetary valuation procedure begs a question that has to be answered beforehand: a decision on what the 'sustainability standards' are and how this issue could be handled within the pragmatic field of statistics. There are three general possibilities: a) science is able to set these standards; b) they are set by political decision (as in the case of the Netherlands' National Environmental Policy Plan); or – failing both these – c) the statistician will take a purely statistical, very pragmatic solution (the target being not to be worse off at the end of the reporting period than at the beginning).

What we need is an appropriate simple and agreed proxy-measure for sustainability targets and the question is whether the dematerialization/material input approach could be such a proxy within the depreciation procedure of calculating environmentally adjusted national income figures.

a)   What we need over the next 30 to 50 years is a profound ecological and structural change, guided by innovative alternatives to business as usual. Both the material inputs approach and the avoidance cost approach focus on improved technologies yielding an increase in resource productivity.

b)   Both approaches focus on the gap between the present environmentally unsustainable and the targeted sustainable state. A calculation of costs of really innovative processes and products, which avoid environmental impacts of rising throughputs, seems to be a common interest of both approaches – although the primary aim of the MI approach is to constantly reduce costs by further de-materializing, and not to calculate the hypothetical costs.

For the sake of a preliminary improvement of the compatibility of the approaches a somewhat modified version might be termed 'wasted costs' (*Verschwendungskosten*). The 'material flows/ecological rucksack' approach as described above teaches us that – compared with a situation of sustainable welfare creation – our production and consumption processes use far too much material and energy. Dematerialization by a factor of 10 within 40 to 50 years requires about 5% per annum increase in resource productivity. It is reasonable to assume that this is possible. If we manage to produce our welfare by using much less material through more recycling, greater longevity of products, and so on, both producers and consumers will save not only materials and energy, but money. Producers save money not only on waste disposal but also on *producing* products which later turn out to be waste (including labour costs). Consumers may need to buy less if the durability of products can be increased. All this adds up to 'wasted costs', which might be deducted from GDP in order to get income figures which are more closely related to our well-being.

Although the greening of GDP seems to be one of the most urgent tasks on the political agenda today (see European Commission 1994), a sound environment nevertheless is only one of several related determinants of 'well-being'. In the next section we turn to examples of more comprehensive approaches for the measurement of sustainable human development.

## 4. Beyond Greening GDP: Indicators of Sustainable Human Development and Well-Being

Well-being can be defined as the state derived from satisfaction of wants evoked by our dealings with both scarce means and non-economic factors. Therefore 'well-being' *includes* green income but goes beyond it. It is positively or negatively influenced by a number of economic factors or conditions, notably:

- the dimension and quality of goods and services produced for the market, by government, and by households and volunteers;
- scarce environmental functions, as mentioned above;
- leisure time;
- income distribution;
- working conditions, including working relationships;
- employment and unemployment;
- security, or relative certainty as to future conditions, insofar as this depends on our behaviour with regard to scarce goods (such as the life-support functions of the environment);

- other factors like levels of health, education and security, which are partly derived from produced goods and services, and partly have other, non-economic causes; and
- influences which are either purely non-economic, or have important non-economic components, for example:

  - relationships, with for example family, friends and Deity
  - freedom and rights to real human development, such as human and political rights, and participation in social and economic decision-making processes.

There has been a continuing discussion since the 1970s ('Social Indicators Movement'), and general acceptance and agreement that neither welfare nor well-being are portrayed by unqualified GDP figures. Therefore it has become customary to look for measurable factors ('economic' or 'non-economic', or both) which can be closely related to welfare and well-being, positively or negatively. A broad range of these, taken together, may be able to give a useful overall impression of well-being, or 'quality of life' (Sen 1983).

One possibility to operationalize this has been developed as the so-called MIPS concept. If the material intensity of a certain standard of living is a good measure of the environmental impact of human activities, the question is how to measure the standard of living. In our view, it is mainly the *utilization* of products that makes up the standard of living, which in many cases can be satisfied by a variety of products. Products give people certain 'capabilities'. The sum of these 'services', or capabilities, makes up a person's living standard (Sen 1983).[8] Here the second part of MIPS comes into the picture (see Hinterberger *et al.* 1994, Femia *et al.* 1995): The concept of calculating MI on a cradle-to-grave-basis allows us to relate the environmental impact of a product to the number of utilizations or services 'provided': the Material Input Per unit of Service. Obviously the environmental impact of a single service can, other things being equal, be reduced if a greater number of 'services' is fulfilled by a single 'service-delivery machine', that is with a single product. Hence, longevity, use-sharing, re-usability and so on are regarded as positive in terms of environmental impact without necessarily reducing the user's standard of living (or utility, in economic terms). But the marginal positive effect of re-using decreases with the number of uses.

The Human Development Index (HDI) is a recent and politically interesting approach in this field. First proposed in 1990, it is still being refined by a team within the UNDP (United Nations Development Programme), which publishes the yearly *Human Development Report* (HDR). This publication has been from the beginning a provocative challenge to both politics and official statistics. Its first issue, in 1990, defined *human development* as 'a process of enlarging people's choices or enabling people to have wider choices' – a framework influenced by Sen's theoretical approach of 'capabilities' (see Nussbaum and Sen 1993), explicitly realizing that human development cannot be promoted by economic growth alone. Although economic growth is treated as important, so, equally, is distribution of growth – whether people participate in it fully. The index is published every year. It is designed as a measure for socio-economic progress, integrating three key components (UNDP 1992, p. 91):

- *longevity* (life expectancy at birth as the sole unadjusted indicator);
- *knowledge* (as measured by two educational stock variables: adult literacy and mean years of schooling). The measure of educational achievement is adjusted by giving a weight of two-thirds to literacy and one-third to mean years of schooling);
- *income* in an innovative way to produce a better yardstick than GDP for measuring a country's progress (assuming diminishing returns from income for human development: the higher the income relative to the poverty level, the more sharply the diminishing returns affect contribution of income to HDI).

This kind of (simple) conceptualization of the HDI is unrelated so far to environmental problems. In their 1992 report the HDR team recognized the urgency of this issue and promised to investigate an 'environmentally sensitive HDI' for future reports.

We now consider whether the material flow approach as presented above could be a helpful tool in making the Human Development Index environmentally sensitive. One advantage is that material input (MI) is a simple universal and standardized measurement of the real total material throughput of material flows, which serves as an estimate for the environmental impact potential. Compared to other statistics, the data requirements are not excessively high. Data is available for Germany (see, for example, Bringezu *et al* 1994; Radermacher and Stahmer 1994) and the methodology could easily be applied to other countries, indicating their environmental impact and its development over time. Integrated into a new environmentally sensitive Sustainable Human Development Index (SHDI), the material input indicator would cover the HDI's environmental deficit. Note that this could change the whole ranking: given that highly industrialized countries are responsible for the main environmental impacts all over the world today, their rankings for SHDI will be lower than for HDI, whereas for less developed countries, with lower environmental impacts, the reverse would be true.

A next step thus should be to investigate the possibilities and difficulties of simple material flow accounts in less developed countries. Probably, the material input calculations of an environmentally sensitive SHDI for countries of the Southern hemisphere will have be modified – a very interesting next task within the North–South dialogue and UN-coordinated environmental research activities.

A further activity is related to the ongoing UN activities in the Rio follow-up process, especially in the CSD process (United Nations Commission for Sustainable Development) for monitoring sustainable development with a core set of *sustainability indicators*. But while a new SHDI has to be calculated from scratch and thus makes possible a radically new approach, this is not the case for the CSD indicators.

At the time of writing, a first, explicitly preliminary 'Work programme on indicators for Sustainable Development' is being developed and submitted to the third session of the Commission for Sustainable Development. The proposed 'core set of indicators for sustainable development' fully recognizes 'that there is need for flexibility as the conditions, activities and priorities for sustainable development differ from country to country'. Nevertheless, the scheme is presented already in a modified 'driving force–state–response' scheme, including not only environmental, but explicitly three other non-environmental indicators, economic, social and institutional ones.

The environmental indicators are designed to emphasize qualitative dimensions of the environmental impacts of economic activities. Would it make sense to add the quantitative material flows approach as defined above to this essentially qualitative core list? (The current set of CSD/OECD indicators include, as environmental indicators of 'driving forces', withdrawals of ground water, land use change, use of fertilizers, emissions, waste disposal, and so on.) In order to be internationally applicable, the core set must be simple and easy to handle, especially in view of the statistical problems of less developed countries. As MI serves as a physical measure for the anthropogenic ecological impact, national MI figures can be compared with GDP figures in order to measure the resource productivity of national economies (see Bringezu 1993, Bringezu *et al.* 1994).

## 5. Efficiency versus Sufficiency?

An 'efficiency revolution'[9] which is based on increasing resource productivity (especially energy productivity) should be designed to raise the wealth we can get out of one tonne of MI, a barrel of oil or one megawatt. Many studies have shown high potential for increasing well-being that way, thus reducing environmental damage caused by the 'throughput' of dangerous material inputs. Such an increase in efficiency is absolutely necessary and feasible. But it will only mean a temporary victory over the entropy-based 'ecology of time', if we delay the historic decisions over the choices in the use of those 'service units' enhancing real wealth. 'Efficiency revolution' and resource productivity without a complementary 'sufficiency revolution' will suffer from blindness towards the 'sustainable' direction humankind must follow in the coming century (Weizsäcker 1994). Otherwise, with the highest efficiency, we may run even in the wrong direction. 'Efficiency without sufficiency is counterproductive; the latter must define the boundaries of the former.' (Sachs 1993, pp. 16-17).

From this follows the *necessity of sufficiency* – even if an ecological safety factor of ten (Schmidt-Bleek 1993, 1994; Factor 10 Club 1995) for resource productivity is established (see Femia *et al.* 1995). To achieve this, we need new models of real sustainable wealth, that is a new (or old?) ethos of a 'de-materialized' kind of well-being, a corresponding new idea of 'eu zen' ('good life') or in other words, an ethical discourse (Seifert and Pfriem 1989, Seifert 1993, 1995) within society and community about our living standards and capabilities as well as our common future and the future of our species.

The relation between efficiency and sufficiency is shown in *Figure 5.1*. Assuming the need to reduce MI by a factor of ten in industrialized economies in order to maintain the stability of the ecosphere, this can be achieved either by a reduction in MIPS (efficiency) or a reduction in S, or any combination of both to give the required reduction of MI.

*Figure 5.1* shows that we have the choice between two extremes, or any combination of the two. If we manage to 'freeze' our well-being in terms of service units at a certain level, we would 'only' need to increase resource productivity by a factor of ten. In order to increase well-being, we would have to do better than that in order to reach the goal of dematerialization in absolute terms. If we cannot do as well, well-being will have to decrease in order to meet the dematerialization standard. We saw from our discussion on 'wasted costs' that this will be partly reflected in the figures for green GDP.

*Figure 5.1 The connections between efficiency and sufficiency*

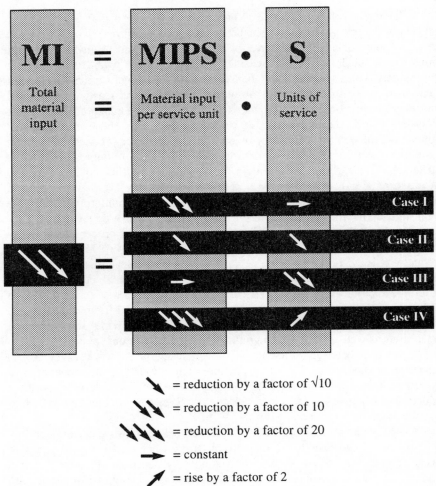

= reduction by a factor of √10

= reduction by a factor of 10

= reduction by a factor of 20

= constant

= rise by a factor of 2

*Source:*    F. Hinterberger, E. Seifert, Wuppertal Institut UM–2308

## Notes

1. This chapter reflects an ongoing discussion process between the two authors concerning the specific focus of their departments at the Wuppertal Institute. We are grateful especially to Renate Aumann, Stefan Bringezu, Reuben Deumling, Manfred Linz, Fred Luks, Juan Martinez Alier, Inge Røpke, Friedrich Schmidt-Bleek, Aldo Femia Simonis, and Jan van der Straaten. The usual disclaimer remains.
2. To some extent this echoes the old physiocratic idea of a real annual net product or income to be consumed without impoverishing the natural stocks (Seifert 1986).
3. In their instructive overview, they   point to the underlying lessons from recent neoclassical literature: 'Those who believe in the capacity   of substitution and innovation to address any problem of natural capital scarcity take comfort in the analyses that highlight the potency of substitution and innovation under certain conditions. Those who question the realism of these conditions will take a less sanguine view, emphasizing the importance of technical progress but also the relevance of constraints on renewable input flows.' (p. 17)
4. Based on the application of thermodynamics to economics, N. Georgescu-Roegen claimed the theoretical impossibility of 'sustainability' and criticized that term as 'snake-oil' as well as describing some basic ideas of substitutability as pure wishful thinking (1994).
5. According to a recent study by the ESSO Company (FAZ 1993) known oil reserves have increased by 51% since 1975 and extraction by 17%. Thus, the increase in world reserves (135.4 bn. tons in 1992, that is 0.6% higher than 1991) was three times higher than the increase in consumption, thus disproving – according to ESSO – previous forecasts of impending scarcity.   The confirmed reserves will last another 42.8 years. But imagine that in only 50 years the fuel to drive our industrial machine will be in permanently short supply!
6. For a full discussion see, for example, Henderson (1991) or the overview in Ekins and Max-Neef (1992, chapter 8).
7. With colleagues from four other European Institutes, one of the authors (Seifert) is engaged in a research project in the field of 'environmental adjusted income' financed by the European Union, results forthcoming, Autumn 1996..
8. The material welfare of a region could then be expressed as the sum of service units available in that region instead of income figures like GDP. Given certain material inputs, material welfare will increase with rising resource productivity. In other words, de-materialized technologies can deliver increasing units of service at a given, or even decreasing, level of material input. Such a development can be assessed as an 'ecological improvement'.
9. Concerning minimizing 'throughput' within the framework  of 'efficiency revolution' see the special issue of the Fresenius Bulletin 8/93; as an example of new 'institutional arrangements' and the problems within the process of creation of new intermediate institutions, a special evaluation of the German 'Dual System' would be very interesting.

# References

Bringezu, S. (1993), 'Measuring Sustainability of Economies: A Conceptual Approach to Regional Material Flow Accounts', in F. Moser (ed.) *Sustainable development - Where do we stand?* (Int. Symposium University) Graz.

Bringezu, S., F. Hinterberger and H. Schütz (1994), 'Integrating Sustainability into The System of National Accounts: The Case of Interregional Material Flows', in *Models of Sustainable Development. Exclusive or complementary approaches of sustainability?* (Vol. II) Symposium International, Université Panthéon-Sorbonne, C 3 E (Metis), Paris.

Brown. L. (1992), *State of the World 1992*, Washington DC : World Watch Institute.

Daly, Herman E. (1991), *Steady State Economics*. 2nd ed. Washington, DC: Island Press.

Daly, Herman E. (1992), *Steady State Economics*: 'Concepts, Questions, Policies'. GAIA 1 (1992) No. 6. 333–8.

Ekins, P. and M. Max-Neef (eds) (1992), 'Real-Life Economics', *Understanding Wealth Creation*, London, New York: Routledge.

European Commission (1994), Directions for the EU on Environmental Indicators and Green National Accounting. The Integration of Environmental and Economic Information Systems, Bruxelles.

Eurostat (1994), 'Contributions of member states and EFTA countries to the SERIEE system', Eurostat Internal Document F3: Environmental Statistics, Luxembourg.

The Factor 10 Club (1995), *Carnoules Declaration*, Wuppertal: Wuppertal Institut.

FAZ (Frankfurter Allgemeine Zeitung) (1993), '51 Prozent höhere Rohölreserven', 12/7/1995, p. 11.

Femia, A. Hinterberger and F.F. Luks (1995), 'Ecological Sustainability, Economic Growth, Individual Well-Being, ... and Eco-Policy', mimeo, Wuppertal Institute.

Franz, A., Stahmer, C. (1993), *Approaches to Environmental Accounting*, 'Proceedings of the IARIW Conference on Environmental Accounting, Baden/Austria 27–29 May 1991', Heidelberg/New York: Springer.

Georgescu-Roegen, N. (1994), 'Thermodynamics and We, the Humans' in J.C. Dragan, E.K. Seifert and M.C. Demetrescu (eds.) *Entropy and Bioeconomics*, Milan: Nagard.

Goodland, R. and H.E. Daly (1992), 'Three steps towards global environmental sustainability I', *Development* (2/1992). pp. 35–41

Henderson, H. (1991), 'Paradigms in progress' in *Life Beyond Economics*, Indianapolis: Knowledge Systems.

Hicks, John (1946). *Value and Capital*, Oxford: Oxford University Press.

Hinterberger, F., F. Luks and F. Schmidt-Bleek (1997), 'Material flows vs "Natural Capital". What makes an economy sustainable?' *Ecological Economics*, forthcoming.

Hinterberger, F., S. Kranendonk, M.J. Welfens. and F. Schmidt-Bleek, (1994), 'Increasing Resource Productivity through Eco-efficient Services', *Wuppertal Papers* (13). Reprinted in Hinterberger and Stahel (eds, 1996) *Eco-efficient Services*, Boston: Kluwer.

Kapp, William K. (1950/1971), *The Social Costs of Private Enterprise,* Cambridge, Mass.: Harvard University Press.

Leipert, C. (1989), *Die heimlichen Kosten des Fortschritts,* Frankfurt/M: Fischer Verlag.

Liedtke, C., C. Manstein, T. Merten (1994), *MIPS,* 'Resource Management and Sustainable Development. Proceedings of the International ASM Conference "The Recycling of Metals",' Amsterdam.

Netherlands Central Bureau of Statistics (1992), *Methodology for the Calculation of Sustainable National Income.*

Nordhaus, W.D. (1994), 'Reflections on the Concept of Sustainable Economic Growth', in Pasinetti, L.L. and R.M. Solow (eds): *Economic Growth and the Structure of Long-Term Development,* New York St. Martin's Press.

Nussbaum, M. C. and A. Sen, (eds) (1993), *The Quality of Life,* Oxford: Clarendon Press.

Pearce, D.W. and R.K.Turner (1990), *Economics of Natural Resources and the Environment,* Baltimore: Johns Hopkins University Press.

Radermacher, W. and C. Stahmer, (1994), 'Umweltökonomische Trends 1960 bis 1990', *Wirtschaft und Statistik* **8**, 658–77.

Sachs, W. (1993), 'Die vier E's. Merkposten für einen mass-vollen Wirtschaftsstil', *Politische Ökologie Special,* 69–72.

Sachs, W. (1994), 'Geschmacksbildung ist wichtiger als Naturschutz'. An interview in *Kunstforum* (128), 78–82.

Schmidt-Bleek F. (1993), '*MIPS* – A Universal Ecological Measure?' Fresenius Environmental Bulletin (2), 306–11.

Schmidt-Bleek F. (1994), *Wieviel Umwelt braucht der Mensch?* – MIPS – Das Mass für ökologisches Wirtschaften. Berlin, Basel, Boston: Birkhäuser.

Seifert, E.K. (1986), 'Zum Problem einer 'Naturvergessenheit' ökonomischer Theorien, Thesen eines Forschungsprogramms zur Zukunft der Erinnerung, in R. Pfriem, (ed.) *Ökologische Unternehmenspolitik,* Frankfurt/M.: Campus.

Seifert, E.K. (1993), 'Sustainable development – From concept to action', in F. Moser (ed.), *Sustainable development – Where do we stand?* (Int. Symposium University) Graz, 263–81.

Seifert, E.K. (1995), 'Sustainable Development – Dauerhaftes Wirtschaften. Für einen umweltverträglichen Wohlstand der Nationen', in E.K. Seifert and B.P. Priddat, B.P. (eds) *Neuorientierungen in der ökonomischen Theorie. Zur moralischen, institutionellen, evolutorischen und ökologischen Dimension des Wirtschaftens,* Marburg: Metropolis.

Seifert, E.K. and R. Pfriem, (eds) (1989), *Wirtschaftsethik und ökologische Wirtschaftsforschung,* Bern/Stuttgart: Haupt.

Sen, A. (1983), 'Poor, Relatively Speaking', *Oxford Economic Papers* (35), pp. 135–69.

Stahmer, C. and E.K. Seifert, (1994), 'Valuation concepts for calculating "green GNP": complementary not exclusive', in: *Models of Sustainable Development. Exclusive or complementary approaches of sustainability?* (Vol. II) Symposium International, Université Panthéon-Sorbonne, C 3 E (Metis), Paris, 699–713.

Tisdell. C. A. (1991), 'Economics of Environmental Conservation' in *Economics for environmental and ecological management*, Amsterdam *et al.*: Elsevier.
Toman, M.A., J. Pezzey and J. Krautkraemer, (1994), 'Neoclassical economics and "sustainability"', in: *Models of Sustainable Development. Exclusive or complementary approaches of sustainability?* (Vol. II) Symposium International, Université Panthéon-Sorbonne, C 3 E (Metis), Paris, 3–18.
Turner, R.K., P. Doktor and N. Adger, (1994), 'Sea-level Rise and Coastal Wetlands in the U.K.: Mitigation Strategies for Sustainable Management', in C. Folke, M. Hammer, R. Costanza and A. Jansson, (eds) *Investing in Natural Capital. The Ecological Economics Approach to Sustainability*, Washington, Covelo: Island Press.
UNDP (1990–1994), *Human Development Reports* 1990, 1991, 1992, 1993, 1994, New York/Oxford: Oxford University Press.
United Nations (1993), *Integrated Environmental and Economic Accounting, Handbook of National Accounts* (SEEA-UN-Handbook), New York: United Nations Publications.
Weizsäcker, E.U. (1994), *Earth Politics*, London: Zed Books.
Welfens, M.J. (1993), 'De-materialization Strategies and Systems of National Accounts', *Fresenius Environmental Bulletin* (2), 431–436.
World Commission on Environment and Development (WCED) (1987), *Our Common Future*, Oxford/New York: Oxford University Press.

# 6. Instituional Learning and Clean Growth

## Björn Johnson

### Introduction

The increasing problems of environmental protection create new needs for technical and institutional change. There is now growing agreement that many environmental problems, both global and local, require multi-level, diversified policy responses, including policies for technical and institutional adaptations. These factors are also coming into focus in environmental economics. We still, however, need a better understanding of the mechanisms and effects of institutional and technical change in relation to environmental problems.

This chapter gives an institutional perspective[1] on the relations between economic growth and environmental protection. Economic growth, regarded as a long-run process of increasing production capacity, is not possible without changes in production structure, product and process technologies and institutions. This is an inevitable conclusion from the analysis of economic growth by Schumpeter (1934), Kuznets (1971) and Abramovitz (1989). Economic growth has never been just plain, balanced growth. It has never been (and could never have been) a simple blow-up of a given economic structure without technical, organizational and institutional change. It has always been fundamentally unbalanced; a process of transformation during which processes and products emerge and disappear and during which institutions change.

It is argued in this chapter that, because of institutional, technical and structural change, the relations between economic growth and the environment change, qualitatively, over time. It is also argued that, because of the important role institutions play in moulding the process of long-run economic transformation, the possibility of economic growth without environmental destruction is to a large extent a question of institutional change, including design and redesign of institutions, in order to stimulate cleaner technologies, habits and values; it is a question not only of technical learning but also of institutional learning.


## 1. Problems of Growth

*The problem of growth and environment*

Globally, we need at the same time both much better protection of the environment and reduction of poverty. Poverty is more easily reduced with economic growth, which implies increasing use of natural resources and more pollution and thus increasing pressure on the environment. Is it possible to have growing material well-being and effective environmental protection at the same time? Brutal growth, that is the old-fashioned, Fordist type of energy – and material intensive growth of production puts pressure on the material and energy 'sources and sinks' of the economy, as earlier chapters have shown.

Even if brutal growth, inevitably, creates environmental problems, zero growth is not in itself a solution. The relationship between economic growth and the environment is neither stable nor reversible over time. Reducing or stopping growth does not remove environmental damage already done, nor prevent current rates of exhaustion of sinks and sources from leading to crisis in the future. Moreover, the political and economic decision systems often react to reduced economic growth in ways which hurt the environment rather than help it. Investments in cleaner technologies, which normally are introduced and diffused quicker in growing industries than in stagnating ones, are postponed, cheaper and more polluting fuels are substituted for cleaner ones, and so on.

These asymmetrical environmental reaction patterns, in combination with some 'classical' economic problems (unemployment, income inequalities, regional imbalances, and so on) which tend to follow reduced growth, make a stop-growth policy a very dubious solution to environmental problems; and yet continued brutal growth is unacceptable. The situation seems to require substantial structural, technological and institutional changes.

*Deep reasons for growth*

It is sometimes said that we, in the industrial world, live in a society that too often tries to solve its problems by expansion: 'Growth has been the dominant behaviour of the socio-economic system for more than two hundred years... It is culturally ingrained and structurally inherent in the global system...' (Meadows *et al.* 1992, pp. 3/14). This suggests that there might be deep reasons for economic growth in capitalist economies, which make it difficult to manage without it.

As Scitovsky (1980) has pointed out, capitalism works best, when it is flexible. As a social and economic system it may not score high in equity and justice, but its capacity to generate technical and, not less important, institutional innovations, and to go on doing so, has been its main advantage. The experimental character of capitalism (Rosenberg and Birdzell 1986), which has to do with its incentive system and its multi-level and multi-head decision structure, has allowed it to expand into new directions, when it was stagnating in the former growth areas. New growth industries have replaced old ones and new organizational and institutional arrangements have been substituted for outmoded ones as responses to mis-match problems between technologies and institutions, and this has permitted and stimulated fast technical change. This is the character of the capitalist development process and economic growth is a consequence of it.

On the microeconomic level the decision-makers are not usually preoccupied with growth as such, but they are locked into a system of dynamic competition in which innovation is a dominant source of profit and instrument of survival. On the macroeconomic level this is registered as economic growth. At the macropolitical level there is also a strong pressure for economic growth even if it is difficult to forecast and almost impossible to control. Income inequalities and social conflicts are often supposed to be easier to handle and social problems more readily solved in a growing economy. At the international level countries lock each other into a global system of economic expansion and a race for growth which is not easy to quit. A country with substantially lower than average growth rates will probably accumulate foreign debt, experience increasing unemployment and public dissatisfaction, and risk losing strategic capital and manpower resources to competing countries. It may well find itself in a vicious circle. For an individual country, there is no obvious alternative to participating in the international growth race.

Economic growth is, thus, built into capitalism. Physical throughput growth arises out of it, without being wanted for its own sake.

*Limits to growth*

It may be of some help to observe that different kinds of growth, which figure in the growth–environment debate, are measured in different units. Throughput growth, that is growth of use of energy and materials and growth of waste disposal and pollution, can from an environmental point of view only be measured in specific physical and disaggregated units. This is also the case for the measurement of welfare growth, which requires disaggregated combinations of different physical as well as psychological and social welfare indicators. Economic growth, on the other hand, is a 'synthetic' concept, which measures the growth of production or income aggregated to the macroeconomic level in money terms with the help of prices in accordance with national accounting conventions. In the short run there are rather rigid relations between throughput growth and economic growth and there may even be some connections between economic growth and welfare growth. In a longer time-perspective, however, when technologies, institutions and values are allowed to change, the connections between different kinds of growth become much looser.

The different kinds of growth may encounter different limits to growth. Since the first publication of the Club of Rome (Meadows *et al.* 1972) it has become usual to recognize 'physical limits to growth'. Non-reproducible natural resources might be used up, the use of reproducible resources might be greater than the rate of regeneration, and for pollutants the rate of emission might be greater than what can be absorbed by the natural environment. We now recognize both 'source limits' and 'sink limits' on materials and energy, and the increasingly global and devastating character of some of them. We also recognize the connection of these limits with population growth and increasingly the additional problems when this leads to urbanization and megacity growth.[2]

Strictly speaking, physical sources and sinks are only limits to throughput growth. The situation is more complicated for welfare growth and economic growth, which may encounter quite a number of different limits. The environmental problems connected to megacity growth illustrate that negative side effects of rapid economic growth might seriously undermine its positive welfare effects. There are several economic and social problems (local unemployment and poverty, housing problems, traffic problems, problems of law and order, and so on) related to the regional and structural dislocation phenomena of rapid, unbalanced growth. We may in this connection talk about 'congestion and dislocation limits to growth'.

Hirsch (1977), however, meant something different when he discussed social congestion effects in relation to economic growth and coined the term 'social limits to growth'. Because of social scarcity and positional competition, economic growth in a market economy generates expectations it cannot fulfil and sharpens, rather than decreases, the distribution conflicts. In addition to these effects Hirsch concluded that capitalist pursuit of economic self-interest destroys the moral foundations, which the market economy depends on, if it is to keep transaction costs within manageable limits. Needless to say, this may become a problem, if society increasingly has to deal with collective environmental values and problems in an institutional set-up in which individual self-interest dominates. It might imply a potential contradiction in using some types of economic incentives in environmental policy. Social limits to growth may be defined as limits to the economy's ability to transform growing economic activity into broadly dispersed welfare growth.

We may also identify limits to the ability of the economy to sustain high degrees of resource utilization during long periods of economic growth. It has been suggested that the slow-down in economic growth and the high level of unemployment since the end of the 1960s was caused by 'institutional sclerosis' (see Chapter 11 in this volume). A growing conflict between an increasing need for change and a decreasing flexibility was assumed to lie behind poor macro-economic performance. According to this hypothesis we may talk about 'institutional limits to growth'.

It has also been suggested that the slow-down was caused by reduced levels of research and development and slower diffusion of new technologies as a consequence of reduced capital investments. This could be termed 'technological limits to growth'. Besides technical and institutional rigidities, rigid consumer tastes may restrict economic growth. In a growing economy without consumer learning stagnation will gradually occur, as consumer demand for different, non-positional goods reaches saturation levels (Pasinetti 1981). This can only be avoided through the emergence of new variants and types of consumer goods and services. The observation that consumers are never satiated depends on product innovation and consumer learning.

Economic growth may, thus, become constrained by many different kinds of factors. When the growth process stagnates for longer periods of time, it is more likely, however, that the problem lies in a combination of several factors. The economy's ability to generate production and income growth in the long run depends mostly on its ability to generate technical change and, at the same time, to adapt its organizational forms, its institutions and its patterns of demand to support this. The concept of a new techno-economic paradigm has been developed by Carlota Perez and Christopher Freeman (Perez 1983, 1985; Freeman and Perez 1988; and see Chapter 9 in this volume) to indicate a radical shift in the entire technological and institutional basis of the economy. Such shifts will lead to long waves in economic development. A techno-economic paradigm will at some point of time run out of steam, mainly as a result of increasing tensions between technical change and the institutional and organizational set-up of the economy, and unless and until a new techno-institutional fit is established, economic growth will be slow. We may define this as 'techno-institutional limits to growth'.

A shift of techno-economic paradigm will change the whole character of economic growth. It is quite clear that economic growth during the Fordist techno-economic paradigm was very resource- and energy-intensive. Yet, resource and energy limits did not restrict growth during the 1950s and 1960s and were not the fundamental cause of the growth slow-down from the beginning ·of the 1970s and onwards, even if the rise of energy prices was a contributing factor. It was, rather, a combined effect of many technological, institutional and economic factors and their interplay. Of course, if the fast economic growth of the 1960s had continued and its resource- and energy-intensive character had prevailed, the Western economies would have moved closer and closer to pure throughput limits. The point is, however, that a new constellation of institutions and technologies in a new techno-economic paradigm has the potential to change the throughput characteristics of economic growth.

In order to see this more clearly it may help to introduce a new perspective on resources and scarcity in the economic process. On ·a general level this point can be illustrated with the help of *Figure 6.1*.

*Figure 6.1: The role of knowledge in the economy.*

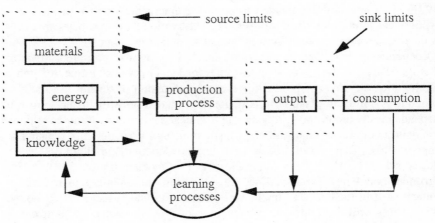

All production is a process in which materials are transformed from one set of physical forms to another. The transformation of materials requires energy and is controlled by knowledge. With the help of a biological analogy (like a chicken produced from an egg; the materials are in the yolk and in the white of the egg, energy comes from the body-heat of the hen and the knowledge is genetically coded) materials, energy and knowledge can be viewed as the basic ingredients of all production processes (Boulding 1981). In the short run production is controlled by a given stock of knowledge. In the long run the stock of knowledge is changed (by various kinds of learning and forgetting in connection with production and consumption) and the character of the growth process changes as a result. We may hope that economic growth may take new, less environmentally damaging, material forms and become less energy intensive.

So what is missing from the discussion of ecological limits to economic growth is 'growth of knowledge'. Knowledge might be regarded as the most important of all resources and the one which goes through the most dramatic changes over time. But even if it also becomes more and more important (Boulding 1981, Lundvall and Johnson 1994), and even if learning is resource-consuming and learning capacities are limited, knowledge is not scarce in the same ways as materials and energy, neither in the traditional economic sense of being limited in relation to human needs and wants, nor in an environmental sense of being non-renewable or exhaustible. From an environmental point of view energy and materials are limiting factors in the growth process, while knowledge is an enabling factor.

The stock of knowledge does not decrease when put to use. On the contrary, the more it is used the more it grows. Of course we would often like to know more than we do, but this is not traditional economic scarcity. While materials and energy are used up in the production process, knowledge is increased. Production is a source of different kinds of learning and the economy can be organized in order to stimulate the growth, diffusion and utilization of, for example, environmentally useful knowledge.

In some ways knowledge is not used to its limits. There is a lot of knowledge about environmental costs and benefits, about source and sink limits, about cleaner technologies and cleaning technologies, about clean products and clean consumption, and so on. Much of this knowledge is, for different reasons, not put to use, however. Consumer preferences and consumer habits may not favour cleaner products. Prices may not stimulate the use of cleaner production processes. Organizational forms and management routines may not be adapted to clean technologies. Product standards may lag behind. Institutions for technological information and service may be inadequate, and so on.

This is to a large extent a question of deficient institutional responses to environmental problems. Knowledge about clean processes and products has not been adequately ingrained into the economy in the forms of norms, routines, standards and habits. If the existence of large amounts of unused resources means that these resources are abundant, then environmental knowledge is abundant; it is the incentives and abilities to use it which are limited. Thus, if suitable institutional changes could be implemented many environmental problems might be solved. Yet new knowledge is required as well. Both a better use of the existing stock of knowledge and the development of new knowledge are central for the 'cleaning' of production and consumption.

The introduction of knowledge as the key resource changes the limits to growth. Technological and institutional learning in combination with consumer learning means that different limits to growth might be, if not removed, at least softened up. New and better-utilized knowledge may make economic growth much less energy- and materials-intensive. A shift from the use of materials and energy towards the use of knowledge as the dominant logic and main characteristic of production has in fact been a trend in the development of the industrialized countries for a long time. New knowledge may also make economic growth more welfare efficient and soften up the social limits to growth. Clearly the absence from the analysis of the most important of the productive resources seriously distorts the picture of the relations between growth and the environment.

## 2. Clean Growth and Lean Growth

*Growth as a policy goal*

Economic growth, defined as growth of the gross national product measured in stable prices, is not a very meaningful economic policy goal in its own right. Most governments would be more interested in 'clean growth', if such a thing was possible. Clean growth is here defined as economic growth, which is not accompanied by growth in the use of materials and energy and which does not move close to any sink limits. Aggregate production in value terms grows, but does not become heavier or more dirty and the sources of specific materials are not exhausted. Completely clean growth is hard to imagine on a macroeconomic level but, with sufficient changes in different forms of knowledge, economic growth may become continuously cleaner compared to the 'brutal growth' of the Fordist techno-economic paradigm. 'Lean growth', that is clean growth with a high level of welfare efficiency, would be even more meaningful as a policy goal – if the social limits to growth could be relaxed, and if some production of 'stimulation' could be substituted for production of 'comfort' (Scitovsky 1980).

Since the 19th century, there has been a gradual change in the bias of technological change at least in the USA (Abramovitz 1994). The shift has been in the direction of less tangible capital-using, less resource-intensive and less scale-dependent technologies. Intangible capital formation, in the form of for example education and R&D, has become more and more important. Thus there seems to be an inherent tendency towards the development of the knowledge-based economy, which makes economic growth less brutal. But clean, and *a fortiori* lean, growth probably also requires a specific additional bias in the growth of knowledge; a systematic and goal-oriented learning process towards environmentally safer and more welfare efficient production and distribution.

## 3. An ICT-based Techno-economic Paradigm as a Solution?

Clean and lean growth, clearly, requires both technical and institutional change. Process and product technologies, the organization of production and distribution, collective consumption standards, consumer norms and habits, and so on, have to be adapted to environmental needs. This is clearly easier in at least some respects within the new information and communication technology (ICT) based techno-economic paradigm, which has been emerging in the second half of the 20th century following the 'Fordist', materials- and energy-intensive, mass production and mass consumption dominated techno-economic paradigm. Has the belief that economic growth is incompatible with environmental protection simply followed from confusing the Fordist type of growth with growth in general? Christopher Freeman (1992b) discusses this question and concludes that there are positive tendencies in the ICT-based new paradigm, but that they are far from sufficient. ICT makes saving of materials and energy possible through more accurate monitoring and control of production processes and through much better quality control and inventory management. The management norms of zero-defects and lean production, and the development of ICT are mutually reinforcing. Networking and R&D co-operation facilitate development of clean production technologies and pollution abatement, which by their nature require much interdisciplinary effort.

We have already seen many changes in these directions, and the environment-friendly potential of ICT and ICT-related organizational and institutional changes is far from exhausted. With the help of already well-established environmental policies – different kinds of economic incentives and penalties and legal regulations – much more of the energy- and materials-saving potential of the new paradigm can be realized. But ICT may also lead the wrong way. So far, for example, the energy-saving potential of ICT applied to transport activities (transporting information rather than people and materials) has not been realized. On the contrary, the ability to co-ordinate production and manage production systems cheaply over great distances has *increased* transport volumes. Freeman concludes that

> the incremental improvement of existing systems will not be enough to achieve the scale of reduction in energy and materials consumption, which will be needed in the industrial countries during the twenty-first century. Radical innovations will be needed including new transport, construction and industrial systems.

(Freeman 1992b p. 207) Technical innovation can contribute to clean growth, but the sheer scale of the problem makes a purely technical solution unlikely. Without radical changes in the present forms of organization of production, of competition, incentive systems, ways of financing and organizing collective consumption and in present consumer norms and habits, it is very hard to imagine economic growth without throughput growth.

What is probably required is a concerted process of incremental and radical technical *and* institutional change. Freeman (1992b) concludes that, in addition to a continuation and reinforcement of already existing policies, there is a need to anticipate and to some degree stimulate the next change of techno-economic paradigm. Prices must be corrected so as to reflect environmental costs (in itself a major institutional reform); long-term, clean technology programmes based on national and international, interactive learning, including networking and user–producer co-operation, and with both government support and participation, must be established; international co-operation organizations with independent, supranational, economic as well as political power must be committed to global environmental protection.

## 4. The Danish Revolution 1500–1800

This is an ambitious list of what one would like, but the fact that a combination of radical technical and institutional changes might be required to solve (or at least postpone) an environmental crisis is exemplified in a recent dissertation on Danish history. Thorkild Kjærgaard (1991) gives an 'ecohistorical' interpretation of how an ecological crisis was provoked and then solved in Denmark in the period from 1500 to 1800.

In the beginning of the 18th century Denmark was a country in the midst of an ecological crisis. In the preceding century a large part of its production capacity had been ruined. The agricultural productivity had been reduced by over-exploitation of the soil, sandstorms, floodings and livestock diseases. The forests had been cut down and there was an acute deficit of fuel and building materials. The standard of living had been reduced for large parts of the population.

According to Kjærgaard the two most important factors behind the crisis were the population growth (from 550,000 in the year 1650 to 925,000 in 1800) and the expansion of state sector consumption, mostly military (Denmark had the biggest army in Europe in relation to its population and a big navy as well). They resulted in both source and sink limits to growth. Wood especially, a crucial resource in the agrarian economy, was extremely scarce, and the cutting down of the forests destroyed many of the ecological systems on which the economy depended. The problems were aggravated by feedback loops: for example, the shortage of wood forced people to use cow- and stable-dung for heating, which reduced harvests and led to more deforestation. In the middle of the 18th century the situation had become almost uncontrollable. Drastic measures were called for and were carried through on different levels. Both central and local governments as well as communities and individual actors were involved. The government initiated measures against the desertification. Foreign experts were called in for advice, and planning and legal regulations which forced local communities to take action were introduced. Floodings and excessive levels of subsoil water were reduced by new systems of ditches and canals, which in turn required new systems for crop-rotation, decision-making and work organization. The excessive acidity of the soil, another result of the over-exploitation, was reduced by marling; knowledge about marl and its effect on crop yields being spread both by private organisations and by government agencies. Much-needed nitrogen was added to the soil by a remarkably fast introduction of domesticated clover in the crop-rotation system, which had a dramatic effect on soil productivity. A common element in these changes was that they required a great increase in working hours. Work norms and habits, in fact the complete institutional regulation of work, changed.

All these measures were effective and necessary. However, the serious energy crisis and the shortage of building materials, which had resulted from the deforestation could not, in spite of many new methods for economizing with wood (the use of clay and straw as building materials and of peat for heating, for example) be overcome without the introduction of a new source of energy, imported coal from England. As a result of all these technological and institutional changes and of the introduction of the new source of energy, agricultural production, forests and energy consumption began to grow simultaneously again. At the end of the process the Danish landscape and its buildings and villages had changed dramatically, a completely new agricultural organization and agricultural technology had been introduced, working hours had increased dramatically, a new social structure and many new institutions had evolved.

Kjærgaard's analysis emphasizes clearly the magnitude and diversity of the measures and changes, which became necessary in order to resume growth. It also shows that many of the institutional responses, first of all the breaking down of the old village communities and the emergence of a new class of independent, freehold farmers and of a centralized bureaucracy, did little to solve the problems and in many respects rather delayed the overcoming of the crisis. On the basis of this case at least, there is not much reason to expect that adequate and rational institutional responses to the encountering of limits to growth will emerge, quickly and automatically.

If clean or, better still, lean growth is to be achieved, technical learning must accelerate. And since institutional change is necessary in order to utilize existing knowledge better, and in order to guide technical innovation towards cleaner technologies and stimulate cleaner consumer habits and norms, institutional learning must quicken too. This is not surprising since, as will be argued in the next section, institutional learning is a fundamental aspect of any process of economic growth.

## 5. The Social Capability for Lean Growth

*Catching-up growth*

The research on catching-up-growth has shown that technical knowledge does not float freely across national borders and that it takes time and effort for laggards to emulate the best-practice techniques (Abramovitz 1989, 1994). It has also shown that countries differ in their ability to catch up and that these differences are related to what Abramovitz calls their social capability.

> As I use it here it is a rubric that covers countries' levels of general education and technical competence, the commercial, industrial and financial institutions which bear on their abilities to finance and operate modern, large-scale business, and the political and social characteristics that influence the risks, the

incentives and the personal rewards of economic activity including those rewards in social esteem that go beyond money and wealth. (Abramovitz 1994)

The research on catching-up-growth has not, however, paid much attention to the fact that the international transfer of technologies also requires institutional adaptations and innovations and that an element of international transfer of institutions tends to accompany economic growth. This means that in addition to Abramowitz's social capability (for absorbing technical knowledge used abroad), we might consider a broader concept of 'social capability for technical and institutional change'. This concept is not limited to the imitation of techniques and products used abroad, for example in the form of import of machinery or procurement of licences. It also includes the capability to adapt to and make minor innovations to the absorbed technologies, to make them compatible with local standards and tastes, to discover and remove faults and deficiencies in design, to make quality adjustments and so on. It also includes a capability for organizational and institutional adaptations in order to get a better fit between the imported technologies and the existing institutional framework. Work organization may have to be adjusted, employees may need education, communication patterns within and between firms may have to change, and so on, in order to realize the potential productivity improvements of new technologies. And it includes a capability to import or borrow suitable organizational forms and institutions from abroad. Changes in the education system, infrastructural reforms, new types of technical service, financial innovations and so on, might be needed in order to absorb the new technologies productively. Finally, the broader concept of social capability includes the capability to adapt both the imported technologies and institutions to the prevailing broader institutional and cultural framework of the country.

## 6. The Need for Institutional Learning

Looked upon in this way it is clear that institutional learning is a crucial factor in economic growth and development. International institutional learning has, for example, been an important factor in Fordist growth: After the Second World War and under the Marshall Aid programme, 'productivity delegations' went from Europe to the USA to study scientific management and the organizational forms connected to the best-practice mass-production technologies. These institutional innovations were then quickly spread to Europe. Not many years later the multi-divisional firm structure, introduced by du Pont and General Motors in the 1930s, with some country-specific modifications, diffused throughout Western Europe (Williamson 1985). The in-house industrial R&D laboratory and the Institute of Technology originated in Germany and in the United States and spread quickly into some other countries, slowly into others. The need for international institutional learning in relation to clean and lean growth is probably much greater than it was for brutal growth. It is needed for at least four reasons:

1. Existing but dispersed knowledge can be diffused and utilized better. Source and sink restrictions can be taken more systematically into account already under present production structure and technologies. In this respect there is a permanent need for institutional learning. For many types of production, there already exist environmentally much safer product and process technologies, which could be better utilized. In many areas consumer habits could become much cleaner with no more than minor adaptations in ways of living. There is a growing international literature on innovations in environmental policy, which reports on experiences with better utilization of existing knowledge (Tietenberg 1992). Sometimes more radical institutional changes might yield rapid gains even without accompanying radical technical changes. Ostrom (1990) has shown that sustainable management of common pool resources is possible under very different institutional and technical regimes, including collective ownership. We should not take for granted that the experiences of the 'socialist' countries have disqualified all sorts of collectivism, or that existing private property institutions are as efficient for clean as for brutal growth.

2. Institutions are needed to take account of the environmental risks which are inevitably connected to technical innovations. Innovations can both solve and generate environmental problems. In this chapter the focus is on the former, but even innovations which are intended to reduce environmental pressures may lead to unexpected problems. The inherent uncertainty element in all innovations requires institutions for risk assessment and risk management in relation to the environment. There is an increasing literature on this topic and there are different experiences in different countries, which could be utilized for institutional learning (Roberts and Weale 1991).

As a consequence of the uncertainty and the potential dangers to the environment connected to technical innovations there is a need for innovating firms to develop an environmental ethics and to exercise responsible environmental judgement. It is not enough just to follow the rules and maximize profits within a set of environmental restrictions, however strict these may be. We never quite know the exact nature of the possible damage, and this makes the processes which define, select and evaluate the dangers connected with innovation important. Formal technology assessment institutions are important but not enough. Effective communication between the scientific community, industry and the public matters in this respect, and the function of the press and other media can be crucial for defining the potential environmental costs and benefits of innovations. Environmental grassroots movements probably play an even more important role in the creation of environmental ethics.

3. There is a need for institutions, which can lead technical development into environmentally safer directions and stimulate the development of cleaner products and processes. National accounting systems, which reflect source and sink costs better, environmental accounting in firms, taxes and subsidies which make market prices reflect long-term environmental costs, government-supported long-term clean technology programmes, national and international networking between firms and research institutions, better identification and organisation of the end users of cleaner products and processes, and development of methods and channels for better communication between users and producers, are important in these respects. The list of relevant institutional innovations is long.

4. If lean as well as clean growth is to be achieved such fundamental technical and institutional changes are needed that they amount to a completely new techno-economic paradigm. Since a new techno-economic paradigm emerges and develops within the old paradigm, and we are dealing with a rather long time-perspective, a programme for institutional learning, designed to shape the institutional set-up so that it promotes technical and organizational learning for the protection of the environment, could be started now.

A techno-economic paradigm contains common-sense guide-lines for organizational and technical decisions and thus shapes technological trajectories. If it is to lock technologies into clean trajectories, it has to introduce environmental considerations into a broad spectrum of social institutions and routines. Standards, textbooks, availability of low-cost components and materials, fashions, training systems, management routines, technological expectations, advantageous infrastructure and scale economies are mentioned by Freeman (1992b). To this can be added government policies, access to information and knowledge, schools and education, relations between private and collective consumption, possibilities and conditions for financing long-term investments, and environmental values in general. The basic rules for competition should be able to take environmental restrictions and priorities into account. For example, process characteristics should in some cases be accepted as elements of product characteristics, so that products produced under stricter environmental rules are fully recognized as different from otherwise identical products.

Of course, not all aspects of institutional change are open for policy-making. From an evolutionary perspective some aspects of institutional learning are, if not totally unpredictable, not politically controllable. Institutions often evolve behind the backs of policy-makers. But in social evolution humans create and shape their own conditions in a way which has no immediate counterpart in biological evolution. In human society social communication results in collective action forming new institutions, which, in turn, affect both the creation and selection of technology (Dalum *et al.* 1992).

In order to assess the possibility of different modes and mechanisms of institutional learning for lean growth we need to improve our knowledge in a number of ways. First, we need a much better mapping of the international institutional diversity in relation to environmental problems. This is a difficult project because of the complexity of most institutional set-ups and because of their largely informal and unregistered character. Second, the problem of institutional compatibility must be better understood. Borrowed institutions have to fit with both domestic technologies and the overall institutional system. How, and how far, this can be done affects the results of institutional learning from abroad. To assess this requires interdisciplinary analysis, in which economists cooperate with sociologists and anthropologists as well as experts on business administration. Even minor institutional changes in the educational system, like a serious introduction of elements of other social sciences and of ecology and environmental science into the  curriculum of economics, might help here.

Third, institutional learning presupposes a degree of institutional openness; a willingness and an ability of policy-makers, firms and households to participate in a process of adapting and renewing the institutional framework through both incremental and radical institutional innovation. To preserve the necessary coherence of the institutional system and avoid creating or increasing social conflicts however, such an openness always has to be restricted. Some of the more successful (in terms of economic growth) examples of institutional borrowing (Korea, Taiwan, Singapore) have combined institutional openness in some respects with institutional conservatism in others. A kind of basic institutional stability, probably, has to be preserved during the process, in order to avoid the institutional system disintegrating and losing its basic, information-signalling functions. The way different institutions complement each other, will affect how much that requirement limits the rate of change.

## 7. Conclusion

Throughput limits to growth can be softened up significantly if it is recognized that economic growth is connected to structural change and that knowledge is the crucial factor in the growth process, a factor which is neither scarce nor exhaustible in the usual meanings of these words. New knowledge develops through different kinds of learning. The focus in this chapter has been on institutional learning, which in a way is more basic than technical learning; institutional learning defines and sets rules for technical learning. The institutional framework has impacts on the resources devoted to technical learning and the directions in which it is pursued as well as the methods used. In this way the institutional set-up influences both production processes and product characteristics and, since it also affects consumer habits and norms, institutional learning is fundamentally important for the possibilities to establish clean and lean growth. Unfortunately our knowledge about the processes of institutional learning is not well developed. Research about both the existing international institutional diversity and mechanisms for its development through learning is needed. Because a new techno-economic paradigm starts to develop from within the old one, we have to look around, screening and mapping, within the existing international institutional diversity for the seeds of the elements of a new, lean institutional set-up. And because of the far-reaching changes in process and product technologies and in consumer norms and habits, which are necessary to implement lean growth, minor institutional adaptations will not be enough. Institutional learning for lean growth will have to include radical institutional innovations including strict restrictions on specific kinds of consumer behaviour. However, if it is realized that modern economies are increasingly becoming learning economies (Lundvall and Johnson 1994) in which the whole institutional framework including the organisational modes of firms are designed to enhance learning capabilities there is reason for hope.

## Notes

1. The concept of institutions used in this chapter is the broad, 'sociological', definition of classical institutional economics, that is institutions are seen as sets of habits,

routines, rules, norms and laws, which regulate the relations between people and shape human interaction (Hodgson 1993).

2. 'In Lima, unsolved sanitation problems recently triggered an outbreak of cholera that spread quickly into neighbouring countries. Studies in Bangkok demonstrate that air pollution is causing irreversible brain damage and loss of IQ in children. Blocked drainage canals in many cities, such as Buenos Aires, not only serve as breeding grounds for malaria but also result in a spate of new urban flooding – a phenomenon that some incorrectly term a "natural disaster" (Cohen 1993).

## References

Abramowitz, M. (1989), *Thinking About Growth*, Cambridge: Cambridge University Press.

Abramowitz, M. (1993), *'The origins of the post-war catch-up and convergence boom'*, paper prepared for the conference on Catching-up, Forging Ahead and Falling Behind, Oslo, May 1993, mimeo.

Abramovitz, M. (1994), 'Catch-up and Convergence in the Post-War Growth Boom and After' in W.J. Baumol, R.R. Nelson, and E.N. Wolff (eds), *The Convergence of Productivity: Cross-National Studies and Historical Evidence*, New York: Oxford University Press.

Boulding, K. (1981), *Evolutionary Economics*, Beverly Hills: Sage Publications.

Cohen, M. (1993), 'Megacities and the Environment', *Finance and Development*, **30** (2).

Dalum, B., B. Johnson, and B.Å. Lundvall (1992), 'Public Policy in the learning Society' Chapter 14 in B.Å. Lundvall (ed.), *National Systems of Innovation*, London: Pinter.

Freeman, C. (1992), *The Economics of Hope. Essays on Technical Change, Economic Growth and the Environment*, London and New York: Pinter.

Freeman (1992a), 'Technology, progress and the quality of life', in *The Economics of Hope. Essays on Technical Change, Economic Growth and the Environment*, London and New York: Pinter.

Freeman (1992b), 'A green techno-economic paradigm for the world economy', in *The Economics of Hope. Essays on Technical Change, Economic Growth and the Environment*, London and New York: Pinter.

Freeman, C. and C. Perez (1988), 'Structural Crises of Adjustment, Business Cycles and Investment Behaviour' in Giovanni Dosi *et al.* (eds), *Technical Change and Economic Theory*, London: Pinter.

Hirsch, F. (1977), *The Social Limits to Growth*, London: Routledge and Kegan Paul.

Hodgson, G. (1993), 'Introduction' in G. Hodgson (ed.) *The Economics of Institutions*, Aldershot: Edward Elgar.

Johnson, B. (1992), 'Institutional Learning', Chapter 2 in B.Å. Lundvall, (ed.), *National Systems of Innovation*, London: Pinter.

Kjærgaard, T. (1991), *Den Danske Revolution 1500–1800. En økohistorisk tolkning*, Aalborg: Gyldendal.

Kuznets, S. (1971), *Economic Growth of Nations*, Cambridge, MA: The Belknap Press of Harvard University Press.

Lundvall, B.Å., (ed.) (1992), *National Systems of Innovation*, London: Pinter.

Lundvall, B.Å. and B. Johnson (1994), 'The Learning Economy', *Journal of Industry Studies*, **I** (2), 23–42.

Meadows, D. H., D. L. Meadows, J. Randers, and W.W. Behrens (1972), *The Limits to Growth*, New York: Universe Books.

Meadows, D. H., D.L. Meadows, and J. Randers (1992), *Beyond the Limits*, Post Mills, VT: Chelsea Green Publishing Company.

Ostrom, E. (1990), *Governing the Commons*, Cambridge: Cambridge University Press.

Pasinetti, L.L. (1981), *Structural Change and Economic Growth*, Cambridge: Cambridge University Press.

Perez, C. (1983), 'Structural Change and the Assimilation of new Technologies in the Economic and Social Systems'. *Futures*, **15** (4), 357–75.

Perez, C. (1985), 'Microelectronics, Long Waves and World Structural Change', *World Development*, **13** (3), 441–63.

Roberts, L. and A. Weale (eds) (1991), *Innovation and Environmental Risk*, London, Belhaven Press.

Rosenberg, N. and L.E. Birdzell (1986), *How the West Grew Rich*. New York: Basic Books.

Schumpeter, J. A. (1934), *The Theory of Economic Development*, London: Oxford University Press.

Scitovsky, T. (1980), 'Can Capitalism Survive? – An Old Question in a New Setting', *American Economic Review*, **70** (2), 1–9

Tietenberg, T.H. (ed.) (1992), *Innovation in Environmental Policy*, Aldershot: Edward Elgar.

Williamson, O.E. (1985), *The Economic Institutions of Capitalism: Firms, Markets and Relational Contracting*, New York and London: Free Press.

# 7. Economic Theory and Environmental Policy Goals

## Frank J. Dietz and Jan van der Straaten

### 1. The Optimization Philosophy of Mainstream Economics

Current environmental economics can roughly be characterized as an extension and application of neoclassical economic theory to environmental problems. Natural resources are an input for human production and consumption processes. Like the scarcity of labour and capital, scarcity of natural resources forces economic agents to decide for which ends they are used. Consequently, given the ends of economic agents, the use of available natural resources is formulated as an optimization problem. Environmental deterioration or, conversely, environmental quality is the result of the aggregated decisions of all individual economic agents, weighing the benefits derived from increasing production and consumption against the benefits enjoyed when the environmental quality is improved.

A complicating factor is, however, that the preferences for environmental quality can only partly be expressed in exchange relations on the market. It is here that the problem of externalities arises. Unfortunately, environmental problems have become outstanding examples of external diseconomies or negative external effects. External diseconomies prevent the available natural resources from being used in accordance with the preferences of economic agents. Since Pigou's *Economics of Welfare* (1920), an external diseconomy has been defined as the production of a negative by-product by one or more economic agents. This by-product, though unwanted and unasked for, is delivered unintentionally and 'behind the back of the market' by one or more economic agents. The loss experienced by the victim is not regarded as a cost-item by the originator of the external diseconomy. As a result, the costs of exploiting nature have consistently been underestimated. Consequently, nature is harmed by production and consumption to a greater degree than the economic agents wish.

In environmental economics, internalization is the central issue. If external effects could be made part and parcel of the transactions in which they are generated, a Pareto optimum use of natural resources would be within reach. Most of the literature is devoted to various internalization procedures. In this chapter it is questioned whether the efforts to develop rather ingenious internalization schemes are truly relevant to environmental policy design. In our view, attempts to deal with the externality problem on the basis of aggregated individual preferences meet with fundamental obstacles, which make them unsuitable and unworkable as a basis for environmental policy design. These obstacles will be discussed in what follows.

This contribution is confined to the issue of goal formation, because it is here that mainstream environmental economic theory – that is, the theoretical literature in the neoclassical tradition of Marshall and Pigou – is most at odds with environmental policy practice. In the literature, the primary focus is on the issue of instrument choice once the policy goals are established. But how do we find out what the social goals for environmental quality are? How do we know the level of environmental quality we prefer? In dealing with this issue in this chapter a distinction is made between (1) the mainstream approach, in which policy goals are reduced exclusively to the preferences of individual economic agents, and (2) alternative approaches, in which policy goals are to a large extent based on ecological insights. The question is whether the optimization philosophy of mainstream economics is of more than heuristic value. In other words, is optimization an option for environmental policy? If not, in which direction do we have to search for alternatives?

It should be mentioned that a broad definition of natural resources is used in this chapter. First, in this definition natural resources are not limited to those traded on a market. A considerable proportion of natural resources used in production and consumption processes do not have a price, for example clean air and the ozone layer. Second, natural resources are included to the degree they have a function in production or consumption. This implies that the deposits of minerals and fossil fuels in the earth's crust are defined as natural resources. The possibility of generating new living organisms is another benefit natural resources provide to mankind. Pollutants of various kinds are neutralized, absorbed and recycled by certain mechanisms within the ecosystem. These absorption capacities are also natural resources.

## 2  Environmental Policy Goals in Mainstream Economic Theory

In the literature, environmental problems are traditionally described as negative externalities. Internalization of these externalities is in line with the optimization philosophy of mainstream economic theory. This is illustrated in *Figure 7.1* for the simple case of pollution varying exclusively with production.

*Figure 7.1: The individual and social optimum level of production.*

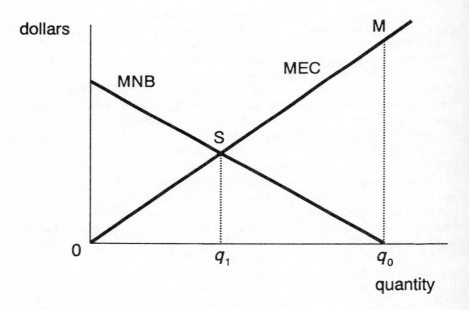

The emissions of an unspecified production process generate damage by environmental degradation which is assumed to rise exponentially with the size of the production (depicted as the rising linear curve for marginal environmental costs MEC). The polluting producer is solely interested in the marginal net benefits of his production (MNB), which by assumption is linear as is depicted in *Figure 7.1*. Profit maximization makes the producer increase the production until the level is reached at which the marginal net benefits are zero ($q_0$ in *Figure 1*.). With regard to the damage a third party suffers from production, a decrease in production is socially desirable. Standard economic reasoning results in the socially optimal level of production $q_1$. Until $q_1$, the marginal net benefits more than outweigh the marginal environmental costs, offering socially beneficial possibilities for production increase. Beyond $q_1$, the marginal environmental costs are higher than the marginal net benefits, requiring a decrease of production from a social point of view. Hence the social optimum, the incorporation of adverse environmental effects in economic decisions, implies a production decrease, from $q_0$ to $q_1$ in this case, which corresponds with the intersection S of the MNB curve and the MEC curve.

*Figure 7.2: The individual and social optimum level of emission reduction.*

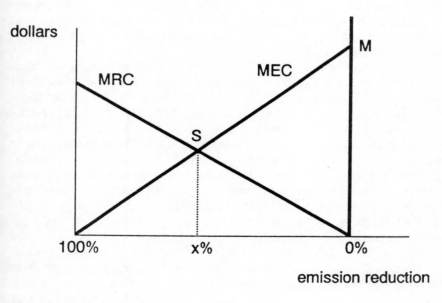

A similar reasoning applies if the polluting emissions can be reduced by adapting the production process or by purifying waste water or filtering waste gases. Instead of diminishing net proceeds due to a production decrease, the producer faces extra costs for emission reduction. A linear relation is assumed between the rate of emission reduction and the level of marginal reduction costs. As depicted in *Figure 7.2*, there are no marginal reduction costs (MRC) when the producer maintains these emissions. The marginal reduction costs are maximized if the emissions are completely eliminated. As long as the marginal environmental costs are higher than the marginal reduction costs, a neo-Paretian welfare improvement can be realized by a further reduction of emissions. The socially optimal reduction rate is $x\%$ and is located below the intersection S of the MRC curve and the MEC curve in *Figure 7.2*.

This analysis enables economists to explain the status quo as a suboptimal state, because it is reasonable to assume that producers will not spontaneously decrease production or reduce emissions to $q_1$. It is, in fact, reasonable to assume that such incentives are often absent in the case of environmental externalities. Prices for emissions or extractions are often implicit or even absent, which presents a necessary condition for policy intervention. According to the partial approach sketched above, polluters tend to produce too much of a specific externality if no adequate prices exist. The social optimum S in *Figure 7.1* can only be attained if society has adequate instruments with which to induce polluters to internalize the externality either through quantity or price-based instruments.

The externality concept is also often used as a normative principle in which the position is taken that the location of the optimum should be based on individual, not political preferences. It follows from the analysis given above that this requires familiarity with the exact location of the social welfare optimum S. In practice, it is hard to locate this optimum, because the shape and position of the MNB curve and, even more so, of the MEC curve are hard to determine. Estimation is hampered by the *evaluation problem*. In particular, problems can arise with respect to the estimation of the damage from an increase in pollution, which is the mirror-image of the benefits of a decrease in environmental damage, for example, if a polluted river is cleaned up. Ideally, the Pigovian framework suggests that these benefits should be derived from individual preferences. Such preferences, and the related benefits, are very hard to discover. Some of these benefits can be derived from market prices, such as the lower costs of producing drinking water and the higher proceeds from fishing. Other benefits, however, are more difficult to estimate, simply because markets do not always exist, for instance, markets for such public goods as valuable ecosystems and landscapes. What is, for example, the price of a square mile of wetlands?

In the absence of markets, other evaluation methods can be used to estimate the benefits economic agents experience if particular environmental damage is decreased or is avoided. In recent decades, a great deal of economic research has been done on alternative evaluation methods, including 'hedonic pricing methods' and 'contingent valuation methods' (CVM).[1] Although some progress has been made, these methods only *indicate* individual preferences. It is, for example, not clear whether CVM underestimates the willingness to pay for a particular environmental quality (Hoehn and Randall 1987) or overestimates this willingness to pay (Crocker and Shogren 1991). In addition, the crucial problem of how to aggregate individual preferences into a collective statement on the value of specific natural resources has proved very difficult to solve. Aggregation attempts meet with problems of the money-metric measurement of utility and of interpersonal comparisons of utility. Hence, the precise shape and position of MEC curves is often hidden. The MNB curve can usually be derived from marginal reduction costs curves, which seem to be less difficult to obtain empirically. However, cost observations are not always available or reliable. In other words, the determination of the optimal policy intervention may imply high agency costs linked with collecting and processing the necessary information, and may even prove impossible due to lack of information.

In conclusion, the use of the externality concept as the basis for setting the goals of policy interventions leads to a number of difficulties. A major reason for this is that the externality concept is based on individual preferences of the population at large. Individuals have to reveal what a particular good or bad is worth to them. Usually economists take this set of preferences as their most important source of information, but in this case it is not available or at best incomplete.

## 3. Ecological Uncertainties

Internalization of externalities appears to be difficult, because there is insufficient knowledge concerning individual preferences. But even in the hypothetical case of familiarity with all individual preferences and, subsequently, the ability to aggregate them into a collective decision on the desired environmental quality, this would still not preclude ecological disasters. This problem is linked to a fundamental limitation of rational choice theory in the context of environmental issues.

In general, the optimization strategy of rational choice theory implies that the production factors available (in most cases this is limited to labour and capital) are allocated according to the preferences of the economic agents, satisfying as many needs as possible. The same strategy applies to the management of the natural resources available. The diagnosis is simple: The present allocation of natural resources is not optimal, as is demonstrated by the generally undesired environmental deterioration. The neoclassical remedy is to restore optimal allocation by price manipulation. However, there is doubt as to whether this optimization philosophy is feasible for the management of the 'ecological utilization space' (Opschoor 1987). What is often lacking is essential information concerning the environmental effects of human actions.

A striking example of this is forests dying on a large scale as a result of acid rain. One of the most important causes of acid rain is the emission of large quantities of sulphur dioxide. Some twenty years ago, the first measures were taken in European industrial areas to reduce the harmful effects of sulphur dioxide on public health. These measures included the increased use of natural gas and nuclear energy and, to an ever greater degree, the construction of tall chimneys. It seemed that adequate measures had been taken, because air pollution in urban and industrial areas did decrease. However, the tall chimneys only dispersed the acidifying substances over large parts of Europe. Acid deposits outside the industrial areas increased rapidly, to the particular detriment of forests in Central Europe and Scandinavia. The acidification of ecosystems was probably foreseeable. Biologists warned at an early stage that tall chimneys would at best shift the problem elsewhere. Society, however, was easily able to dismiss these warnings as exaggerations, because it was not known for certain what the effects on nature would be.

Another example is the extensive ecological damage caused by the use of DDT and other persistent agricultural pesticides. The emission of carbon dioxide may also lead to unpleasant surprises later, since the climatological effects of an increased $CO_2$ content in the atmosphere are not clear. The same holds for the relation between the emission of CFCs and the hole in the ozone layer. From these and many other serious and less serious examples, it can repeatedly be seen that the effects of human (industrial) actions on nature are underestimated, minimized, or even ignored.

If the effects of so many interventions in and influences on nature are not sufficiently known or are consistently disregarded, an optimal use of natural resources for human production and consumption, such as is presupposed by neoclassical analyses and policy recommendations, becomes a problem. The point is that neoclassical optimization requires insight into the effects of alternative actions on nature (or into the availability of natural resources) with a probability bordering on certainty, or at least with a probability that can be calculated using the theory of probabilities. The former is the familiar assumption of the existence of fully-informed agents, whereby the problem of inadequate ecological knowledge is simply neglected. The latter seems more advanced, but still requires far better ecological knowledge than is generally available for constructing a distribution of probabilities of ecological states occurring as a result of a particular human intervention (for comparison, see Drepper and Manson 1993).

In general, processes in nature, and hence human interventions in these processes, appear to be very difficult to predict for at least three reasons. First, *synergetic effects* increase the impact of separate emissions on the environment. For example, laboratory experiments have made clear that the combined impact on plant growth of the acidifying substances $SO_2$, $NO_x$, $NH_3$ and $O_3$ is substantially more severe than would be the (linear) total of the impacts of each of these substances separately (Tonneijck 1981). Second, *thresholds* are very common in ecosystems. Again acidification serves as an excellent example. The sudden acceleration of the deterioration of forests and the subsequent dying off of large sections of European forestlands at the beginning of the 1980s was, for most people, including a large number of scientists, a rude awakening. It appeared that the buffering capacity of the soil had protected trees from serious damage for decades. Once a saturation point had been reached, acidifying substances could damage trees considerably and kill them within a couple of years. Third, many emissions have a *delayed effect* on the environment. It takes decades, for example, before the nitrogen from manure and chemical fertilizers is washed from the top soil into deeper layers, causing severe nitrate pollution of the groundwater, which is in most countries the primary source of drinking water. Even if nitrogen leakages into the groundwater could be halted instantaneously, the nitrate pollution of groundwater would continue to increase considerably for several decades.

In short, synergetic effects, thresholds, and delayed reactions cloud the issue of the relations between emissions and the deterioration of nature. As a result of human actions, ecosystems change far more capriciously than economists normally assume. The neoclassical approach to optimizing the use of the natural resources available is unsatisfactory as long as the quantity of the natural resources at our disposal cannot be accurately assessed. In other words, we cannot optimize our ecological utilization space without knowing the concrete limits that must not be crossed if irreversible effects on nature are to be avoided.

## 4. An Alternative Approach

From the preceding sections, it is clear that neoclassical approaches fall short in analyzing environmental issues and, consequently, provide a flawed basis for developing goals for environmental policy. Too much reliance is placed on the idea that the use of natural resources is a normal optimization problem. Internalization of externalities is the key to an optimum use of the natural resources available. Consequently, the question arises whether an alternative theoretical approach could be developed providing a more appropriate basis for descriptions and analyses of various environmental problems, and, if this is the case, does this imply that the link between economic theory and environmental policy could be restored? This section deals with the contours of an alternative approach to natural resources.

Various alternative starting points for adapting economic theory are suggested in the literature. Boulding (1966) has the concept of 'spaceship earth' in mind, Goudzwaard (1974) proposed economization within the limits set by nature, Sachs (1984) advocates ecological development, Söderbaum (1980; 1982) suggests ecological imperatives for governmental policies, Opschoor (1987; 1990) wants to keep economic activities within the ecological utilization space available, and the WCED (1987), finally, opts for the now famous concept of sustainable development. All these concepts have in common that ecologically bounded possibilities for using natural resources are taken as a starting-point for the development of economic theory.

Sustainable development is a normative concept. Indeed, the heart of the argument deals with a fair distribution of the natural resources available among different generations, as well as among the populations of the First, the Second and the Third Worlds of our own generation. Though the concept is given massive support throughout the world, the realization of sustainable development is highly problematic (Opschoor 1990). One of the greatest problems is the operationalization of the concept. In this respect, many questions arise which still remain unanswered. What are, for instance, the limits nature sets to human production and consumption processes? Are these limits related to current ecological quality, which has already vastly deteriorated, or should we aim at an improved ecological quality? At what pace can we use stocks of exhaustible natural resources if we employ a maximum recycling of materials? It is impossible to answer such questions on the basis of current knowledge.

In our view, the character of the relations between the ecological system and the economic system determines to a large extent the direction in which the answers to these questions should be sought. In order to develop a framework for research, a closer look at ecological cycles (or ecocycles) is needed. For too long, production and consumption processes have been portrayed as completely closed cycles, suggesting they are independent of ecological processes. If ecological insights are to be integrated into economic theory, which we think is necessary in order to grant nature a full-fledged position in economic theory as the third production factor, then the traditionally closed character of economic cycles in economic theory has to be opened up. In ecology, the notion of the 'ecocycle' describes the character of ecological processes. In general, the course taken by various substances in the ecological process is analysed, and the points in the ecocycle at which they accumulate or decompose or are blocked are determined. The description of an ecological process is complete only if the flow of information and energy in the ecosystem is also indicated. Without energy from the sun the system would not function. Furthermore, some sort of information must be present in the ecosystem on the basis of which events can take place within the system. This information causes, for example, the decomposition of organic matter or the generation of new cells. Each economic model in which an attempt is made to describe how production and consumption could be fitted into ecological processes, should take these relationships into account.

*Figure 7.3* helps to distinguish between several kinds of effects of human production and consumption on the ecological system.[2] A system of human production and consumption is based on, among other things, the need to use natural resources from ecological cycles – the active part of the ecosystem. Agricultural production provides a good example of this relation. Organic matter is formed under the influence of the sun and serves as food for animals and humans. These natural resources are, in theory, inexhaustible and therefore eternally flowing. Since the beginning of the nineteenth century man has been using fossil natural resources on a large scale. However, these resources are exhaustible. For example, the hydrocarbons of which petroleum is composed are denoted as 'stock quantities', because the stock of crude oil available in the earth's crust cannot increase within a human time horizon. The fossil part of the ecological system is hardly, if at all, affected by the flow of waste products originating from the economic system. Pollution of the environment occurs in that part of the ecological system in which cycles function. These cycles can be disturbed by the discharge of waste products.

There is a vast difference between the dumping of organic materials and the dumping of inorganic and synthetic materials into the ecocycles. Organic materials are normal elements of functioning ecocycles, while inorganic and synthetic substances are foreign to them. Among the latter are the waste products from fossil resources. When dumped into the ecocycles they are likely to cause disturbances, even in low concentrations, in the absence of mechanisms available

*Figure 7.3: Interactions between the economic system and the ecological system.*

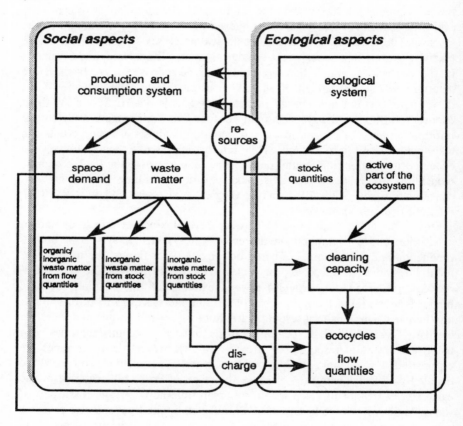

for processing or decomposing these waste products. On the other hand, the dumping of decomposable organic matter does not necessarily disturb the ecocycles. Such matter is already a natural part of the ecocycles and can be decomposed by bacteria in the normal fashion. However, if excessive quantities of decomposable organic matter are dumped into, for example, surface water, the water's self-cleaning capacity can be impaired to the extent that only stinking, rotting and deoxidized expanses of water will remain. Similarly, pollution from fossil matter is worse than pollution from organic, decomposable matter. Whereas the latter occurs locally and may be neutralized over a period of time, pollution from undecomposable stock matter is irreversible. It is almost impossible to restore the cycle in this case. Substances foreign to ecocycles accumulate, causing long-term effects on the environment across large areas. Thus, when heavy metals are discharged into surface water, the flora and fauna in it will be seriously affected. Heavy metals do not just disappear when the organisms die, but accumulate in the ecocycles.

Finally, there is one category of effects on nature by human actions that has not yet been focussed on: the use of land. Yet this very seriously violates the ecocycles. The process began when people became settled in one place, took up agriculture and began to change the natural layer of vegetation. In Europe, the process has reached the point where there is almost nothing left of the original vegetation. Modifications in the layer of vegetation do not necessarily lead to unacceptable changes in the ecocycles, but they do interfere with the cyclical processes. Further attacks on the natural vegetation through the construction of houses and factories and the construction of roads and other infrastructural elements have seriously affected the ecosystem. Their effect is different from that of the discharge of waste products, however, in that they threaten the functioning of the ecocycles much faster and more directly, without complicated intermediary processes. For instance, ecocycles may be changed if natural woodland is turned into arable land or cut down because of road construction.

The box 'production and consumption system' in *Figure 7.3* represents the human impulse to exploit natural resources. The price mechanism only partially informs individuals about the quality and availability of natural resources. The recommendation made by (neoclassical) economists to remedy this lack of information by price manipulation using levies and subsidies, does not appear to be feasible (see Section 2 above). This implies that the lack of information about the environmental effects of economic activities continues to exist. A (Pareto) optimum exploitation of nature seems to be nearly impossible due to the unpredictable effects of human activities on nature (see Section 3 above). Under these circumstances, there is a real danger that the burden of proof for the ecological sustainability of human activities will rest squarely with nature. If that is the case, environmental problems are likely to increase rather than decrease.[3]

In our view, existing mainstream economic theory is not the proper starting point for the development of economic theories concerning environmental problems. It would be better to take the insights of ecologists as a starting point, despite the often imperfect and contradictory nature of these insights. It is this uncertainty concerning what and how much can be taken from nature without creating irreversible effects, which should encourage us to act carefully.

If our aim is an ecologically sustainable society, it is necessary that we use ecocycles in such a way that their functioning is not damaged irreversibly. It is not easy to operationalize this requirement. Certainly, the discharge of materials which are alien or rarely found in ecocycles and are mainly extracted from the stocks of fossil resources, should be minimized or, preferably, stopped. This imperative implies that the speed at which fossil resources are depleted, must be reduced sharply by switching to the recycling of minerals and synthetics. However, it is impossible to recycle all materials completely. During production, consumption and recycling processes a certain part of the materials will be 'lost', and, therefore, end up in the ecocycles. Technological development should be directed to a continuous decrease of the percentage of 'lost' materials.

Ultimately, the sustainable solution is to convert completely to renewable resources. Renewable resources, if carerefully exploited, can be extracted from the (on a human timescale) eternally functioning ecocycles, and subsequently, after being used in production and consumption processes, they can be disposed of without disturbing ecocycles (so long as the carrying capacity is not exceeded). The same recommendation holds for the extraction and use of energy. Fossil stocks of oil, natural gas and coal will eventually be depleted. This implies that a complete conversion to the use of energy derived from flow quantities is inevitable in the long run.

As was demonstrated previously, traditional cost–benefit analysis cannot solve the problem of the determination of the optimal pollution point. Indeed, the price mechanism does not provide sufficient information for this purpose. In our view, there is only one way of preventing overexploitation of the ecological utilization space: specified standards which are sustainable from an ecological point of view. This implies that standards be derived directly from the functioning of the ecocycles. Such standards have to be established by the government or other authorities. Critical loads, emission standards, and extraction quotas are the policy goals in this respect. Subsequently, both 'command and control' instruments and economic instruments could be used to attain these policy goals. The choice between these instruments, or better, a specific combination of them depends on the standard criteria, such as effectiveness and efficiency.

## 5. Sustainability, Economic Theory and the Institutional Framework

In the previous sections it became clear that fundamental shortcomings are present in the neoclassical optimization approach to dealing with environmental issues. This is to a large extent due to the origin of neoclassical economics. Neoclassical economics can be seen as a scientific description of the economic expansion process, which started in the period of the Industrial Revolution. In the neoclassical framework, the availability of natural resources was not generally seen as a fundamental hindrance to economic growth; this represented a common societal viewpoint in the second half of the nineteenth century and the first half of this century. Hence, hardly any categories and concepts can be found which are suitable for analysing environmental problems occurring on a large and global scale. In the neoclassical framework, environmental problems are only described as negative externalities, meaning effects on economic agents external to the centre of the theory, the market itself.

Neoclassical economics suggests that values are found exclusively in the market and are based on the individual preferences of economic agents. Martinez Alier (1991) demonstrates that already over a hundred years ago this starting point was criticized from an ecological point of view. If the preferences of individual economic agents are taken as the sole basis for valuation, ecological disasters could easily be the result. The early critics argued that economists should pay more attention to the flow of energy in the economy. The flow of energy provides more insight into the value of economic goods than is the case using traditional valuation methods based on market prices. This approach has reappeared in what is now called ecological economics (compare Christensen 1989).

Our view on the contours of an alternative approach to natural resources was sketched in the previous section. In short, standards which are sustainable from an ecological point of view must be imposed on economic activities. These ecological standards should be derived from insights into the functioning of the ecocycles, combined with ethical views regarding the quantity and quality of natural resources we would like to leave behind for future generations. Attempts of this sort must be elaborated and developed into a more encompassing theoretical framework than neoclassical economics can provide.

In our view, this alternative theoretical framework has to meet at least three requirements. First, the economic process is seen as an open system which has various impacts on the ecological system and *vice versa*. Economic theory must be built on the notion that production and consumption possibilities completely depend on the current quantity and quality of the natural resources available, while the current and future quantity and quality of the natural resources available is affected by current production and consumption processes. Second, there must be room in the theoretical framework for ethical judgements concerning the quantity and quality of the natural resources we would like to leave behind for future generations. This implies, for example, the adoption of the principle that irreversible effects on nature cannot be permitted. The introduction of ecological standards also brings about distributional issues: which countries, industries and individuals may use which part of the (shrinking) ecological utilization space? Third, the theoretical framework must be suitable for analysing the forces in society obstructing sustainable development. In other words, institutional barriers to attaining sustainability must be analysed.

Söderbaum (1987; 1991) makes similar demands for a theoretical framework. Referring to the specific and complex characteristics of current environmental problems (multidimensional, multidisciplinary, non-monetary as well as monetary, often irreversible, and a cause of conflict between interests and ideologies in society), he argues for a more multifaceted approach than neoclassical economics can offer. In his view, the holistic context of institutional economics offers such an approach.

Those institutionalist economists involved in environmental issues generally focus primarily on the issue of how essential ecological knowledge can be incorporated in economic theories. Swaney, for example, is of the opinion that 'a holistic systems approach to environmental problems starts with the recognition that social systems coevolve with natural systems' (Swaney 1987a, p. 295; see also Norgaard 1984). He formulated the principle of 'coevolutionary sustainability', which can be seen as an environmental application of Foster's principle of institutional adjustment (Foster 1981). According to Swaney 'coevolutionary sustainability means simply that development paths or applications of knowledge that pose serious threats to continued compatibility of sociosystem and ecosystem evolution should be avoided. Coevolutionary sustainability explicitly recognizes that environmental systems evolve interdependently along development paths that may or may not be sustainable' (Swaney 1987b, p. 1750). Referring to the uncertainty of the impacts of human activities on the environment he is of the opinion that 'far more research is needed to assure that institutional adjustment is consistent with a sustainable coevolutionary development path' (Swaney 1987b, p. 1750).

Swaney (1987a) argues that the development of coevolutionary sustainability requires that individuals, interest groups and companies be educated in the practice of environmental conservation. Furthermore, an increase of scientific knowledge is a prerequisite for improving the prevention of environmental disruption. According to Swaney, only a flexible and responsive social system can guarantee a rapid adjustment to new knowledge concerning the causes of environmental problems. Therefore, the rapid penetration of new knowledge in the field of environmental protection is of utmost importance in order to ensure a sound environmental policy.

In our opinion, the prerequisites for coevolutionary sustainability mentioned by Swaney should be adopted. There is, however, at least one more prerequisite which should be taken into consideration. Knowledge is continuously produced, thereby improving our insight into the process of environmental degradation. However, new knowledge and improved insights are not applied in environmental policy as a matter of course, due to the opportunities open to the vested economic interests to query new knowledge and to hamper a stricter environmental policy. Consequently, environmental economists have to pay special attention to the balance of power in society concerning environmental issues.

Despite the previous efforts of a number of authors, adequate incorporation of natural resources in economic theories will not be an easy process. It will prove to be especially difficult if mainstream economists continue to view the economy as a closed system, operating independently from nature. Should an environmental problem emerge, its analysis and the development of an abatement strategy is thought to be a matter for specialists in the subdiscipline of environmental economics. All critical remarks about the non-incorporation of natural resources in economic theory can be neutralized by referring to this subdiscipline. In this way an alibi is created to maintain the closed system view of society.

The consequences of an adequate incorporation of natural resources in economic theory cannot be stressed enough. For instance, the traditional system of National Accounts will be untenable in the long run, as it is based on the neoclassical approach of measuring almost exclusively economic market variables. Such a system cannot provide insights into the unpriced scarcity of various natural resources.[4] Likewise, a cost–benefit analysis can only provide partial insight into environmental problems, if important benefits such as environmental quality have no market price. As a third example, the exclusion from the expression of the national debt in dollars of the national debt caused by the degradation of natural resources, makes this figure an inadequate indicator of the solvency of a country in the long run. Furthermore, discussion of industrial relations should no longer neglect the position of employees in industries which destroy or irreversibly affect the environment on a large scale. Finally, the concept of the optimal growth path, as it is defined in macroeconomics, should be regarded as a nonsense if the effects of environmental factors are not included in the concept itself.

If economists succeed in giving natural resources their due position in economic theory, there is a real chance that the link between economic theory and environmental policy can be restored. However, this does not guarantee a successful environmental policy, aimed at and attaining sustainability. Industries with major interests in the pollution and overexploitation of nature, are well organized and are well represented in the state, which gives them the power to weaken, retard, or even prevent the design and execution of a sound environmental policy. Polluting industries have, indeed, built up their position by appropriating ecological utilization space without payment. If this space decreases, as is currently the case in all industrialized countries, these industries will be confronted with increasing costs, which in turn will lead to an intensification of the struggle for the remainder of the shrinking ecological utilization space. It will become even harder to impose strict ecological standards which limit economic activities than it has proved in the last decade. Vested economic interests will continuously stress their economic importance by pointing out their substantial contribution to traditional economic variables (GNP, employment, balance of payments, and so on). In this case, employees will often take the same attitude as their employers as they will fear unemployment or a reduction in income. This occasional coalition between capital and labour has paralysing effects on environmental policy. All this time, there is no countervailing power to break down these obstructive forces in society.

The way society wrestles with the environmental problem bears a remarkable similarity to the way in which the 'social question' was dealt with at the turn of the century. The social conflicts concerning the rights of employees could only be 'solved' after a considerable shift in the balance of power in society, a process which took several decades. In our view, the same holds for the 'environmental question'. The old balance of power has to be broken down before the principle of sustainable development can penetrate all branches of society and a strict environmental policy can be designed and executed to manage the ecological utilization space in a sustainable manner. The environmental movement, consumer organizations, and political parties without strong relations to capital or labour must take the lead. For the sake of future generations, it must be hoped that the required shift in the balance of power will not take as long as it did in the case of the  social question.

## Notes

1.  Surveys of these methods can be found in Mäler (1985), Freeman (1985), and Anderson and Bishop (1986).
2.  Ecological systems can be described on a global level (higher air layers, including the ozone layer in the stratosphere) in which processes regulating radiation and temperature take place, on a continental level (continents and oceans) where processes take place such as air and ocean currents, on a fluvial level (large river-basins and coastal seas) comprising various processes related to the water ecology, on a regional level (landscapes) involving various processes within the soil, and on a local level (work and living environment) dealing with the environment made by man.
3.  This is one of the explanations for the lack of linkages between mainstream environmental economic theory and current environmental policy (see Dietz and Van der Straaten 1992).
4.  Here we encounter the discussion concerning the possibilities of a green GNP; see for a recent state of the art Ahmad *et al.* 1989. However, attempts to calculate a green GNP meet with the fundamental problems discussed in Sections 2 and 3. In our view, a much more promising initiative in this context is the attempt to develop indicators of sustainable development, by which the 'extent of sustainability' of a whole nation, economic policy or specific sectors could be determined (see Kuik and Verbruggen 1991, for potentials and pitfalls).

## References

Ahmad, Y.J., S.E. Serafty, and L. Lutz, (1989), *Environmental Accounting for Sustainable Development*, Washington DC. World Bank.

Anderson, G.D. and R.C. Bishop, (1986), 'The Valuation Problem', in D.W. Bromley (ed.), *Natural Resource Economics; Policy Problems and Contemporary Analysis*, Dordrecht: Kluwer Academic Publishers.

Boulding, K.E. (1966), 'The Economics of the Coming Spaceship Earth', in K. Jarret (ed.), *Environmental Quality in a Growing Economy*. Baltimore: John Hopkins Press 13–14.

Christensen, P.P. (1989), 'Historical Roots for Ecological Economics: Biophysical versus Allocative Approaches', *Ecological Economics*, 1 (1), 17–36.

Crocker, T.D and J.F. Shogren, (1991), 'Preference Learning and Contingent Valuation Methods', in F.J. Dietz, F. van der Ploeg and J. van der Straaten (eds), *Environmental Policy and the Economy*, Amsterdam: North-Holland, 77–93.

Dietz, F.J. and J. van der Straaten, (1992), 'Rethinking Environmental Economics: Missing Links between Economic Theory and Environmental Policy', *Journal of Economic Issues*, **XXVI** (1), 27–51.

Drepper, F.R. and B.A. Månson, (1993), 'Intertemporal Valuation in an Unpredictable Environment', *Ecological Economics*, **7** (1), 43–68.

Foster, J. (1981), 'Syllabus for Problems of Modern Society: the Theory of Institutional Adjustment', *Journal of Economic Issues*, **15**, 932–3.

Freeman, A.M. (1985), 'Methods for Assessing the Benefits of Environmental Programs', in A.V. Kneese and F.L. Sweeney (eds), *Handbook of Natural Resource and Energy Economics*, Vol. 1., Amsterdam: North Holland, 223–70.

Goudzwaard, B. (1974), *Schaduwen van het Groeigeloof* (Shadows of the Belief in Growth), Kampen: Kok.

Hoehn, J.P. and A. Randall (1987), 'A Satisfactory Benefit Cost Indicator for Contingent Valuation', *Journal of Environmental Economics and Management*, **14**, 227–47.

Kuik, O. and H. Verbruggen (1991), *In Search of Indicators of Sustainable Development*. Dordrecht: Kluwer Academic Publishers.

Mäler, G.K. (1985), 'Welfare Economics and the Environment', in A.V. Kneese and F.L. Sweeney (eds), *Handbook of Natural Resource and Energy Economics*, Vol. 1, Amsterdam: North Holland, 3–60.

Martinez Alier, J. (1991), 'Ecological Perception and Distributional Effects: A Historical View', in F.J. Dietz, F. van der Ploeg and J. van der Straaten (eds), *Environmental Policy and the Economy*, Amsterdam: North Holland, 117–37.

Norgaard, R.B. (1984), 'Coevolutionary Development Potential', *Land Economics*, **60**, 160–73.

Opschoor, J.B. (1987), *Duurzaamheid en Verandering* (Sustainability and Change), Inaugural Speech, Amsterdam: Free University Press.

Opschoor, J.B. (1990), 'Ecologische duurzame ontwikkeling: Een theoretisch idee en een weerbarstige praktijk', in P. Nijkamp and H. Verbruggen (eds), *Het Nederlandse milieu in de Europese ruimte*, Leiden: Stenfert Kroese.

Pigou, A.C. (1952[1920]), *The Economics of Welfare*, London: MacMillan.

Sachs, I. (1984), The Strategies of Ecodevelopment. *Ceres, FAO Review on Agriculture and Development*, **17**, 17–21.

Söderbaum, P. (1980), 'Towards a Reconciliation of Economics and Ecology', *European Review of Agricultural Economics*, **7**, 55–77.

Söderbaum, P. (1982), 'Ecological Imperatives for Public Policy', *Ceres, FAO Review on Agriculture and Development*, **15**, 28–32.

Söderbaum, P. (1987), 'Environmental Management: A Non-traditional Approach', *Journal of Economic Issues*, **21**, 139–65.

Söderbaum, P. (1991), 'Actors, Roles and Networks: An Institutional Perspective to Environmental Problems', in C. Folke and T. Kåberger (eds), *Linking the Natural Environment and the Economy: Essays from the Eco-Eco Group*, Dordrecht: Kluwer Academic Publishers, 31–42.

Swaney, J.A. (1987a), 'Building Instrumental Environmental Control Institutions', *Journal of Economic Issues,* **21**, 295–308.

Swaney, J.A. (1987b), 'Elements of a Neoinstitutional Environmental Economics', *Journal of Economic Issues,* **21**, 1739–99.

Tonneijk, A.E.G. (1981), *Research on the Influence of Different Air Pollutants Separately and in Combination in Agriculture, Horticulture and Forestry Crops,* IPE Report No. R 262, Wageningen.

WCED (1987), *Our Common Future.* Cambridge: Cambridge University Press.

# 8.  Environmental Law, Environmental Globalization, and Sustainable Techno-Economic Evolution

## Klaus Lindegaard

---

### 1. Introduction: Environmental globalization and the PPP

Environmental problems have changed character from instant and temporary effects on the local environment to cumulative, lasting and pervasive effects with a multitude of complex causes and contributors – some affecting the entire globe. The standard text-book 'innocence' of the polluted stream in the local countryside is if not entirely lost then severely in need of an up-date. Little, however, is being done to address these increasingly complex problems; least, to address the global ones. The lack of common cause for global environmental agreements may have something to do with the fact that the environmental problems generated in the developing countries (the South) are predominantly of a local nature while the causes of the global environmental problems are to be found in the developed countries (the North) (Pearce *et al.* 1992) – though the contribution of the South is rapidly increasing. This holds for the problems of the global climate and the ozone layer as well as for the depletion of exhaustible resources. Nonetheless, the policies of the individual nation states are still of great significance: global problems are after all the sum of the effects of local activities.

The Polluter Pays Principle (PPP) and the implied maxim that pollution prevention pays (!) have, during the past twenty years, gained international status as a primary guiding principle for environmental policy at all political levels. The PPP is today a common feature of the national environmental programmes in almost all industrialized countries. OECD has played an important role in this development with the organization's recommendation in 1972 regarding the PPP as an uniform political principle for pollution control in the member states (OECD 1991). The European Community made a similar recommendation in 1975 and the PPP was formulated as a basic rule in Article 130r(2) of the Single European Act of 1987 (Krämer 1992).

The purpose has in both contexts been to declare and implement a uniform cost internalization strategy – a 'level playing field' that would make it unnecessary for states to subsidize pollution control in their industries. It is indeed fundamental to the PPP that polluters should not be subsidized (OECD 1991); and there have up to now apparently existed very strict limits on the use of such subsidies by OECD member states. (Even government support for R&D has been kept to a rather low level: the share of environmental protection in total government R&D appropriations has been estimated to have grown from an OECD average of 1.6% to 2.3% over the period 1980–90 (OECD 1992).) In 1989 OECD applied the PPP to accidental pollution, linking the principle with the legal principles relating to damage compensation (tort law). This development of the PPP is mirrored by both the latest environment programme from the Commission of the European Communities (1992) and the United Nations programme for the global environment (the UNCED Rio Declaration of 1992), where principle 16 states:

'National authorities should endeavour to promote the internalization of environmental costs and the use of economic instruments, taking into account the approach that the polluter should in principle bear the cost of pollution, with due regard to the public interest and without distorting international trade and investment.' (Johnson 1993 p. 120).

The other OECD trend in the development of the PPP is found in principle 13 of the Rio Declaration:

States shall develop national law regarding liability and compensation for the victims of pollution and other environmental damages. States shall also cooperate in an expeditious and more determined manner to develop further international law regarding liability and compensation for adverse effects of environmental damage caused by activities within their jurisdiction or control to areas beyond their jurisdiction. (Johnson 1993 p. 120)

This obligation towards the development of international law regarding liability between different independent jurisdictions should be related to the obligation of principle 15 to take a precautionary approach to the protection of the environment: 'Where there are threats of serious or irreversible damage, lack of full scientific certainty shall not be used as a reason for postponing cost-effective measures to prevent environmental degradation.' (Johnson 1993 p. 120), with the addition of due regard to the capabilities of the states in question. Besides the usual divergence between words and action, why has little progress been made towards implementing the Polluter Pays Principle, and least of all at the global level, when all these declarations are considered? After giving a tentative answer to that, this chapter goes on to explore the possibilities of one expression of the PPP, environmental tort law. After outlining them in principle, we proceed to look at developments in the US, Denmark and the European Union. We then discuss how any vigorous implementation of environmental liability could be expected to affect the direction and speed of technological change. The chapter concludes with a discussion of the most difficult and important issue: how and how far can environmental liability be used to deal with global environmental problems?


## 2. Mismatches between awareness and action

Many environmental problems are characterized by highly uncertain knowledge of causes and effects. We do not know what would happen if we did apply the Polluter Pays Principle, because of uncertainty over the sources of pollution, the ultimate destination of emissions, the physical impact of the emissions, the human valuation of the realized impacts, the physical and ecological impact of policy responses including the question of human reactions and economic behaviour and, finally, the trade-off between damage costs and the cost associated with the policy response (Bromley 1989). These uncertainties are exploited by polluters: they not only take advantage of them as they find them, but work to increase them, by 'contra-research', for example, casting doubt as to whether they are doing any serious ecological damage. (See Dietz and Van der Straaten Chapter 7.) They are helped by the fact that information is generally asymmetrical: polluters know better than victims or governments what they are doing. This strategic attitude can explain the mismatch between the economic consensus in favour of cost internalization and the continuing dominance in real life environmental policy of direct, command and control regulation and voluntary, negotiated agreements. Vested economic interest groups can secure and even increase their rents quite easily under such a regime: sometimes they will simply evade regulations, sometimes they will appeal to private sunk costs and international competitiveness, employment and economic growth to get them eased or their implementation delayed (Dietz and van der Straaten 1992); sometimes they will seek to use them as protection against competitive pressure. Such opportunistic behaviour – 'self-seeking with guile' – has a key role in Williamson's (1985) explanation of the organization of economic activities, by increasing transaction costs in certain market relationships. In this case something similar is going on: a sort of market relationship in which the polluter would be induced to pay a price, to someone, for his pollution, is being blocked by opportunism. One important difference is that the opportunist is not merely taking advantage of the character of the market but adopting a sophisticated strategy to shape it to his advantage. The parties generating the environmental problems have the opportunistic incentive of raising the costs of potential transactions, negotiations and regulations (Minsch 1991); agents take account of both the costs imposed on them by others and their own cost-imposing opportunities.

The global nature of many environmental problems makes both the uncertainty about them, and polluters' strategic behaviour towards it, worse. One simple and popular ploy is to follow a dilution strategy towards emissions – send smoke up a high enough chimney and no one will know exactly what damage you did and where: the more you can globalize your environmental impacts the greater the uncertainty about them. Nations are to global impacts as individuals are to local ones: although they may share the general concern, they have an individual incentive to avoid the costs of restraint. If they are particularly heavy contributors to a problem – as for example the US with global warming – they have a strong incentive to cast doubt on its severity and even existence. However even the recognition of a global problem may not necessarily be helpful. The perception that problems are global raises expectations of some kind of common global action towards them – as promised in the Rio Declaration of 1992. The global perspective then becomes an excuse for business as usual at the local and national levels, even though there is a strong case for immediate action at those levels. Everybody is waiting for the 'proper' global action to be taken.

## 3. Liability and transaction costs

The 'globalizing' behaviour described above directs attention to the question of the underlying rights, responsibility and liability structures of the economy: the legal regime and habits of thought (Veblen 1898). Law, as Katz (1986) has put it, may be regarded as 'the infrastructure of economic thought'. Liability rules serve the purpose of both allocation of restoration costs and of compensation costs to damage sufferers. The present international interest in liability rules arises from the fact that under proper conditions they could serve as a key part of a cost-internalization strategy.

Such a strategy must be based on one or both of two elements:

1. direct government-initiated corrective taxes – *ex ante* in the sense that they are announced beforehand on the basis of current knowledge of impacts. This *taxational* approach rests on a social entitlement to keep public goods undisturbed by negative externalities of economic significance, and is supported by the Pigovian tradition within mainstream economics.
2. governmentally- or privately-initiated *ex post* compensation with the aim of *ex ante* deterrence. Damage compensation involves tort law, distinguished from both contract law and property law by its focus on third-party effects. This is consistent with the equally-mainstream Coaseian tradition, which distrusts the capacity of government to act as an impartial, omniscient assessor and apportioner of externalities. The Coaseian view is simply that individual entitlements must be clearly set out in law – whether in this case entitlements for the polluter to pollute, or the 'victim' not to suffer damage, may not matter. Then the individuals concerned can *negotiate* with one another, on the basis of entitlements, as to how much pollution there will be, and how much compensation. If one *infringes* the entitlement of the other, then of course the latter can sue for compensation.

The two approaches are in a sense combined within any regime which (a) imposes liability on the environmental damage generator – there is no right to pollute, which accords with the taxational approach, and (b) insists that damage compensation must be assessed – for example, by the courts – and paid to the sufferer, which accords with the negotiational approach:

Taxational:
liability for injurer

PPP: : Environmental torts

Negotiational:
compensation to injured

This is achieved by what could be described as the emerging *environmental tort synthesis*. In effect this combines the two historically opposed traditions of taxation and negotiation, partly, as we shall see below, in response to the irreversible environmental effects now emerging at the global level. Torts, in general, depend traditionally on liability rules assigning the responsibility of the injurer to compensate the victim. Liability rests on the assignment of entitlements and is fundamentally one way of protecting an individual entitlement whereas property rules are another (Calabresi and Melamed 1972). While interference with your entitlement under a property rule needs your explicit *ex ante* consent, interference and third-party effects under a liability rule give you the right to compensation. The liability concept is basic for tort law, but so are the actual rules which assign liability in specific situations, determining which party in the conflict should bear the (transaction) costs associated with a claim for compensation and which party has the responsibility to compensate. Traditionally, the victim and injured party must in the court room establish culpa (fault) and provide evidence for the causal connection between the action of the defendant (cause) and the damage suffered by the plaintiff (effect). The tort is a public damage valuation which can be seen as most relevant in situations where *ex ante* bargaining costs are high and the parties therefore cannot enter into a contractual relationship about the (potential) harm (Cooter and Ulen 1988).

Traditional tort law has three limitations which restrict its usefulness for environmental problems: First, it requires that negligence be proved – which in view of the uncertainties discussed above, will usually be extremely difficult. Second, it (at the very least) prefers that an individual be identified as solely responsible for specific damage, rather than jointly with others who may at that point not be identifiable. Third, it requires an injured party who can sue. Otters and trees cannot bring legal actions, let alone the ozone layer; I can sue for damage to my back garden, but not for acid rain damage to the wood at which I look, or for loss of biodiversity. All of these limitations can be and are being removed, with the United States (as we shall see below) taking the lead. The requirement to prove negligence can be replaced by *strict* or 'no fault' liability, where only the causal connection need be established. Liability can be made *joint and several*, so that any one (or more) of the parties responsible can be sued, as may be convenient, and if any party or parties sued blame others not sued for part of the damage, it is for them through 'recourse' to seek to pass on a due share of the costs. And some agent of the state may be given the right and duty to sue on behalf of the public interest. Since there is no way to compensate the public (or the otters and trees) for the harm inflicted on them, this agent (agency) has to be given the responsibility for restoration of damage, or 'clean-up'; and then the damages awarded will be paid to it and assessed on the basis of its costs. This last change represents a shift from traditional tort/civil liability to 'statutory clean-up' liability.

In one way the widening of liability may need to go beyond the 'joint and several' rule. A remaining problem is that companies are, in law, the 'persons' which – jointly and severally or individually, as the case may be – are liable. If they have *limited* liability, then the worst that can happen to them and their employees and shareholders is bankruptcy – a limited sanction, and the less frightening, the longer it happens after the event.   There is no reason in principle why a director or manager of a company should not have some degree of personal liability in an environmental tort, in addition to the company's liability. Liability also needs to extend beyond national boundaries. As they have independent jurisdiction it is essential for the nation states to give equal access for plaintiffs from other nations to seek compensation for international damages. This possibility is at present restricted to the developed countries of the North (Birnie and Boyle 1992).

Three other factors affect the effectiveness of environmental liability rules. First, their impact depends on the way in which damage estimation is conceived and monetary valuations of losses are conducted in practice, who pays the legal costs; and how high these are. The magnitude of American tort awards has tended to deter policy-makers in Scandinavia and other European countries from implementing strict liability; but different rules and practices could yield lower awards. The second factor is their treatment of *time*. The most restrictive approach is to impose a new regime in year 0 which allows a subsequent suit in say year 10 to claim damages only for harm inflicted between years 0 and 10. The US practice is already firmly retroactive – it takes account of harm inflicted before year 0 – and there are calls there for a switch from the current post-damage recovery approach to a more 'anticipatory' one, which would include future income losses of third parties due to existing environmental damage in the awards made (Clites *et al*. 1991). The third factor is the burden of proof: with what degree of certainty and accuracy must damage be established? Within limits, a relaxation of the burden of proof increases the probability of conviction for a given enforcement effort and thus makes the system more effective in deterring offences (Kaplow and Shavell 1994); on the other hand, clearly, there is a cost in terms of justice and equity so far as (alleged) offenders are concerned.

Clearly the environmental tort system is not the only 'legal regime' which can be brought to bear on the environmental problem. 'Command and control' regulation is an alternative legal regime which can be compared with environmental tort. Entitlements and liabilities are less explicit in this regime: one could say that normal regulatory limits on pollution resemble liability where negligence is proved, and outright prohibition resembles strict liability, since the polluter must pay for any pollution at all. In the same way, liabilities are implicitly present in the design of economic instruments, such as eco-taxation or tradeable permits. In both cases the liabilities and their enforcement are left to the political process and public authorities. With the modifications described above, the litigation and enforcement/transaction costs associated with liability rules may be low compared with other regulatory approaches, at least where the damage is unlikely to occur or the information is asymmetrical and in favour of the potential damage generator (Shavell 1987). Clearly the switch to strict and joint and several liability plays a crucial role in preventing the use of uncertainty to make the regime expensive and ineffective. (A danger arising from such a shift is the possible incentive for strategic moves *by sufferers*: for example, refraining from relatively cheap measures to clean up, in order to get a massive increase in damages award. However this could be prevented if the courts were known to respond unfavourably to evidence of such sub-optimal behaviour.)

We can see that the implementation of the Polluter Pays Principle through such environmental tort law may be supportive of a 'PSP': Polluter Says Principle – putting pressure for openness, instead of the incentive to conceal the direct and indirect costs of a firm's actions given by taxation of pollution. The pressure will come from many sides. It will be felt from insurers, investors and potential merger partners (Simmons 1993). The 'green' (final) consumer's altruistic desire to buy from a 'green' firm will be matched by industrial customers' quite un-altruistic desire to do so, to avoid joint liability. In turn, the firm will know its best chance of reducing its future liabilities will be to give its customers the maximum information about any danger they might run. To the extent that its employees are individually liable for their actions on its behalf, it will be under pressure for openness from them. At the same time it will depend upon them individually to alert it collectively to harm it may be doing. The question of firms' credibility and trustworthiness will seem ever more important (Christensen and Remmen 1994).

It is therefore not surprising that the recent emergence of environmental liability (see below) coincides with environmental audit schemes and generally improved information access to companies. This development is both self-initiated by private business organizations and companies and supported by the promotion and standardization initiatives of the public. At the European level there is the Council Regulation No. 1836/93 of 29 June 1993 allowing voluntary participation by companies in the industrial sector in a Community Eco-management and audit scheme (Commission of the European Communities 1993a). In Denmark a law of 1995 on the publication and approval of green audits, makes them mandatory in 1996 for companies in selected industries with especially strong environmental impacts. (Unfortunately the audit methods and reporting practices still leave much to be desired in terms of informational content and value.) In the United States, the states of Colorado, Idaho and Mississippi have passed so-called audit privilege legislation, which gives companies immunity from prosecution and criminal and civil penalties if they conduct environmental audits, voluntarily disclose any violations found and correct them in compliance with existing rules (Parkin 1995). While this principle of self-notification and correction is awaiting federal approval and implementation, it is in force to some extent already in the Environmental Protection Agency's enforcement practice, where cooperative companies are met with less strict penalties in case of breaches. The practice of rewarding cooperation with relevant authorities is not unfamiliar in the European context and has precedents outside environmental law. While the audit privilege in the absolute form described may seriously weaken overall deterrence, in a diluted form it could strengthen compliance with existing environmental norms and standards, reduce enforcement costs and enhance the technical consultative role of environmental authorities. It could be useful in situations where private compensation claims for, for example, personal injuries and property damages are triggered by information releases during publicly or privately initiated clean-up processes. This initiative clearly shows the need the public authorities now have for dialogue, interaction and negotiation with private parties on environmental issues.

We now proceed to examine the principles found in some new legal liability rules in the environmental field, which are either in operation or proposed.

## 4. A new total system of strict, joint and several environmental liability: two examples

### United States: CERCLA

Strict liability is implemented in the United States in the environmental field, in the area of hazardous industrial waste, under the statutes of the Comprehensive Environmental Response, Compensation, and Liability Act (CERCLA) from 1980, revised 1986. This is a classic case of statutory clean-up liability rather than traditional tort/civil liability: CERCLA gives the Environmental Protection Agency (EPA) the right to take immediate actions to restore environmental damages and to seek compensation for the action from the involved parties that are strictly liable. The actions are explicitly directed towards releases from sites containing hazardous substances. The CERCLA statutes do not contain any direct formulation of joint and several liability, but refer to 'potentially responsible parties' in §107 with reference to present owners and operators, owners and operators at the time of disposal, generators of the hazardous wastes and materials and companies that have transported the waste to the site in question (Jacoby and Eremich 1991). The CERCLA rule of joint and several liability, as applied by the courts, extends the compensation claim from the direct producer to suppliers, lenders and other major actors around the damaging activity. The court judgments have shown the CERCLA to be retroactive in its scope and to make liabilities personal and directed to parent/successor companies and lenders in some cases. A problem of the liability-based regime arises in cases where no party can be found liable for environmental damages and remedial action needs to be undertaken. The 'Superfund' which finances EPA's clean-up operations is funded, accordingly, not only by compensation awards but by a tax on the chemicals industry. Waste management practices in the US since the imposition of the CERCLA rules show some striking changes in behaviour. A survey of the members of the Chemical Manufacturers Association has shown that while chemicals shipments in the US rose from $180.5 billion in 1981 to $214 billion in 1985, waste generation decreased over the period by 51.8%. The use of landfills for disposals in the period 1981 to 1987 decreased by 64% while the use of incineration increased (Dewees 1992). Increases in waste exports from the United States are not reported here, but they probably help to explain these figures, which reminds us that even local waste problems of the North are becoming local problems in the South under the present conditions of trade and international law.

The EPA's strategy under CERCLA is typically to sue only a few of the potentially liable parties – usually the ones with the deepest pockets. This simplifies and cuts the cost of the legal processes for the EPA but then obliges those which are sued to 'take recourse': to sue the other potentially liable parties and pass on part of their costs. It is certainly desirable that the others be forced to pay up, otherwise neither equitable and efficient compensation nor the full preventive effect of *ex ante* deterrence can be secured (Tietenberg 1989). However, from the recourse system follow both higher insurance costs on an imperfectly functioning risk market and especially high legal costs in cases of recourse. Among five very large industrial firms in the US it was found that expenditures related to inactive hazardous waste sites tripled between 1984 and 1989 and that 21% of the total outlays were transaction costs for legal representation, leaving 79% to investigation and remediation. A sample of American insurers involved in inactive hazardous waste sites experienced in the same period a rise in both claims and actual outlays. Transaction costs were here estimated to amount to 88% of total expenditures on average divided between roughly 42% used on coverage disputes and 37% used on defending policyholders against other potentially responsible parties, government agencies and private parties (Acton and Dixon 1992 pp. xff). To this should be added the possible reduction in deterrence due to considerable time lags in the legal process from the point at which claims are raised to their final resolution. The above study found that two-thirds of the claims raised during the period 1984–

89 were still open three years later. The transaction cost share of closed claims was 69% of outlays for the insurers (Acton and Dixon 1992 p. xi).

We should be wary of reaching an unfavourable judgment of CERCLA on the basis of legal costs so far. There are two reasons for expecting the ratio of legal costs to compensation awards to fall over time. First, now that firms know the regime, they are likely in future to go to considerable trouble to clarify the responsibility of one firm to another. Second, the courts and those who plead before them, are learning, and can be expected to operate more quickly and cheaply as precedents are established and ways of assessing damage and liability become accepted. Meanwhile it should be remembered that the raising of money for remediation is less important in the long run than the encouraging of preventive behavioural effects. Even if most of the cost to the damage-generator is in the form of legal and other transactions costs, the incentive to pollute less, remains. We may still conclude, however, that improvements could be made to the system. The statute that sets up such a system could at the same time set out more precise rules than CERCLA has about assessing damage and allocating damages. This would imply a greater role for the legislature relative to the judiciary – more in keeping with the European tradition than that of the US. (It might even be possible to economize – here and in traditional tort claims – by giving a more activist role to the judge and relying less on the adversarial arguments of the advocates. That would be in keeping only with the *continental* European tradition.) But the most important task is not so much to reduce legal costs as to establish a clearer and more certain link between polluting behaviour and subsequent sanctions.

## The European Community

Denmark provides an example of new legislative developments at the national level. A committee appointed by the Danish Ministry of Justice recently recommended the implementation of strict liability for private and public activities of specially damaging or polluting character. With the liability followed a proposal for a compulsory insurance obligation for the parties involved. Liabilities are recommended to cover compensation of income and property losses and clean-up costs. The proposal included both private and public initiation of claims for compensation, but only for directly affected parties (Justitsministeriet 1992). In a modified version this proposal was passed by the parliament as Danish Law no. 225 on compensation for environmental damages (Folketingstidende 1993–94), which came into force in July 1994. The law states that only reasonable expenses are to be covered and that the concept of damage includes only significant disturbances of ecological balances with respect to the existing situation and state of the environment in question. Damage sufferers are obliged to take remedial action from the time the damage is discovered to limit the consequences. On the grounds that no insurance market yet exists in this area, the law excludes insurance obligations for the present. It is not retroactive: it applies to harm done after its enactment. Of course where no one liable can be found the liabilities fall on present and future taxpayers.

The new Danish liability legislation supplements existing laws on waste deposits enacted in 1990 as a widening of the scope of earlier legislation on chemical waste deposits and waste from oil products from the mid and early 1970s (Basse 1990). These call for the registration of polluted land and make polluters liable for the expenses of remediation. However, partly because they are recent and not retroactive, it is generally though implicitly accepted that no liable parties can be found in most cases (though no comprehensive record or investigation of the problem yet exists) and the problem is commonly refered to as the 'sins of the past'. The remedial activities have, accordingly, become a public task, potentially imposing a considerable financial burden on government budgets. Meanwhile, between registration and remediation property owners are *de facto* excluded from the housing market, causing much private agony and public concern about distortion of housing markets. (It is possible to shorten this period by making a voluntary clean-up agreement in some cases.) Pleas have been made for public compensation for the private loss of property value, for example by a suspension of property taxes (Ilsøe 1994). The response has been to hold back and slow down the registration of polluted property. Another proposal is to establish a fund financed by a special tax on present polluting activities that could finance a systematic scheme of clean-up measures (Andersen 1994). Since 1992, a special tax on oil and petrol products has financed a fund for the clean-up of the grounds of old service stations, which is administered by the industry itself.

At the European level progress is relatively slow. Like the Danish legislation, present European proposals in this area find their inspiration both in product liability law and American environmental law. Directives of the European Union on product and service liability are examples of strict, joint and several, no-fault liability, with reversed burden of proof in the case of some services (Geddes 1992). But the EU is well behind the US. A recent Green Paper suggests that a 'horizontal approach' to environmental liability should be developed jointly for the member states: that is, a civil liability system of the traditional type. For civil liability action to be possible, as the Commission points out, several conditions have to be met regarding environmental damage. The environmental damage is required to be measurable and immediate, resulting from a finite act or incident, potentially liable parties must be identifiable, a causal link must be established and a party with legal interest who can bring action must exist. If these conditions are not fulfilled, the Commission suggests that a joint compensation mechanism be established to compensate for the damage, which mirrors the 'Superfund' associated with the CERCLA and similar systems. (Commission of the European Communities 1993b). The Green Paper proposal was a further development and generalization of a draft Directive on civil liability for waste from 1989 (Club de Bruxelles 1992), which has not yet been implemented at the Community level.

Another example of European legislation that remains to be implemented is the convention from the Council of Europe on damages resulting from activities dangerous to the environment, adopted in 1993, that also operates with strict liability rules applicable to compensation for income losses and restoration costs for damages from hazardous activities, which imposes a complicated process of harmonization of existing national rules of environmental compensation schemes in and between the member states (Bianchi 1994). As commonly in Europe, 'harmonization' involves restraining the more progressive as well as spurring on the others. It remains to be seen whether the next (6th) European Community action programme on the principles for common policies towards the environment for 2000 and onwards signals any progress in the formulation of ambitious targets for harmonization as well as any indication that common strict environmental liability rules may be implemented in the near future. This would be a necessary first step towards international rules on compensation for past and future environmental damage in general.

## 5. Environmental liability and innovation costs

How can the general implementation of the PPP through liability rules be expected to affect technological change and innovation?

The innovation process can be characterized as a process of potentially economic advantageous applications of new knowledge and inventions, which are realized through their introduction into actual processes and as actual products. Hence: 'The economic logic prevails over the technological.' (Schumpeter 1934 pp. 14–15): innovations are only introduced if they are expected to be profitable, and are only adopted, if they turn out to be. Economists studying innovation have directed much of their attention towards the analysis and determination of the complex feedbacks between the wide range of activities involved from the initial initiation of the development process to the final launching of the result. Innovation is here best described as an uncertain and 'chain-linked' (Kline and Rosenberg 1986) process of interactive learning (Lundvall 1992) between research, marketing, design, test, production and distribution or implementation activities involving to a varying degree both user and producer linkages. Economic considerations affect decisions whether to finance an investment in innovation, as well as the organization and carrying out of the research and development activities themselves.

Innovation is not a simple process of rational decision-making and internal selection of promising ideas. It is a highly social process. The innovation system's perspective stresses the importance of extra-market interaction including publicly-provided technical services and information. Processes of institutional learning and borrowing between countries and between actors and companies are necessary to secure flexible habits, routines and patterns of interaction for the stimulation of the introduction and diffusion of new technologies and innovations (Johnson 1992). Interaction costs and capabilities therefore affect the overall cost of innovation. It is also a process dominated by uncertainties and risks. (The process of innovation has been described as a process of turning uncertainty into risk (Schon 1967).) The uncertainties are typically divided into technical, market and general business uncertainty, which in practice are subdivided into long checklists of specific factors affecting the technical and commercial success of a research and development process (Freeman 1982).

Innovation proceeds in a context of external selection environments, whether natural, built or institutionalized (Freeman 1992). Individual research and development processes are influenced and given direction by quite general 'climatic' factors, including specific historical trajectories of dominating key technologies. The incentive to take advantage of falling costs of key factors – and to make them fall further – may be an essential element in the establishment of these technological trajectories (Biondi and Galli 1992). However, selection environments do not entirely determine the conduct of individual firms: they can to some extent either ignore external pressures or act to change them.

On the face of it any moves to implement the PPP should alter the selection environment in such a way as to increase the profitability and encourage the diffusion of relatively 'green' technologies. One could say that they would do so by altering the relative cost of the factors of production, in the broadest sense of the term. The longer the time period considered, the greater, and the more beneficial the resulting change: for the only quick way of reducing pollution is what is called 'bolt-on' pollution abatement technology, which necessarily involves extra cost. The longer-term alternative is of course to redesign the product and/or the process of production. This is very likely to result in the improvement of materials and energy productivity: all pollution is waste of a kind and if it can be designed out, costs can be reduced. In the medium to long term, such changes may be profitable, even allowing for the cost of the R&D and ignoring the impact of the PPP – that is they might have been worth making without it. Thus in the Danish dairy industry considerable production-cost reductions have been achieved in recent years through effective environmental management practices of resource input minimization and of turning waste products into valuable resources. When faced with increases in water prices and waste water charges, liabilities can be turned into assets: investments in pollution prevention together with general reductions in water consumption due to the involvement of employees and better housekeeping led to considerable savings for the companies. A representative dairy had an increase in production of 59% in the period 1988–92 together with an increase in water consumption of only 10% and more than a 50% reduction in pollution annually discharged during the same period (Remmen and Nielsen 1994 p. 149). Similar achievements can be found in other branches of the Danish food processing industry and in other industries, where substitution of harmful substances has proved possible. The gains are not only in process costs: in fact the distinction between process and product innovation in the environmental field is becoming less meaningful, because process characteristics make a clear difference to the qualities of final products. Organic farming, for example, involves a change in process – economizing on at least some production factors – and a change in product, up-market.

Such a 'win-win' outcome may seem too good to be true: if these changes were worth doing anyway why were they only done under pressure? The answer may be that firms are not profit-maximizers but 'satisficers' in Simon's (1959) sense: they are not constantly searching in all directions for ways of increasing profits but respond to pressure. Moreover they may also be 'short-termist' in various ways, applying time rates of discount which are inappropriately high either with reference to their own or the social opportunity cost of capital (Tylecote 1987; Demirag and Tylecote 1992), and thus refraining – until forced – from some investments which would be profitable at an 'appropriate' rate of discount.

Clearly the regime of cost internalization chosen will affect the direction of innovation. Under the 'traditional system' of direct regulation, the incentive is to reduce the cost of a given degree of pollution abatement. The taxational approach of pollution fees provides an incentive to increase the effectiveness and efficiency of abatement (Nentjes and Wiersma 1988) – so long as the harmful nature of the activity has been identified and is being monitored. The regime of strict liability (and so on) provides a constant incentive not only to reduce such recognized pollution but to identify and abate as yet unrecognized forms of potential damage generation. Other differences between the effects of pollution taxes and strict liability are not all in the latter's favour. The internalization of cost to the polluter in the former case is early and known at the time: you either have to pay for your pollution now – definitely – or not. In the latter case it is uncertain and at all events in the relatively distant future. Therefore a risk-averse and 'long-termist' firm will be more sensitive to strict liability; a risk-happy and short-termist firm will be more sensitive to pollution taxes.

There is, however, an argument that the PPP as implemented through environmental tort liability may have a perverse effect: since innovators risk being liable for any damages caused by their new products or processes, they will have to incur additional expenditure for testing, control and monitoring in connection with research and development, production and distribution, as well as insurance costs. This is bound to raise innovation costs, and may do so to the extent of discouraging even 'green' innovations.[1] This argument follows from the finding that the American system of strict product liability has deterred more radical innovations in favour of incremental ones (or none at all) in the case of for example vaccines and small aircraft (Huber 1988). The riposte to this is that any tightening of the liability regime will raise the cost of the less-green status quo even more, thus increasing the attraction of the 'green' innovation. The perverse effect can only arise where the pollution caused by the status quo is not covered by environmental tort liability, probably because it is too diffuse: thus for example the development of a new fuel which would reduce $CO_2$ emissions – which are not covered or soon likely to be – may be discouraged because of fears that the plant which made it would cause relatively local pollution which *would* be liable to environmental tort action.

Another possible disadvantage of environmental tort liability as a motivator of 'green' innovation relates to the position of small firms. In most cases cleaner technology solutions are highly dependent upon the provision of information through interaction with a wide range of actors outside the individual company. Still, it makes a difference whether the firm is a big one with internal R&D activities or a small one relying on the supply of pollution abatement technology from specialized firms. The big firm can be expected to respond to either type of cost internalization, through tort or taxes; the small firm depends on the initiative of others. One can be confident that such initiative will be forthcoming when pollution taxes are levied, since the existence of a market for a 'greener' technology becomes clear to the supplier. Where the pressure arises from the more uncertain prospect of a tort action, the response of firms faced by it, and therefore their suppliers, is less certain; and if the small firm is to wait until it is faced with a tort action, it may be crippled by the costs and unable then to pay for change. Where small firms are subjected to a strict liability regime there is thus a particularly strong case for public policy to help them identify polluting activities early, to promote stronger interaction between users and producers and to assist them in devising solutions. Different innovation capabilities thus need to be considered and promoted to enhance the technological dynamism of strict liability.

## 6. A new total system of environmental liability

Let us make it clear what are the objectives we have in mind – much more than merely compensation and collection of financial means for ex post restoration, which is effectively what CERCLA is for. In many cases no restoration is in fact possible; even where it is, one may seek to go much further. The purpose should then be to properly deter actions harming the environment, and to redirect the trajectory of technological change in a sustainable direction. The particular contributions of environmental tort law are to *decentralize* regulation and enforcement, since the initiative on any incident of damage is not left to government, and to reduce or even reverse the advantage *uncertainty* may otherwise give to the polluter, since even if the occurrence and impact of damage becomes known long after the event, punishment can follow. We have seen that in order to make the most of these contributions, a system of environmental liability should involve:

- strict liability
- joint and several liability with recourse
- diminution of burden of proof
- total environmental scope
- clear damage evaluation principles
- access for private organizations and government agencies
- free and equal access

It is the requirement of total environmental scope that is most important and most difficult. We have seen that if scope is limited – let us say to local impacts – the incentives for behavioural change and innovation may move perversely: a large amelioration of a problem like greenhouse gas emissions which remains outside the scope of law may be discouraged because of the prospect of a small worsening of a problem within its scope. However, in widening scope we hit real difficulty. Liability rules are traditionally regarded as most efficient where only two or a few parties are involved and the court system then can produce detailed and well-specified solutions to the case, while the involvement of many plaintiffs or defendants raises the legal costs associated with the case. Rules of strict liability help by considerably lowering legal costs and increasing effectiveness in comparison with rules of negligence and culpa. Still, there are obviously limits to the numbers of plaintiffs and defendants one can involve, and this creates problems when harm is diffuse. One response is to bring in an agent of the state, like the US Environmental Protection Agency, to act on behalf of 'the public interest', that is an infinite number of plaintiffs whose view, air or biodiversity has been harmed. This still requires a limited number of defendants, and accordingly cannot cope directly with problems like emissions from car exhausts – only pollution charges, perhaps supplemented by regulations, will do here. Moreover any legal liability regime requires that harm and consequent damages be assessed at a distance in time from the pollution incident or incidents. Toxic waste which accumulates in a certain land area, from a reasonably identifiable source, is an appropriate subject for a liability regime. Gaseous emissions which go on over a long period of time and disappear into the distance, are more difficult to deal with: at the very least they will need to be monitored continuously, even if the harm they do is only assessed *ex post*. Once again the State, which the Coaseian tradition distrusts and wants to keep in the background, is obliged to step in as monitoring authority. An alternative or supplementary solution is to allow citizen groups to monitor and take legal action according to some specific lines of strict global liability – which would imply relaxing the concept of 'directly affected party' and of damage suffering, which at present still resembles traditional property rules.

The problems of information and uncertainty-raising behaviour at sectoral level are, however, an obstacle to the clear identification of the internal distribution of damage generation within each nation. Recent Responsible Care Programmes of the American and European chemical industries focus on self-regulation to improve performance regarding the environment and other issues. They seek to go beyond mere compliance with regulations and to develop the industries' responsiveness to public concerns. Furthermore, some national chemical industry associations are working with systems of collecting and publicizing performance indicators for the industry and to involve local community interest. In the American case these efforts were initiated as the consequence of the Superfund Amendment and Reauthorization Act (SARA Title III), the 'Emergency Planning and Right-to-Know Act' from 1986. The enforcement capabilities of the national associations are, however, very questionable and the industry has yet to come to terms with public concern and public accountability (Simmons and Wynne 1993). Still, as the PSP – Polluter Says Principle – moves towards standardization and public control, we shall get more information on relative contributions by different sectors which we need to impose a total and dynamic system of strict environmental liability.

When we consider scope beyond the nation state – as we must if we are concerned with the ozone hole or the greenhouse effect, or even acid rain – the problems are compounded. Traditional civil liability has little to offer because most cross-boundary effects are diffuse. Who are the owners of Swedish forests and lakes to sue for the acid rain that stunts their trees and kills their fish? The civil liability system proposed by the European Commission might make it possible for them to sue major individual polluters like electricity generating companies, but most sources of acid rain are too small and the nature of their past emissions too uncertain to be effectively sued. At most it may be possible to establish that such and such a proportion comes and has come from Poland, so much from Germany, so much from Britain, so much from Denmark. What then? Legislation is needed which can provide sufferers from cross-boundary acid rain with identifiable parties they can sue, in an international environmental court. It can only be the governments of the countries from which the pollution comes. If they were made liable to be sued, then they in turn would be inclined to pass on the cost to those who could be found responsible. How? If the liability related to past pollution the conventional approach of pollution taxes would not be feasible. Had the government managed to monitor emissions while they were taking place, it could, however, impose a retrospective charge; and of course once it became clear what had to be paid for past pollution, it would be possible to anticipate fairly accurately what would have to be paid in future, and impose continuous charges accordingly. At this point it becomes difficult to distinguish the environmental liability regime from the pollution taxes regime: Coase and Pigou mingle. At the international level it is Coase, with a judicial decision on damages against a background of agreed entitlements; at the national level it is Pigou, with the national government levying taxes and monitoring emissions, with the important qualification that revenue collected should in principle exclusively be spent on compensatory and remedial actions.[2]

Regional problems like acid rain involve not only large numbers of generators and sufferers, but reciprocity – a large proportion of sufferers are generators and vice versa. There is also reciprocity in global problems such as greenhouse gases, where the situation is further complicated by the diffuse and future potential damage effects involved. Does the tort synthesis of liability and compensation offer any feasible solutions here? The application of a total liability system to the global, diffuse and reciprocal cases of present and possible future environmental damage would challenge the overall structure of vested interests, rights and duties, expressed in existing priorities and policies. The legal system is of course best suited to cases with a clearly identifiable damage effect as well as parties involved; so in reciprocal cases the total system should be viewed more as a supplement and guiding principle than a complete alternative to direct regulation and economic instruments.

Strict national liability seems to be an appropriate starting point here. The collection of damages and allocation of means for compensation to sufferers should be carried out according to an internationally sanctioned scheme for the individual nation states. The distribution of the means collected for compensation among the sufferers poses a special problem here in that the sufferers are either not yet present or damage generators themselves to a varying extent and, furthermore, most of the damage will take place gradually in future, so that cost estimates are difficult to make with any confidence. To the extent that the individual contributions of the nation states can be estimated, then (within states) a mix of taxation and tort awards could deter, and raise funds for preventive action. However, before the scope and means of international environmental obligations could be agreed, a consensus would be required on which of the many divergent principles of global justice should be chosen (Arler 1995). Tort law usage provides us with the principle of contribution in the case of joint and several liability, that suggests that the individual nations' share of (for example) $CO_2$ emissions should determine their liability share.

Once liability is assigned, the next question is how damage is evaluated. It seems in the spirit of this chapter, and indeed of this book, to relate damage evaluation as far as possible to *dynamic remediation*, that is, preventive measures aimed at the enhancement, development and introduction of environmentally friendly technologies and substitutes. Dynamic remediation costs could be defined as the minimum cost of reducing future damage by the amount of the damage done. For pragmatic reasons it may be advisable to let 'bygones be bygones' and base the damage award on the annual rate of emissions after the system takes effect. The consequent accelerated diffusion of clean technologies will help to make them more cost-effective and competitive. Successive generations of clean technology will lower the compensation claim imposed on emitters together with the emission problems themselves. The dynamic remediation principle gives us some chance of 'sugaring the pill' for big contributors to global pollution (like the US). Rather than have to compensate other countries – when all are offenders and all are sufferers – or hand over eco-taxes to an international authority (which at present looks politically unthinkable in the US), the damage generator, whether a nation or a firm, can be given a choice: undertake your own activities (R&D and so on) to resolve the problem or pay others to do so.

The solution proposed for the greenhouse effect solution could also be applied to other global effects such as unwanted side-effects of releases of genetically modified organisms or even resource degradation and future depletion. Here again the dynamic and action-oriented perspective of total liability imposes a political responsibility to collect and invest resources in proactive solutions based on some mechanism of deterrence together with the compensation principle. The purpose is in general to stimulate ways out of all the ecologically damaging 'lock-ins' of present industrial society. Those found liable would have to compensate by carrying out R&D activities and implementing preventive measures, clean technologies, and so on – which is what one would hope to achieve by deterrence anyway. Thus the total system would involve interaction between *publicly* stated preferences via internationally negotiated compensation programmes and *privately* initiated performance criteria due to deterrence.

To sum up: The recommendation of the 1986 Brundtland Report on 'Our Common Future' was to integrate environmental concerns in decision-making at all levels and across all sectors of society. Some piecemeal progress has been made towards doing so: we can best speed up our progress, and challenge present 'globalizing' practices, by adopting the total liability system proposed above. The particular advantage of this system is that it reduces reliance on government knowledge and action and stimulates the initiative of individual persons and firms, in finding ways to use and improve clean and sustainable production technologies and consumption practices.

## Notes

1.  Note that such a rise in innovation costs would make it appear, *cet. par.*, that the rate of innovation was increasing, if judged by the 'input' measure of R&D spending. This must be assumed already to be the case with the strict product liability schemes aimed at enhancing consumer safety.
2.  This principle of compensation should not be confused with the 'compensation' paid to groups of firms subjected to new environmental legislation or standards, or redirected to firms subject to green taxes as is the case with the present Danish $CO_2$ tax. Here the revenues collected are returned to the firms in a mixed form of tax reliefs and support schemes for energy savings. This was nevertheless the condition under which it was politically possible at all to implement the $CO_2$ tax in Denmark and the support scheme aspect points in exactly the direction advocated here.

# References

Acton, J.P. and L.S. Dixon, (1992), *Superfund and Transaction Costs. The Experience of Insurers and Very Large Industrial Firms*. Santa Monica: RAND.

Andersen, M.S. (1994), 'Lad afgifter betale for oprensing (Make taxes pay for clean-up).', in *Der Mangler en plan! En debatbog om forurenet jord,* Lyngby: Akademiet for de tekniske Videnskaber, 120–26.

Arler, F. (1995), 'Justice in the Air. Energy Policy, Greenhouse Effect, and the Question of Global Justice', *Human Ecology Review*, Winter/Spring, 2, 1–24.

Basse, E. M. (1990), *Fourenet jord-hvem baerer ansvaret?* Copenhagen: C.E.C.Gad.

Bianchi, A. (1994), 'The Harmonization of Laws on Liability for Environmental Damage in Europe: An Italian Perspective', *Journal of Environmental Law*, 6 (1), 21–42.

Biondi, L. and R. Galli (1992), 'Technological Trajectories', *Futures*, July/August, 580–92.

Birnie, P.W. and A.E. Boyle, (1992), *International Law and the Environment*. Oxford: Clarendon Press.

Bromley, D.W. (1989), 'Economic Interests and Institutions', in *The Conceptual Foundations of Public Policy,* Oxford: Basil Blackwell.

Calabresi, G. and A.D. Melamed (1972), 'Property Rules, Liability Rules, and Inalienability: One view of the Cathedral', *Harvard Law Review*, 85 (6), April, 1098–128.

Christensen, P. and A. Remmen (1994), 'Solutions, Strategies and New Incentives. Danish experiences and perspectives with cleaner technologies', *Centre for Environment and Development Papers* no. 6. Aalborg University.

Clites, A.H., T.D. Fontaine and J.R. Wells, (1991), 'Distributed costs of environmental contamination', *Ecological Economics*, 3, 215–29

Club de Bruxelles (1992), *Environment in the Single European Market,* Brussels: Club de Bruxelles.

Commission of the European Communities (1992) *Towards Sustainability*, A Community Programme of Policy and Action in relation to the Environment and Sustainable Development. COM(92) 23 final, Brussels, 27 March.

Commission of the European Communities (1993a) *Council Regulation No. 1836/93 of 29 June 1993 allowing voluntary participation by companies in the industrial sector in a Community Eco-management and audit scheme. OJ L168, Vol. 36, 10.7.93.*

Commission of the European Communities (1993b), *Green Paper on Remedying Environmental Damage*. COM(93) 47, Brussels, 17 March.

Cooter, R. and T. Ulen, (1988), *Law and Economics,* Illinois: Scott, Foresman and Co.

Demirag, I. and A. Tylecote (1992), 'The Effects of Organisational Culture, Structure and Market Expectations on Technical Innovation: a Hypothesis', *British Journal of Management*, 3 (1), 7–20.

Dewees, D. (1992), 'Tort Law and the Deterrence of Environmental Pollution', in T.H. Tietenberg (ed.), *Innovation in Environmental Policy*, Aldershot: Edward Elgar.

Dietz, F.J. and J van der Straaten (1992), 'Rethinking Environmental Economics: Missing Links between Economic Theory and Environmental Policy', *Journal of Economic Issues*, **XXVI** (1), 27–51.

Folketingstidende (1994), *Forslag til Lov om erstatning for miljøskader. Lovforslag nr. L 123, Folketinget 1993–94, København (Proposal of Law on Compensation for Environmental Damages. Proposal no. L 123)*, The Parliament 1993–94, Copenhagen.

Freeman, C. (1982), *The Economics of Innovation*, London: Pinter

Freeman, C. (1992), *The Economics of Hope: Essays on Technical Change, Economic Growth and the Environment*, London: Pinter.

Geddes, A. (1992), *Product and Service Liability in the EEC: The New Strict Liability Regime*, Eynsham: Sweet & Maxwell/Information Press.

Huber, P.W. (1988), *Liability: The Legal Revolution and Its Consequences*, New York: Basic Books.

Ilsøe, J. P. (1994), 'Værditab på private boliger som følge af jordforurening' (Value Loss of Private Habitations as a Consequence of Ground Pollution). 84–94 in *Der mangler en plan! En debatbog om forurenet jord*, Lyngby: Akademiet for de tekniske Videnskaber.

Jacoby, D. and A. Eremich (1991), 'Environmental Liability in the United States of America', in *Environmental Liability*. International Bar Association Series. London: Graham & Trotman.

Johnson, B. (1992), 'Institutional Learning', Chapter 2 in B. Å Lundvall (ed.), *'National Systems of Innovation. Towards a Theory of Innovation and Interactive Learning'*, London: Pinter.

Johnson, S. P. (1993), 'The Earth Summit: The United Nations Conference on Environment and Development (UNCED)', *International Environmental Law and Policy Series*, Cornwall: Graham & Trotman/Martinus Nijhoff.

Justitsministeriet (1992), *Betænkning om erstatning for miljøskader. Afgivet af Justitsministereiets udvalg om erstatning for miljøskader*. Betænkning nr. 1237, København: Statens Information. (Danish Ministry of Justice 1992: Report on Compensation for Environmental Damages by Committee appointed by the Ministry of Justice. Copenhagen.).

Kaplow, L. and S. Shavell (1994), 'Accuracy in the Determination of Liability', *Journal of Law and Economics*, **XXXVII**, April, 1–15.

Katz, M. (1986), 'The Role of the Legal System in Technological Innovation and Economic Growth', in R. Landau and N. Rosenberg (eds), *The Positive Sum Strategy. Harnessing Technology for Economic Growth*, Washington DC: National Academic Press.

Kline, S.J. and N. Rosenberg (1986), 'An Overview of Innovation', in R. Landau and N. Rosenberg (eds), *The Positive Sum Strategy. Harnessing Technology for Economic Growth*, Washington DC: National Academy Press.

Krämer, L. (1992), *Focus on European Environmental Law*, London: Sweet & Maxwell.

Lundvall, B.Å. (1992), 'User-Producer Relationships, National Systems of Innovation and Internationalization', Chapter 3 in B.Å. Lundvall, (ed.) *National Systems of*

*Innovation. Towards a Theory of Innovation and Interactive Learning*, London: Pinter.

Minsch, J. (1991), 'Kausalität und externe Effekte. Ein Beitrag zu einer problemorientierten Weiterentwicklung der Externalitätenkonzeption' (Causality and External Effects. A Contribution to a Problem Oriented Development of the Conception of Externalities) in F. Beckenbach (ed.), *Die ökologische Herausforderung für die ökonomische Theorie*. Marburg: Metropolis-Verlag.

Nentjes, A. and D. Wiersma (1988), 'Innovation and Pollution Control', *International Journal of Social Economics*, **15**, issue and 51–70.

OECD (1991), *The State of the Environment*, Paris.

OECD (1992), *Technology and the Economy. The Key Relationships*, The Technology/Economy Programme, Paris.

Parkin, W. P. (1995), 'Audit Privilege Advocates should not Celebrate Yet', *US Environment Watch*, Blaine: Speciality Technical Publishers.

Pearce, D., S. Frankhauser, N. Adger, and T. Swanson (1992), 'World Economy, World Environment', *The World Economy*, **15** (3), May, 295–313.

Remmen, A. and E.H. Nielsen (1994), 'New Incentives for Pollution Prevention. Environmental Strategies for Companies and Public Regulation', in S.P. Maltezou *et al.* (eds), *Selected papers from the Third International IACT Conference on Policies and Incentives for Clean Technology*, Vienna: Federal Ministry for Economic Affairs and International Association for Clean Technology.

Schon, D.A. (1967), *Technology and Change: The New Heraclitus*, London: Pergamon Press.

Schumpeter, J.A. (1934), *The Theory of Economic Development: An Inquiry into Profits, Capital, Credit, Interest, and the Business Cycle*. Cambridge MA: Harvard University Press (originally published 1911/1926).

Shavell, S. (1987), *Economic Analysis of Accident Law*, Cambridge, MA: Harvard University Press.

Simmons, P. (1993), 'EC Civil Liability Proposals and the Environmental Responsiveness of Industry', *European Environment*, **3**, Part 1. 2–5.

Simmons, P. and B. Wynne (1993), 'Responsible Care: Trust, Credibility and Environmental Management' in K. Fischer and J. Schot (eds), *Environmental Strategies for Industry. International Perspectivess on Research Needs and Policy Implications*, Washington DC: Island Press.

Simon, H.A. (1959), 'Theories of decision-making in economics and behavioral sciences', *American Economic Review*, **49**, June, 253–83.

Tietenberg, T.H. (1989), 'Indivisible Toxic Torts', *Land Economics*, **65** (4), November, 305–19.

Tylecote, A. (1987), 'Time Horizons of Management Decisions: Causes and Effects', *Journal of Economic Studies*, **14** (4), 51–64.

Veblen, T. (1898), 'Why is Economics not an Evolutionary Science?' *The Quarterly Journal of Economics*, **XII**, July, 373–97.

Williamson, O.E. (1985), *The Economic Institutions of Capitalism: Firms, Markets, Relational Contracting*, New York: The Free Press.

PART THREE

Ecology, Technology and Long Fluctuations in
Economic Growth

# 9.   The Political Economy of the Long Wave

## Chris Freeman

---

### Introduction

The last quarter of the 20th century has seen a revival of interest in theories of long waves (or Kondratieff cycles) and in particular with the role of technical change in these cycles. This paper deals with technical change in the trough of the 'Fourth Kondratieff' (1970s to 1990s) and the possibilities of a new 'Fifth Kondratieff' upswing in the early part of the next century.

The first section of the paper argues that the 1990s' recession was more serious than any other since the Second World War. It has stimulated a faint-hearted resurgence of Keynesian ideas among policy-makers. Although this is welcome, Keynesian ideas are not enough since this recession takes place in the trough of a long wave. Section 2 discusses Schumpeter's theory of long cycles and argues that this is not sufficient either, even though it adds an important dimension which is lacking in most Keynesian analysis. Section 3 suggests that the theory of change in 'techno-economic paradigms' advanced by Carlota Perez represents a major advance on Schumpeter's formulations. Section 4 attempts to apply this theory to the present change of techno-economic paradigm and, finally, Section 5 considers briefly the prospects for the future.

### 1. The Recession of the 1990s: Why Keynes is not enough

It is now widely agreed that the recession of the early 1990s was the most serious since the 1930s. Already in the 1970s and 1980s the cyclical fluctuations became more severe than in the previous quarter-century and large-scale unemployment re-appeared as a persistent problem in most of the industrial countries (*Table 9.1*) as well as the Third World. In the 1990s however, the scope and duration of the recession surpassed earlier downturns and many analysts began to observe features of the recession which distinguished it from its milder predecessors. The OECD (1993) 'Interim Report' on Unemployment described the situation as 'disquieting, perhaps alarming'.

That the 1990s recession was not even more severe was due in no small measure to the Keynesian 'stabilisers' built into the socio-economic system in the main industrial countries following the catastrophe of the 1930s. Among the most important were the social security systems including unemployment benefit arrangements, which helped to cushion the fall in consumer expenditure. Also important, especially in the USA, were the various systems for protecting the weaker banks from collapse and the stabilization of farm prices and incomes. Stagnation and persistent unemployment were thus more characteristic of the early 1990s than the vicious downward spirals of the early 1930s. Nevertheless with average unemployment exceeding 10% in the EEC in 1993 and still worse levels in some East European and Third World countries, the need for new policies at both national and international level became increasingly apparent.

However, what is needed is not a return to Keynesian orthodoxy of the 1930s, still less a return to the pre-Keynesian economics of the 1920s, but a post-Keynesian prescription which takes into account new developments of his theory as well as the fundamental (and still valid) core. This involves a debate which has hitherto been lacking. Such a debate should, in particular, take into account some Schumpeterian ideas. Schumpeter argued that a satisfactory theory of business cycles should embrace long-term structural and technical change, as well as the shorter cycles analysed by Keynes. The rather savage criticisms of Keynes' 'General Theory' made by Schumpeter should not obscure the fact that Schumpeter's theory of Kondratieff cycles has something to add to Keynesian theory.

The period from the late 1890s to the First World War became known as the 'Belle Époque' and was one of prosperity and relatively low unemployment. It was followed in the 1920s by a period of great instability and high unemployment, and in the 1930s by the Great Depression. The quarter-century following the Second World War was again a period of high growth – probably the fastest period of world economic growth ever known – and of relatively full employment in the OECD countries and the socialist countries. The final quarter has once more been a period of much greater instability, higher levels of unemployment and slower growth. These long swings correspond rather well to Van Gelderen's metaphor of 'spring tides' and 'ebb tides' of economic development, each phase lasting about a quarter of a century.

*Table 9.1: OECD unemployment, 1959–93 (% of Labour Force)*

|             | 1959–67 Average | 1979 | 1992 | 1993 |
|-------------|:----:|:----:|:----:|:----:|
| Belgium     | 2.4  | 8.7  | 10.3 | 12.1 |
| Canada      | 5.0  | 7.4  | 11.3 | 11.2 |
| Denmark     | 1.4  | 5.3  | 11.1 | 12.1 |
| France      | 0.7  | 6.0  | 10.4 | 11.7 |
| Germany     | 1.2* | 3.4* | 8.9  | 10.1 |
| Ireland     | 4.6  | 7.5  | 17.2 | 17.6 |
| Italy       | 6.2  | 7.5  | 10.7 | 10.2 |
| Japan       | 1.4  | 2.0  | 2.2  | 2.5  |
| Netherlands | 0.9  | 4.1  | 6.8  | 8.3  |
| UK          | 1.8  | 5.3  | 9.8  | 10.6 |
| USA         | 5.3  | 5.8  | 7.4  | 6.9  |
| Finland     | 3.0  |      | 13.1 | 18.2 |
| Spain       | 4.5  |      | 18.4 | 22.7 |
| Sweden      | 1.4  |      | 4.5  | 9.2  |

*Source*: OECD

* Federal Republic only

Van Gelderen (1913), Kondratieff (1925) and Schumpeter (1939) argued that these long cycles were an integral feature of world economic development, as well as the more familiar medium-term (Juglar) business cycles. They insisted that long cycles merited some attention and explanation in addition to the shorter cycles on which most economists concentrated. Furthermore, they argued that the shorter-term cycles were themselves strongly influenced by the long waves.

Despite the fact that outstanding economists, such as Pareto and Tinbergen, took the long wave idea seriously, mainstream economics has generally been uneasy about this somewhat unorthodox concept. However, the leading exponent of neo-Keynesian theory (and author of a widely acclaimed economics textbook), Paul Samuelson, did hazard the following comment (now proven accurate):

> It is my considered guess that the final quarter of the 20th Century will fall far
> short of the third quarter in the achieved rate of economic progress. The dark
> horoscope of my old teacher Joseph Schumpeter may have particular relevance
> here. (Samuelson 1981)

Apart from a few such odd remarks, most economists have continued to neglect
long cycles, except for the occasional attempt (Weinstock 1969; Solomou 1987)
to demonstrate statistically that they did not exist. This statistical debate will
probably rumble on indefinitely since the statistics for the 19th century are very
poor and not available for more than a few countries. Moreover, there are
problems in precise dating of turning points both nationally and internationally
and some long wave theorists have discredited the idea by attempting to insist on
an exact period of years – 54 years was popular at one time – for the duration of
each cycle, instead of recognizing as Schumpeter did that the very nature of the
cycles meant that they could vary in length, just as Juglar cycles do. Moreover,
as Tylecote (1992) has shown, the feedback effects during the cycle itself may
dampen the upswing or the downswing in particular national economies.

The rather sterile controversy about statistics is regrettable because it has
tended to obscure the main positive outcome of long wave theory – its attempt to
account for the uneven assimilation of pervasive new technologies in the
economic and social system (Perez 1983). Schumpeter spoke of 'successive
industrial revolutions' and it is evident that when we are thinking of steam
power, electric power or computer systems which affect almost every industry,
they have profound and changing consequences for investment behaviour as they
are diffused throughout the system.

Although there is no consensus among economists about business cycles, there
*are* actually some areas of substantial agreement within the profession in the
analysis of investment behaviour and its influence on cycles. As interest in
technical change continues to grow it offers the prospect of widening this area of
agreement. Almost all economists agree that whilst consumer confidence and
consumer behaviour strongly influence investment and are important in their
own right in influencing business cycles, it is investment which is subject to the
greatest fluctuations and is the main source of instability in the system
(Samuelson 1980).

There is also a broad consensus that 'confidence' is a strong influence on
investment behaviour. Whilst neo-classical economics is still somewhat
reluctant to accept the idea of 'bounded rationality' and to recognise fully the
role of uncertainty in investment decision-making, none have succeeded in
refuting the central propositions of Keynesian investment theory, enshrined in

the oft-quoted passage comparing investment with an expedition to the South Pole, emphasising the role of 'animal spirits' and the impossibility of exact calculation of future returns on investment. However, confidence is related not only to such factors as political stability and government policies but also, as Schumpeter emphasized, to band-wagon effects associated with the diffusion of new technologies, new products, new services and the opening of new markets. In a passage which is seldom referred to, Keynes fully acknowledged the significance of these influences on investment behaviour.

> In the case of fixed capital, it is easy to understand why fluctuations should occur in the rate of investment. Entrepreneurs are induced to embark on the production of fixed capital or deterred from doing so by their expectations of the profits to be made. Apart from the many minor reasons why these should fluctuate in a changing world, Professor Schumpeter's explanation of the major movements may be unreservedly accepted. (Keynes (1930), Vol. 2, pp. 85-6.)

It is true that this strong endorsement of Schumpeter's analysis of investment behaviour was often forgotten by the followers of Keynes, and even by Keynes himself, when they later began to concentrate on short-term fluctuations and counter-cyclical policies. This should not obscure the importance of Keynes' comment or Schumpeter's theory of investment behaviour. Nevertheless, Schumpeter's theory too is inadequate.

## 2. Why Schumpeter is Not Enough

Although Schumpeter was right to stress the role of 'Successive industrial revolutions' in the development of capitalism, his theory was deficient in several important respects (Kuznets 1940; Sweezy 1943; Ruttan 1959).

In the first place, his theory of entrepreneurship ascribed the central role in technical and organizational innovation primarily to exceptional individuals. Almost all contemporary research on innovation, as well as much historical research, emphasizes also the importance of the accumulation of knowledge within firms and within scientific and technical institutions and universities and the plurality of inputs to the innovation process (for example Pavitt 1984, 1986; Teece 1988; Dosi 1982; Dosi *et al*, 1988). This does not deny the importance of entrepreneurial initiative in combining inputs in new ways, nor the important distinction between invention and innovation, but a theory which emphasizes almost exclusively the outstanding 'heroic' individuals is not merely one-sided but deficient in historical perspective since it tends to ignore the changing nature of the entrepreneurial functions in the successive phases of development. It also understates the importance of incremental innovation, learning by doing, by using and by interacting in the process of technical change and diffusion of innovations (Arrow 1962; von Hippel 1976; Rosenberg 1982; Lundvall 1988).

The changing nature of entrepreneurship is especially important in relation to the present wave of technical change involving many forms of networking, partnerships, new relationships between firms and much stronger transnational corporations.

In the second place, Schumpeter's theory is deficient with respect to the notion of *profit*. As is well known, he took from Marx the idea of exceptional profits as a driving force stimulating innovation and as a signal to imitators to move into new profitable areas ('swarming'). He also followed Marx in suggesting that the profits of the innovators would gradually be eroded by these competitive pressures. However, unlike Marx (and most other economists) he defined profit as deriving *only* from innovative entrepreneurship and rejected the idea of profit as a social surplus or rent derived from the monopoly of *ownership* or *power*.

Although Schumpeter's theory of the erosion of profitability during the diffusion process is helpful in understanding waves of technical change and their relation to business cycles, it obscures the role of other ways of sustaining or increasing profitability. It also neglects the wider problem of income distribution in society as a whole and the extent to which inequality may hinder growth (Tylecote 1992). Social conflicts cannot be ignored in cycle theory. For example, attempts to increase work intensity in various ways are a constant source of social conflict although they may sometimes be successful, at least temporarily, in raising profitability. Since the first industrial revolution, the resistance to increased work intensity and long hours of work has grown and this has increased the pressures to use technical and organizational change as the main methods of maintaining or raising profitability. But the two can often go together as in some forms of 'Taylorism' or 'just-in-time' and it is an unnecessary over-simplification to neglect entirely the issue of work intensity, which is so obviously a matter of daily concern to both employers and employees. Methods of work organization and work supervision were and are a very important aspect of social change in each successive Kondratieff wave and are often intimately related to attempts at increasing work intensity. This was particularly the case with Taylor's 'scientific management' and other related ways of reorganizing production which emerged in the 1880s, even though Taylor always denied that his system involved higher work intensity. To find a man who was capable of loading 45 tons of metal per day rather than 15 tons led to Barth's 'Law of Heavy Labouring' and Schmidt became the most famous of Taylor's anecdotes (Nelson 1980 p. 172). To be fair to Schumpeter he did stress the importance of organizational and managerial innovations as well as technical.

There are still other ways of attempting to maintain or increase profitability and these cannot be neglected either, although they too are often closely intertwined with processes of technical change more narrowly defined. Historically, capital investment in areas of the economy (or whole countries) which had not previously been drawn into the capitalist mode of production was certainly important (Mandel 1972). The commodification of information services is a major contemporary example.

By the same token the renewed extension of capitalist relationships to the former Communist countries cannot be ignored. Finally, although Schumpeter gave a fairly plausible account of the upswing of the long wave based on the diffusion of a cluster of major innovations through the economic system and of the erosion of profitability at the peak of the wave, he did not give an equally plausible explanation of depression or of recovery from depression. His obsession with Walrasian equilibrium theory, his tendency to regard business cycles as 'natural' phenomena and his reluctance to consider socio-political measures to deal with depression all prevented him from developing an integrated theory of technical and institutional change in relation to long waves.

For all these reasons (and others too) Schumpeter's theory of long waves, although an advance on Kondratieff's own theory in some respects, does not provide a satisfactory starting point. There are certainly many valuable comments and insights to be found in his work, particularly in the historical chapters of *Business Cycles,* but a different starting point is needed for a satisfactory discussion of the main problems.

## 3.  Towards a New Theory of the Long Wave

Among the various attempts to develop a more satisfactory theory of the relationship between technical change and long waves, the ideas of Carlota Perez (1983, 1985, 1989) are particularly interesting. There are several original features of her exposition which seem to overcome some of the main weaknesses of other explanations in the Schumpeterian tradition.

She suggests that each wave is characterized by a dominant technological style or 'techno-economic paradigm' which influences not just one or two leading sectors but almost all branches of the economy to a varying extent. Thus, her explanation is not just based on a cluster of major innovations occurring in a particular decade (as Mensch (1975) and Kleinknecht (1986) at one time suggested), nor yet on a few leading sectors, but on a pervasive technological style embracing a whole constellation of technically and economically interrelated innovations and influencing almost all industries and an entire phase of economic development.  These constellations of innovations do not emerge suddenly just before a new Kondratieff upswing but crystallize over several previous decades.  This chapter will explore this concept in relation to the trough of the fourth and the upswing of the fifth Kondratieff wave.

A number of economists have pointed to the importance of 'technological trajectories' (Nelson and Winter 1977) and of 'constellations of innovations' (Keirstead 1948) which are both technically and economically interrelated. Several have also extended Kuhn's (1961) notion of scientific paradigms to the concept of 'technological paradigms' (Freeman 1979;  Dosi 1982).  Nelson and Winter (1977) suggested that some trajectories could be so powerful and influential that they could be regarded as 'generalized natural trajectories'.  They suggested electricity as one such example.  Freeman, Clark and Soete (1982) and other economists have stressed the interdependence of technical innovations in 'new technology systems'.  Carlota Perez, however, takes these ideas one step further.  Her idea of 'techno-economic paradigms' relates not just to a particular branch of industry but to the broad tendencies in the economy as a whole.  Her model may be described as a 'meta-paradigm' or a 'pervasive technology' theory.

Perhaps the expression 'techno-economic paradigm' conveys too great an air of precision.  She has also used the expression 'technological style' and this may rather better convey her meaning.   We shall use both expressions interchangeably.   A change of techno-economic paradigm or 'technological style' is based on a whole range of new products and processes and many others which are redesigned to take advantage of the new technical and economic possibilities.  She suggests that, underlying this paradigm change is a change in the dynamics of the relative cost structure of all possible inputs into production. In each new techno-economic paradigm, a particular input or set of inputs, which may be described as the 'key factor or factors' of that paradigm, fulfil the following conditions:

1.       Clearly perceived low and rapidly falling relative cost.  As Rosenberg (1976) and other economists have pointed out, *small* changes in the relative input cost structure have little or no effect on the behaviour of engineers, designers and researchers.  Only major and persistent changes have the power to transform the decision rules and 'common sense' procedures for engineers and managers (Perez 1985;  Freeman and Soete 1987).

2.  Apparently, almost unlimited availability of supply over long periods. Temporary shortages may of course occur in a period of rapid build-up in demand for the new key factor, but the prospect must be clear that there are no major barriers to an enormous long-term increase in supply. This is an essential condition for the confidence to take major investment decisions which depend on this long-term availability.

3.  Clear potential for the use or incorporation of the new key factor or factors in many products and processes throughout the economic system; either directly or (more commonly) through a set of related innovations, which both reduce the cost and change the quality of capital equipment, labour inputs, and other inputs to the system.

Perez maintains that this combination of characteristics holds today for microelectronics, and few would deny this. It held until recently for oil, which underlay the post-war boom (the 'fourth Kondratieff' upswing). She suggests that previously the role of key factor was played by low cost steel in the third Kondratieff and by low cost coal in the second.

Clearly, every one of these inputs identified as 'key factors' existed (and was in use) long before the new paradigm developed. However, its full potential was only recognized and made capable of fulfilling the above conditions when the previous paradigm and its related constellation of technologies gave strong signals of diminishing returns and of approaching limits to its potential for further increasing productivity or for new profitable investment. This slow-down in productivity growth was clearly evident for both labour and capital productivity in the 1970s and 1980s.

The most successful new technology systems gradually crystallize as an 'ideal' new type of production organization which becomes the common sense of management and design embodying new 'rules of thumb', restoring confidence to investment decision-makers after a long period of hesitating, at first in a few industries and later in many. This renewal of confidence and resurgence of animal spirits was clearly evident in the 'Belle Epoque' leading up to the First World War, especially in Germany and the United States, which adapted their institutions to exploit the new technology more rapidly than the UK. It was apparent again in the 1950s and 1960s, based on cheap oil and Fordist mass production.

The full constellation – once crystallized – goes far beyond the key factor(s) and beyond technical change itself. It brings with it a restructuring of the whole productive system. Among other things, as it crystallizes, the new techno-economic paradigm involves a wave of new infrastructural investment as well as explosive growth of new products and services using this infrastructure. It also requires a new skill profile, new organization of production and new management systems.

It is evident that the period of transition – the downswing and depression of the long wave – is characterized by deep structural change in the economy and Perez insists that such changes require an equally profound transformation of the institutional and social framework. The onset of prolonged recessionary trends as in the 1970s, 1980s and early 1990s, indicated the increasing degree of *mismatch* between the techno-economic subsystem and the old socio-institutional framework. It showed the need for a full-scale reaccommodation of social behaviour and institutions to suit the requirements and the potential of a shift which had already taken place to a considerable extent in some areas of the techno-economic sphere. This reaccommodation can occur only as a result of a prolonged process of political search, experimentation and adaptation, but when it has been achieved, by a variety of social and political changes at the national and international level, the resulting 'good match' could facilitate the upswing phase of the long wave. A climate of confidence for a surge of new investment would be created through an appropriate combination of political changes, regulatory mechanisms and infra-structural investment which foster the full deployment of the new paradigm. The emphasis on institutional and political change in the downswing of the long wave distinguishes the theory of Carlota Perez from most other long wave theories including Schumpeter's own. However, the two most original and innovative books on long waves appearing in the 1990s both follow her ideas on this point as well as on her theory of dominant 'technological styles' (Tylecote 1992; Berry 1991).

We turn now to describe the pattern of technical and organizational innovations which led to the emergence of a new paradigm based on cheap micro-electronics, computers and telecommunications in the second half of the 20th century. This constellation of innovations may be conveniently summarized as 'information and communications technology' (ICT).

## 4. The Emergence of a New Techno-Economic Paradigm

There are many economic advantages based on the use of ICT but some of the most important can be grouped under four headings:

1. Speed of processing and transmitting information
2. Storage capacity for vast quantities of information

3.    Flexibility in organizing manufacturing, design, marketing and administration
4.    Networking within and between firms and other individuals and organizations

The first of these characteristics – speed – was there from the beginning of computers and of telephony and was indeed the main purpose in developing computers at all from Babbage and Zuse onwards.    Storage capacity also developed rapidly from the very early days of computing.    The other characteristics developed only during the diffusion process as a result of linking computer technology with telecommunication technology and numerous related and complementary innovations in software, in peripherals, in computer architecture, in components and integrated circuits, in optical fibres and in telecommunications technology.    The characteristics which will be discussed in this section already give a coherent pattern for a new style of management, which is in conflict with the old style based on mass production and often described as 'Fordism'.    An over-simplified and schematic contrast between these two styles is shown in *Table 9.2*.

This is not technological determinism.    Technologies are developed and diffused by human institutions;    the processes of development, selection and application are *social* processes.    In the OECD (and most other) contemporary economies, the selection process is heavily influenced by perceived competitive advantage, expected profitability and (intimately related to these factors) time-saving potential.    It is for this reason that we prefer the expression 'techno-economic paradigm' to the more commonly used 'technological paradigm'. However, it is also true that some technological trajectories, once launched, tend to have their own momentum and to attract additional resources by virtue of past performance.    Finally, both the technological system and the economic system get 'locked in' to dominant technologies once certain linkages in supply of materials, components, and sub-assemblies have been made, economies of scale realized, and training systems and standards established.    Consequently individuals, firms and societies are not quite so 'free' in their choice of technology as might appear at first sight (Arthur 1989; Dosi 1982; Perez 1985).

In fact, in its early days computing was in no way a dominant technology and had to struggle for survival in a world geared to very different technologies and systems.    Even very well-informed industrialists, such as T.J. Watson, the head of IBM, did not believe that there would be any large commercial market for computers (Katz and Phillips 1982) and thought that the only demand would be for a few very large computers in government, military and scientific applications.    Early computer users had great difficulties in obtaining reliable

*Table 9.2: Change of techno-economic paradigm*

| Old 'Fordist' | New ICT |
| --- | --- |
| Energy-intensive | Information Intensive |
| Design and engineering in 'drawing' offices | Computer-aided designs |
| Sequential design and production | Concurrent engineering |
| Standardized | Customized |
| Rather stable product mix | Rapid changes in product mix |
| Dedicated plant and equipment | Flexible production systems |
| Automation | Systemation |
| Single firm | Networks |
| Hierarchical structures | Flat horizontal structures |
| Departmental | Integrated |
| Product with service | Service with products |
| Centralization | Distributed intelligence |
| Specialized skills | Multi-skilling |
| Government control and sometimes ownership | Government information, co-ordination and regulation |
| 'Planning' | 'Vision' |

*Source*: Adapted from Freeman and Perez (1988)

peripherals and appropriate programmes and in recruiting people with the necessary skills. However, even in these early days, computers did already demonstrate those revolutionary *technical* advantages, which enabled such far-sighted pioneers as Norbert Wiener (1949) or John Diebold (1952) to forecast their ultimate universal diffusion.

In the 1950s, the electronic industries generally were still 'fitting in', albeit somewhat uncomfortably, to the old, world Fordist, paradigm. Computers became part of the departmental, hierarchical structures of the large firms which adopted them. Their main advantages at this stage were the time-savings in *storing and processing* of enormous volumes of information in standardized applications such as pay-roll, tax, inventories, and so on. They certainly did not yet revolutionize the *organization* of firms, for example, by making available information at all levels in all departments. Radio and television fitted in well to the paradigm of cheap, standardized consumer durables supplied on hire-purchase to every household, like washing machines, cars or refrigerators.

However, by the 1970s the role of computers was changing. The speed of processing vast quantities of information was reduced by orders of magnitude (see *Table 9.3*). In the 1950s and 1960s new technical advances still further enhanced this extraordinary speed by even more orders of magnitude and these advances still continue.

A major characteristic of the semi-conductor and computer industry from the 1960s onwards was the very rapid change in the successive generations of integrated circuits. The number of components which could be placed on one tiny chip doubled every few years until it has now reached many millions and still continues to expand. This meant that all those firms making the numerous products which used these chips were also obliged to make frequent design changes. Rapid changes in design and product mix thus became a characteristic feature of the electronic industry and they increasingly used their own technologies to meet this requirement (CAD, networks of computer terminals, integration of design, production and marketing, and so on). Speed, storage capacity, flexibility and networking thus emerged in the 1980s as strongly inter-related characteristics of the new techno-economic paradigm (*Table 9.3*). Organizational and technical change became inextricably connected.   There were strong pressures for greater flexibility in working hours which interacted with the potential of ICT to deliver this flexibility.

Now it was no longer a question of 'stand-alone' computers or numerically controlled machine tools or other items of equipment, or of separate data-processing departments or separate machine shops with a few CNC tools. Increasingly, it was a question not of 'islands' within an alien and quite different manufacturing system or service delivery, but of the whole organization being tuned in to what was previously stand-alone equipment or experimental plant. Flexible manufacturing systems (FMS and 'systemation') or computer-integrated manufacturing (CIM) became the name of the game rather than the diffusion of individual items of equipment.

Numerous case studies of diffusion of robots, CNC, lasers, CAD and so forth in manufacturing (for example Fleck 1988) or of computers and ATM in banks or of EDI (electronic data interchange) in retail firms testify to the systems integration problems and the site-specific problems which arose and still arise in a widening range of firms and industries: operating and maintenance skills do not match the new equipment;   management cannot cope with the inter-departmental problems, changes in structure and industrial relations;   sub-contractors cannot meet the new demands;   the software does not run properly, interface standards do not exist, and so on and so on.   Nevertheless, the small

*Table 9.3   Change of techno-economic paradigm in OECD countries: a summary*

| Area of Change | (1) Late 1940s-Early 1970s | (2) Early 1970s-Mid 1990s | (3) Mid 1990s Onwards "Optimistic" Scenario |
|---|---|---|---|
| **I. Information and Communication Technology** | | | |
| A. Electronic Computers | Early valve-based machines mainly in military applications. Future potential often under-estimated. Big improvements in architecture, memory, peripherals lead to take-off in commercial market in 1950s. Huge improvements in reliability and performance from use of transistors and integrated circuits. Main-frame computers in large firm data-processing dominant but mini-computers take off in 1960s. | From 1971 the micro-processor leads to small, cheap, powerful personal computers diffusing to households as well as huge numbers of business users change the nature of the computer industry. Large main-frames and centralised data-processing departments play diminishing role as work-stations and PCs gain greater share of market. | Universal availability of PCs and of portable and 'wallet' type computers linked to networks. Computers so unobtrusive in so many applications that they pass unnoticed (like electric motors in the household today). Super-computers and parallel processing for RD and other applications such as data banks where truly vast memory capacity and speed of processing is needed. |
| B. Computer Software | First programming languages in 1950s. Hardware companies developing and supplying software to own standards. As applications multiply scientific users in R&D do their own software programming. Big DP departments develop software teams working with hardware suppliers. Emergence of independent software companies giving advice and support to users and designing systems. | Very rapid growth of software industry and consultancy especially in United States. Packaged user-friendly software facilitates extraordinarily rapid diffusion of computer hardware, especially to SME, but customised software and modified packages business also grow very rapidly. Movement to Open Systems in the late 1980s facilitates inter-connections and networking. Shortages of software personnel acute in 1970s and 1980s but abating in 1990s. | Reductions in requirement for software labour from (1) standard packages, (2) automation of coding and testing, (3) reduced mainframe support, (4) improved skills of users. But these trends offset by new software demand from (1) Parallel processing, (2) Multi-media and virtual reality and expert systems, (3) Changing configurations because of continuing organisational and technical change. Renewed surge of demand for more skilled software design and maintenance. |
| C. Semi-Conductors and Integrated Circuits | From valves to transistors in 1950s and integrated circuits in 1960s to large-scale integration (LSI) in 1970s. Orders of magnitude improvement in reliability, speed, performance almost doubling the number of components per chip annually and drastically reducing cost. | From LSI to VLSI and wafer-scale integration. With the micro-processor from 1970s onwards, many small firms enter computer design and manufacture. Huge capacity of VLSI circuits leads to vastly increased capacity of all computers and huge reductions in cost. | Chips have become a cheap commodity. Both technical and economic limits to present stage of miniaturisation reached in early 21st Century leading ultimately to 'Bio-chips' or other radically new nano-technology. |

| D. Tele-communications Infra-structure | Electro-mechanical systems predominate in 1950s and 1960s. Traffic mainly voice traffic and telex limited by coaxial cables (plus microwave and satellite links from 1960s). Large centralised public utilities dominate the system with oligopolistic supply of telephone equipment by small ring of firms. | Massive R&D Investment leads to fully electronic stored-programme-controlled switching systems, requiring less maintenance and permitting continuous adaptation to new traffic, including a wide variety of voice, data, text, and images. Many new networking services develop. Optical fibres permit orders of magnitude increase in capacity and cost reduction. Break-up of old monopolies. | Widespread availability of bandwidths up to a million times that of the old 'twisted pair' in coaxial cables. 'Information Highways' using access to data banks and universal ISDN providing cheap networked services for business and households and permitting tele-commuting on an increasing scale for a wide variety of activities. Mobile phones and videophones diffusing very rapidly, linked to both wireless and wired systems. |
|---|---|---|---|

*Estimated of Increase in ICT Capacity*

| | | | |
|---|---|---|---|
| OECD Installed Computer Base (Number of machines) | 30,000 (1965) | Millions (1985) | Hundred Millions (2005) |
| OECD Full-time Software Personnel | >200,000 (1965) | >2,000,000 (1985) | >10,000,000 (2005) |
| Components per Micro-electronic Circuit | 32 (1965) | 1 Mega-bit (1987) | 256 Mega-bit (late 1990s) |
| Leading Representative Computer: Instructions per Second | $10^3$ (1955) | $10^7$ (1989) | $10^9$ (2000) |
| PCs ips | – | $10^6$ (1989) | $10^8$ (2000) |
| Cost:Computer Thousand ops. per $US | $10^5$ (1960s) | $10^8$ (1980s) | $10^{10}$ (2005) |

*Table 9.3 continued*

## II. Industries and Services

| | | |
|---|---|---|
| A. Manufacturing | Mass production industries based on cheap oil, bulk materials and petro-chemicals predominate in 1950s and 1960s boom. Electronic capital goods industries still small though very fast growing. Consumer goods (radio and TV) fit into general pattern of household consumer durables. Early CAD and CNC introduced as 'islands' of automation mainly in aerospace and promoted by government. | Electronic industries become leading edge in 1980s. Rapid diffusion of CAD, CNC and Robotics in metal-working and later other industries. Productivity increases and diffusion slowed by learning problems, site-specific variety, skill mis-matches and lack of management experience. Integration of Design Production and Marketing slow to take off. FMS and CIM have big teething troubles. | Generalisation of electronic-based equipment and control in all industries. "Systemation" of various functions within firms through CAD-CAM, etc. Flexible manufacturing systems in most industries. Larger labour and capital productivity increases in OECD countries. Layered incorporation of Third World countries in expanding world manufacturing output and trade. |
| B. Services | Mass production style spreads to many service industries, especially tourism (packaged holidays, cheap air and bus travel, etc.) distribution and fast food. Rapid growth of (public) social services and of central and local government employment. Hierarchical centralised management systems in large organisations, whether government or private. | Many services become capital-intensive through introduction of computer systems, especially financial services. Service industries also begin to do R&D and more product innovation. 'Diagonalisation' of services based on capability in ICT (tourism companies into financial services and vice-versa; banks into property services, etc.). Big learning problems and software failures. Word processors become universal. | Vast proliferation of inter-active networking services, producer services, consultancy and information systems. Tele-shopping, tele-banking, tele-learning, tele-consultancy, tele-commuting, based on cheap universal computing and very cheap telecommunications (Fax, E-mail, video-phones, mobile phones, etc.). Growth of labour-intensive craft services, 'caring' services and creative services on personal customised basis and local networks. |
| C. Scale Economies, Firm Size and Industrial Structure | Increasing size of plant in many industries in 1950s, and 1960s (steel, oil, tankers, petro-chemicals). Big scale economies facilitate growth of large firms and concentration of industry. MNCs spread investment world-wide especially in oil, automobiles and chemicals. In late 60s and early 70s increasing evidence of 'limits to growth' of energy-intensive mass production style. | Production scale economies sometimes reversed but scale economies in R&D, Marketing, Finance, etc. still important. In 1980s and 1990s intense competition, computer systems and cultural revolution lead to 'down-sizing' of some large firms – with reduction of both white and blue collar employment. Many new SMEs side by side with high mortality in recessions. | Continued high rate of small firm formation especially in new technology and new service areas. Some re-concentration in capital-intensive and R&D-intensive sectors, leading to world-wide oligopolies in symbiosis with myriads of small networking firms at local level. Conglomerates with complex and shifting alliances in various regions. |

| | | | |
|---|---|---|---|
| D. Organisation of Firms | Hierarchical departmental structures with many management layers and vertical flow of information typical of large firms. Computers fit into existing structures and often into existing data processing departments based on tabulating machines. In manufacturing computers introduced as process control instruments of existing processes or as 'islands' in existing production systems. | Cheap widespread computer terminals lead to 'cultural revolution' in firms based on de-centralisation of some functions, horizontal information flows, lean production systems and networking within and between firms. Acute stress and conflict attends clash of cultures, reorganisation of production and systemation, and out-sourcing of many functions. | New flexible management style predominates. More stable employment for core personnel with networks of smaller firms and part-time workers. Greater participation of work-force at all levels of decision-making. |

### III. The Macro-Economy and Employment

| | | | |
|---|---|---|---|
| A. Economic Growth and Business Cycles | 'Golden Age of Growth' in mass production industries, services and systems. Rather stable Keynesian regulation of 'vertebrate' economy providing stability and confidence for investment and consumer spending. Inflationary pressures and social tensions of late 60s and early 70s herald structural crisis of this paradigm as it reaches limits. Bretton Woods system provides fairly stable international framework until it breaks down in early 1970s. | First structural downswing crisis of mid-70s leads to desire to 'get back on course' (e.g. McCracken Report). Second crisis of early 80s leads to recognition of structural problems but only in the third crisis of early 90s is their depth and difficulty appreciated. Huge productivity potential of ICT offset by rigidities in social system. The conflict of alternative paradigms is increasingly fought out in the political sphere as governments search for solutions and as public opinion tires of the invertebrate economy with its excessive turmoil. | Combination of technical and social change together with political reforms leads to new pattern of sustainable growth, renewed confidence for investment and new pattern of consumer spending. Changes in UN and Bretton Woods family of international economic institutions lead to stable global framework of expansion. 'Forgotten' elements of Keynes' 1940s vision restored and provide greater resources for Third World 'catching up'. A new 'vertebrate' world economy emerges. |
| B. Employment and Unemployment | 'Full employment' policies rather successful based mainly on full-time adult male employment 16-65. Relatively low but rising female participation rates. Very low structural unemployment. Recessions of relatively short duration. Low levels of youth unemployment. Expanding secondary and tertiary education systems. | Structural unemployment becomes more severe with each recession. Big increase in part-time employment and in female participation. Big increase in training and re-training to change skill profile of work-force but problems remain especially for less skilled and less educated. Long-term and youth unemployment become major problems. | Economy reverts to shallow recessions with much lower levels of structural unemployment. More self-employment and more flexible part-time work and life-time education and training for both men and women. 'Active Society' providing work for all who seek it. Labour-intensive craft, caring and creative occupations and services proliferate. Shorter working hours for all and greater male participation in child care and house-work. |

Source:   Freeman and Soete (1994), pp 48–51

minority of firms that succeed in coping with all this turbulence can reap great advantages in flexibility yielding economies of scope, better quality and image of products, customization of design and rapid response to market changes.   These problems are intensified when it comes to the interaction of entire industries with different regulatory regimes as well as different cultures and go a long way towards the explanation of the 'Solow Paradox' (computers everywhere but where is the productivity?).

The old national telephone utilities and their equipment suppliers grew up with an entirely different culture and system of regulation from the younger computer and software firms with whom they must now collaborate.   The culture, traditions and behaviour of both are again entirely different from the entertainments industry, television and film companies with whom they are now forming or contemplating strategic alliances, partnerships and mergers.   The boundaries of all of them are being re-drawn and even more radical changes are on the horizon, as was clearly indicated by the spectacular merger negotiations in the US cable, computer and telecommunications industries.

What kind of society emerges from this turmoil depends of course on many social and political changes, as well as on the technical changes which are in many cases easier to foresee.   The social changes involve the birth of new institutions as well as the death of old ones, the rise of new forms of regulation as well as the de-regulation of older services and industries.   The right hand column of *Table 9.3* suggests an 'optimistic' scenario for the future but whether or not a much darker future comes to pass depends on social and political conflicts whose outcome cannot be predicted.   The value of scenarios is that they can generate the imaginative capacity to consider alternative futures.

A hundred years ago, or even fifty years ago, very few people would have imagined that most households in Western Europe would have a car, a television, a refrigerator, a washing machine and many other appliances that we now take for granted.   Nor would they have imagined that the industries which produced these goods, the services which sold, repaired and delivered them, and the infra-structures which they used would employ tens of millions of people.

It is comparably hard today to imagine the future patterns of manufacturing and services in fifty or a hundred years' time.   Only with a long-term historical perspective is it possible to avoid the poverty of imagination which sees only the contemporary job-reducing side of technical change.   The final section of this paper considers briefly some pessimistic and optimistic views of future employment prospects.   It argues that despite the recent wave of down-sizing in large firms and despite the labour-saving techniques diffusing in software as well as hardware, there is nevertheless enormous scope for a vast process of job generation.

## 5. Prospects for the Growth of Employment in the Fifth Kondratieff

Writers on technical change and long waves have generally argued that the process of job destruction in the down-turn phase is ultimately more than compensated by a process of job creation in new occupations, firms, services and industries during the upswing. But this is by no means an automatic process and is heavily dependent on a process of institutional change as well as on more narrowly economic factors, such as productivity and profitability. Historically, the argument has proved a valid one but it is only necessary to recall the 1930s, the early resistance to Keynesian policies, the events of the Second World War and the subsequent general adoption of full employment as a policy goal, to recognize the complex processes of political and social change which led to the success of job creation. There are few reasons to suppose that it will be any easier on this occasion. Indeed, in some respects the situation appears more threatening.

However, despite all the turbulence and all the re-structuring, the ICT industries and services have been the fastest growing group of activities in world production, world trade *and* world employment. They have also shown the highest rates of productivity increase both in capital productivity and in labour productivity. People sometimes tend to think that employment and labour productivity move in opposite directions, that a high growth rate in labour productivity would be associated with declining employment. This is sometimes true in mature or declining industries, such as mining. However, historically, the evidence is strong that with new products and services a 'virtuous circle' of high output growth, high employment growth and high labour-productivity growth tend to go together and to reinforce each other. This was the case, for example, with textiles during the industrial revolution and with steel and automobiles earlier this century. This is because the rapid diffusion of *new* products and processes is strongly associated with cost reduction. Whilst ICT *hardware* prices have indeed been falling dramatically because of the falling cost of chips, (bucking the world-wide inflationary trends), *software* costs and prices have tended to rise, thus acting as a brake on the diffusion of ICT systems. Consequently, there are good reasons to believe that rising software productivity would generate an even faster increase in software employment and not a reduction, as might appear at first sight.

We shall take the example of software employment to illustrate the general problem of assessing the *future* potential impact of ICT on employment growth. Official estimates understate total software employment because of the difficulties of measuring software activities in *user* firms. In the United States the number of employees in 'computational data processing services' grew from 304,000 in 1980 to 835,000 in 1991 (*Statistical Abstract* 1992), but the *total* number of people working in software activities of all kinds (that is the software industry, plus hardware firms, plus user firms) is two or three times as great as the official figures for the software 'industry'. In the United States where the specialized industry is strongest, there are probably now (1993) about two million people employed in software work. In Japan there are nearly a million and in the European Community well over two million. These estimates can be cross-checked with many consultants' reports and independent industry estimates even though there are no official figures. There is thus no doubt that software and information services have been one of the fastest growing categories for new employment in the past decade and that the *total* employment gains were much greater than those registered in the software industry itself. World-wide there were well over 10 million people working in software activities by 1993. Many estimates of *future* employment growth forecast a continuing high growth rate for software, although not quite so rapid as in the 1980s. Thus the US Department of Labor (1992) in its forecasts for the year 2005 puts the projected growth for 'computer scientists and systems analysts' as 79% from 1990 to 2005 and for 'computer programmers' as 56%. No other occupations except 'home health aides' show such high growth. No similar official forecasts exist for the European Community but many similar national forecasts were made in the past.

However, some well-informed comentators have cast doubts on these estimates of future employment growth in the service industries, particularly for software. For the first time in the 1990s' recession, there have been significant redundancies among software employees and it has been suggested that software employment has reached a plateau and might even decline in the future because of the automation of coding, the availability of standard packages and the improved skills of users.

If it were true that for the above reasons software employment would level off or decline in the next decade, this would be a very important change in the labour market. However, there are also some good reasons to believe that employment growth will continue both in Europe and the US.

The main reasons for a more optimistic forecast are the following:

1.      ICT will continue to diffuse at a very high rate over the next decade. There are still innumerable applications of computers and all of these require software for their implementation. As we have already argued, rising labour productivity in software would accelerate rather than

retard diffusion, so that output and employment growth would outstrip labour productivity growth.   Parallel processing, expert systems and multi-media are all likely to experience extraordinarily rapid growth in the next decade and all will make huge new demands on software applications skills.

2.        Even though it is perfectly true that standard software packages have vastly improved and diffused very widely, the needs, the technology and the organization of firms are changing all the time and will continue to do so.   To achieve a good 'match' between technology, organization and software is not a matter of static 'maintenance' but a creative activity which will continue to make new demands on software skills. However, it is true that the balance of employment growth will probably shift from 'programmers' to 'systems design' or even to managers and hybrids who may not be designated as 'software' people at all.

3.        Most important of all, there is a vast new area of potential employment growth associated with the infra-structural investment in cable and both wired and wireless telecommunications, which is taking off in the US, in Europe and Japan.   This growth will be in many new interactive services to *households* as well as to business.   Part of it will initially be 'edu-tainment'.   The demand for home education to complement the formal education system is potentially almost limitless, as is the learning capacity of most human beings.   This market will be opened up by enterprising companies and educational organizations all over the world but it will require extraordinary software skills, linked to multi-media and entertainment skills.   Even greater demands could arise in the public education sector given appropriate policies.

It is not difficult of course to generate a far more pessimistic and cynical scenario for the future of software employment and all the related service activities.

Even if the 'optimistic' scenario shown in *Table 9.3* could be realized, only a minority of the new jobs needed would actually be in the ICT industries and services themselves, or indeed in ICT occupations in other industries and services. Most new jobs would be in many other service industries as well as in the manufacture of computers, telecommunication equipment and other electronic products. The main effects would be in the area of information services, data banks, publishing, education, training and health services. Software professionals could seldom provide the type of interactive services which are needed, except in collaboration with experienced professionals in these other fields, just as they have to collaborate with engineers and managers in the design of manufacturing systems. Creative hybrid professionals would play an important role. The success of such new employment generation would of course depend on world-wide expansionary policies for the economy and there are reasonable grounds for pessimism on this score. The outcome will depend on politics more than on technology.

Another important arena of political conflict and political choice would be in the relationship between the formal education system and the new services which may often be based on commoditization of information. The maintenance and enhancement of quality standards and avoidance of cultural degeneration will be major issues in the future regimes of regulation, as also will be the question of universal access.

A new pattern of consumption cannot of course be forced on consumers but the pattern of long-term change shows a strong secular rise in demand for education and health services, as well as other social services.

When we come to consider the actual methods of provision of these services and the employment which may be generated, then again there are some grounds for cautious optimism. To satisfy future demand in these areas will require a lot of labour-intensive activity. Much health care, child care and education depends completely on personal involvement – the personal caring is the essence of what is being provided. The same is probably true of many leisure, catering and entertainment services. Nevertheless, there will be strong pressures to use new technology as a *substitute* for personal care rather than a *reinforcement* for people.

The scope for ICT in home education as well as in laboratory and class-room education is almost infinite. This should not mean that teachers will be displaced. They will be needed more than ever because personal caring attention is essential to most educational processes, as well as to health services. What ICT can do is to free teachers to give this personal attention to their pupils and to relieve them of much boring routine repetition of information which can be assimilated far more quickly and reliably by computer edu-tainment, or other interactive educational ICT-based services.

ICT-based services will not (indeed cannot) replace personal caring services, including most health and education. What they can do is improve and enhance these services and in some cases make them more accessible to people who otherwise could not enjoy them. The extent to which they do so will depend on political choices. The growth in demand for education, health and many other personal caring services can indeed generate also a great increase in employment, including professional ICT-related employment, as well as educationists and health professionals who are also skilled in ICT.

These expanding services can vary greatly in quality and in the skill with which they use ICT. The response from consumers will depend very much on these factors. Clearly there is an extremely important role for public policy in setting and achieving high standards in health and education. There is also a major role for public policy in stimulating research, development and demonstration. The combination of jobs which are created may be a high proportion of low skill, low pay, low quality, insecure jobs or a high proportion of skilled, high value-added, higher quality and more secure jobs.

Advocates of reduction in wages and social provisions for unskilled workers in Europe believe that this is necessary to generate employment more quickly, as they believe has already occurred in the United States. However, as the OECD (1993) Interim Report points out there is a danger of being caught up in a low wage trap on a long-term basis. To avoid this danger of a permanent large low wage, low skill underclass it is essential to press forward with policies for training and high quality services, so that high skill jobs become a steadily higher proportion of the total. The diffusion of ICT can contribute a great deal to this process, but the extent to which it does so depends on the understanding and capability of the contending political and social forces.

Successful strategies for full employment, for structural competitiveness and for economic growth will thus increasingly depend on social and institutional change of the type indicated in *Table 9.3*. The scope of these changes will vary in different countries but they will have in common, both at national level and at firm level, the assimilation and effective use of ICT and the new ICT infrastructure.

# References

Arrow, K. (1962), 'The economic implications of learning by doing', *Review of Economic Studies* **29**, 155–73.

Arthur, W.B. (1989), 'Competing technologies, increasing returns and lock-in by historical events', *Economic Journal* **99** (1), March, 116–31.

Berry, B.J. (1991), *Long-wave Rhythms in Economic Development and Political Behavior*, Baltimore: Johns Hopkins University Press.

Diebold, J. (1952), *The Advent of the Automatic Factory*, New York: Van Nostrand.

Dosi, G. (1982), 'Technological paradigms and technological trajectories: a suggested interpretation of the determinants and directions of technical change', *Research Policy* **11** (3), June, 147–62.

Dosi, G., C. Freeman, R. Nelson, G. Silverberg, and L. Soete (1988), *Technical Change and Economic Theory*, London: Frances Pinter; New York: Columbia University Press.

Fleck, J. (1988), 'Innofusion or diffusation? The nature of technological development in robotics', ESRC Programme on Information and Communication Technologies (PICT), Working Paper series, University of Edinburgh.

Freeman, C. (1979), 'The Determinants of Innovation: Market Demand, Technology and the Response to Social Problems', *Futures*, **11** (3), 206–15.

Freeman, C. (1990), 'Schumpeter's Business Cycles revisited', in A. Heertje and M. Perlman (eds), *Evolving Technology and Market Structure*, Ann Arbor: University of Michigan Press.

Freeman, C. (1993), 'Technical change and future trends in the world economy', *Futures*, **25**, July–August, 621–35.

Freeman, C., J. Clark, and L. Soete (1982), *Unemployment and Technical Innovation*, London: Frances Pinter.

Freeman, C. and L. Soete (1987), *Technical Change and Future Employment*, London: Pinter.

Freeman, C. and L. Soete (1994), *Work for All or Mass Unemployment*, London: Pinter.

Freeman and Perez (1988), 'Structural Crises of Adjustment, Business Cycles and Investment Behaviour', in G. Dosi, C. Freeman, R. Nelson, G. Silverberg and L. Soete (eds), Technical Change and Economic Theory, London: Pinter, 38–66.

Katz, B.G. and A. Phillips (1982), 'Government, technological opportunities and the emergence of the computer industry', in H. Giersch (ed), Emerging technologies: consequences for economic growth, structural change and employment, Tubingen: Mohr, 419–66.

Keirstead, B.S. (1948), *The Theory of Economic Change*, Toronto: Macmillan.

Kleinknecht, A. (1986), 'Long waves, depression and innovations', *De Economist*, **134** (1), 84–107.

Kondratieff, N. (1925), 'The major economic cycles' *Review of Economics and Statistics*, **XVII** (6), 105–15.

Kuhn, Thomas (1961), *The Structure of Scientific Revolutions*, Chicago: University of Chicago, Bess.

Kuznets, S (1940), 'Schumpeter's Business Cycles', *American Economic Review*, **30** (2), 257–71.

Lundvall, B-Å. (1988), 'Innovation as an interactive process: from user-producer interaction to the national system of innovation', in Dosi, G *et al.* (eds), *Technical Change and Economic Theory*, London: Pinter.

Mandel, E. (1972), *Late Capitalism*, London: NLB.

Mensch, G. (1975), *Das technologische Patt*, Frankfurt: Umschau.

Nelson, D. (1980), *Frederick W. Taylor and the rise of scientific management*, Madison: University of Wisconsin Press.

Nelson, R.R. and S.G. Winter (1977), 'In search of a useful theory of innovation', *Research Policy*, **6** (1), 36–76.

OECD (1993), Interim Report by the Secretary-General on Employment/Unemployment, *The OECD Response*, Paris: OECD.

Pavitt, K. (1984), 'Patterns of technical change: towards a taxonomy and a theory', *Research Policy*, **13** (6), 343–73.

Pavitt, K. (1986), 'International patterns of technological accumulation', in N. Hood (ed.), *Strategies in Global Competition*, New York: Wiley.

Perez, C. (1983), 'Structural change and the assimilation of new technologies in the economic and social system', *Futures,* **15** (5), 357–75.

Perez, C. (1985), 'Microelectronics, long waves and the world structural change: new perspectives for developing countries', *World Development,* **13** (3), 13 March, 441–63.

Perez, C. (1989), 'Technical change, competitive restructuring and institutional reform in developing countries', *World Bank Strategic Planning and Review, Discussion Paper 4*, Washington DC: World Bank.

Rosenberg, N. (1976), *Perspectives on Technology*, Cambridge: Cambridge University Press.

Rosenberg, N. (1982), *Inside the Black Box*, Cambridge: Cambridge University Press.

Ruttan, V. (1959), 'Usher and Schumpeter on innovation, invention and technological change', *Quarterly Journal of Economics,* **73** (4), November, 596–606.

Samuelson, P. (1980), *Economics*, 11th Edition, New York: McGraw Hill.

Samuelson, P. (1981), 'The world's economy at century's end', *Japan Economic Journal,* **10**, March, 20.

Schumpeter, J.A. (1939), *Business Cycles: A Theoretical, Historical and Statistical Analysis of the Capitalist Process*, 2 vols, New York: McGraw-Hill.

Solomou, S. (1987), *Phases of Economic Growth, 1850–1973*, Cambridge: Cambridge University Press.

*Statistical Abstract 1992*, Statistical Abstract of United States, US Department of Commerce, Economics and Statistics Administration Bureau of the Census, Washington DC.

Sweezey, P. (1943), 'Professor Schumpeter's Theory of Innovation', *Review of Economics and Statistics,* **25**, February, 93–6.

Teece, D.J. (1988), 'The nature and the structure of firms', in G. Dosi *et al.* (eds), *Technical Change and Economic Theory*, London: Frances Pinter.

Tylecote, A. (1992), *The Long Wave in the World Economy*, London: Routledge.

Van Gelderen, J. (alias J. Fedder) (1913), 'Springvloed' (Springtide), *De Nieuwe Tijd* **18**, 253, 269 and 445ff. English translation by B. Verspagen in C. Freeman (ed.), *Long Wave Theory*, Aldershot: Elgar.

von Hippel, E. (1978), 'A customer-active paradigm for industrial product idea generation', *Research Policy,* **7**, 240–66.

Wiener, N. (1949), *The Human Use of Human Beings*, New York: Houghton Mifflin.

Weinstock, U. (1969), *Das Problem der Kondratieff-Zyklen*, Munich: Duncker und Humblot.

# 10. Information Age – Deformation Age – Reformation Age: An Assessment of the Information Technology Kondratieff

## Gerhard Hanappi and Edeltraud Egger

---

### Introduction

This chapter tries to bring together several lines of argument brought forward by quite different and distinct research communities in recent years. The first of these streams of thought is the one preoccupied with the long-term socio-economic behaviour of the world economy, in particular with the existence of long swings, so-called Kondratieff cycles, in economic activity. Each of these cycles, so goes the argument of the proponents of this research, is connected with a certain set of basic technological innovations, which is thought to be so influential that it can stimulate and shape the socio-economic development of half a century. There has been an extensive discussion concerning the question of what comes first, the set of basic technological innovations or the new social context in which it appears[1]. In our reading the strong interdependence between the two phenomena necessarily undermines any strong conclusion on this matter, though we tend to see the socio-economic contexts driving technological innovations as dominating the feedback forces, at least in the first phase of a Kondratieff cycle. The interesting point is how the contemporary state of the world economy, the current socio-economic context, and the basic innovative technology, which we propose to be information processing, work together in stimulating a new long-term upswing. Section 1 tries to throw some light on this 'information technology Kondratieff'.

But information is a very special kind of commodity. To grasp its characteristics we have to study the ways in which information becomes relevant for micro-behaviour, which necessarily leads to the consideration of individuals as model-builders. This goes beyond the generally accepted view that expectation formation is a pivotal issue in economics – even the tools with which expectations are formed are socially produced and sold. How individual model building is influenced and shaped, be it through the influence of central 'ideological institutions'[2] or be it through the unconscious influence of technical carrier systems like computer games, becomes crucial for any forecast of the current development. Clearly such an approach goes beyond the narrow borders of mainstream economic reasoning, where the concept of information enters only in the form of commodity prices. Economists should be urged to take a closer look at theories of ideology, philosophical research on the essence of information, and the like. Section 2 surveys what we think to be the large turn from the emphatic aspirations of the progressive role of information distribution starting with the French enlightenment towards the contemporary deformation of individual models by cheap technology steered by conservative groups in power.

The third section evaluates how and where this rather sinister scenario can breed contradictions which are strong enough to lead to resistance. In other words we try to find areas in which sustained reformation of the social context seems to be possible, since there is a social group which is pushing for this reform. Social groups, in particular social classes (to use the classical term), have to share mental models to act as conscious agents in the socio-economic development. It is this common world view, which acts as catalyst for mass action and which again strongly depends on the use of technical means for information production and information destruction. As a consequence Section 3 has to draw on political theory, organization theory, comparative studies of institutional solutions and similar research areas.

Needless to say the high aspirations set out in this introduction will not be fully satisfied by what follows. This chapter is rather a guide through a larger research project, than an in-depth study of the questions concerned[3]. As such the concluding section tries to give some hints on future research rather than presenting decisive results of individual problems.

## 1. Is there an 'Information Kondratieff'?

In our view Nikolai Kondratieff's[4] major point in explaining the long-term behaviour of the economy was that all relevant phenomena have to be explained endogenously in the long-run[5]. As a consequence (applying our contemporary knowledge about the  behaviour of deterministic dynamic systems not available at his time)  the existence of any type of economic laws governing this motion 'naturally' should give long swings of slowly changing variables. At this point Joseph Alois Schumpeter stepped in and propagated Kondratieff's work for Western economists, since it fitted well with his own view.  His vision was that the interplay of two countervailing types of forces lies at the heart of the motion of a capitalist economy – on the one hand the equilibrating forces of markets working via the price and quantity reactions of supply and demand and on the other hand the disequilibrating forces of swarms of innovative entrepreneurs. Coupling these two types of forces responsible for long-term behaviour evidently could lead to a fully endogenized system of long cycles[6]. This is what fascinated Schumpeter when he read Kondratieff. Periodic pushes of entrepreneurial activities could produce waves in Walras' 'smooth lake' of equilibrium.

Market equilibrium as envisaged by Walras was already a standard concept in Schumpeter's time. What was exciting about his economic theory was the new concept of swarming of innovations. To assume that capitalism is constituted by special types of disequilibrating activity directs research in two different directions. First, the agents carrying out these activities can be studied, in particular the dynamics of the social context they are part of have to be described. Second, one can investigate how the effects of their activities cumulate at certain times in economic history to produce what can be termed 'swarming' – a set of basic innovations. It is the latter question which involves the study of the technical nature of certain types of innovations and which until recently preoccupied long-wave theorists[7]. In our view, the social context of entrepreneurial activity and the technological features of candidates for basic innovations have to be studied *simultaneously*. This is so, because they condition each other.

Let us look at the phenomenon from one perspective – the technological one – first, and from the other - the socio-economic one - only afterwards. We state that there has been a long wave in global economic activity after World War II and that this long cycle reached its lower turning point in the early 1980s. Without going into the questions of economic history concerning existence, timing and nature of observed Kondratieff cycles, we think that at least this recent motion is quite obvious[8]. The question now under consideration is whether we are already witnessing a new upswing.

Consider *Figure 10.1*, which presents a five-year moving average of real GDP growth rates of the US[9]. There is some evidence – though some would prefer to call it plausibility – that there have been three business cycles superimposed

*Figure 10.1 Growth of GDP in the US, 1949-91*

(5-year moving average of real growth rates)

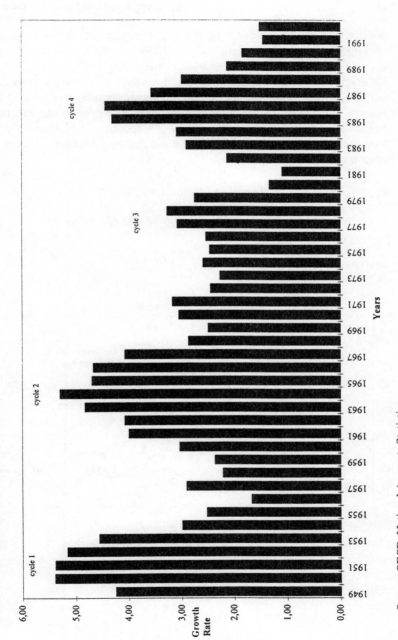

Source: OECD, National Accounts Statistics

on the post-war Kondratieff of the US economy. Moreover, after the lower turning point of the long wave – the year 1981 for the US – there seems to have been a first Juglar cycle[10] of a new long wave.

The growth pattern of the USA, the hegemonial economy of this century, is paralleled by the development of its two major competitors: Europe and Japan (see *Figure 10.2*). Long waves clearly are a global phenomenon, though the country-specific characteristics can be important. Evidently the post-war Kondratieff saw an immense growth of the Japanese economy, strengthening its position relative to the US[11].

*Figure 10.2: Growth of GDP in Japan, Europe and the US compared*

(5 year moving average of real growth rates)

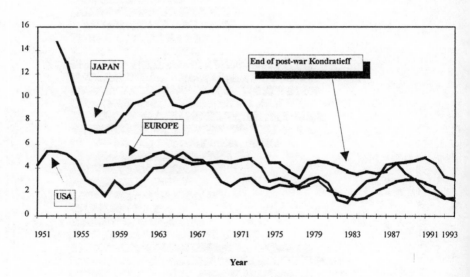

*Source*: OECD, National Accounts Statistics

The second big competitor, Europe, also improved its position: business cycles in Europe have been less dramatic than in the US. The more developed socio-economic integration of European nations in that respect seems to have played an important role. In the meantime post-war Europe not only became an economic giant, but under the less and less hidden leadership of Germany also challenges the political hegemony of the US. As *Figure 10.2* shows all three competitors experienced quite a fierce first Juglar cycle of the new Kondratieff. We will come back to the socio-economic implications of the increased international competition later on.

*Figure 10.3: National patent applications, 1973–90*

### National patent applications

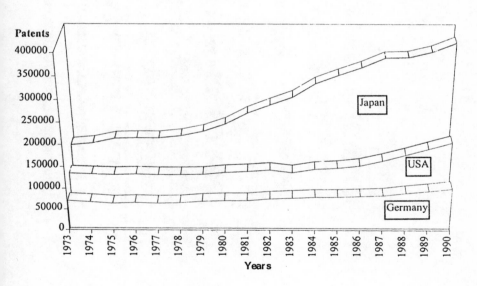

*Source*: OECD, Science and Technology Indicators

According to Schumpeter, and many neo-Schumpeterians like Kleinknecht follow him in this respect, innovative activity starts at the lower turning point. It is a reaction to low and unprofitable production. That is, an increase in patent time series might be used as indicator. *Figure 10.3* shows the increase in national patent applications during the 1980s. Though there are different patenting rules in different countries, which means that absolute levels should not be compared, there still remains the fact that growth rates of absolute numbers where highest in Japan.

*Figure 10.4    R&D expenditure of firms for electronic equipment, 1981–91* (US$ millions; real 1985)

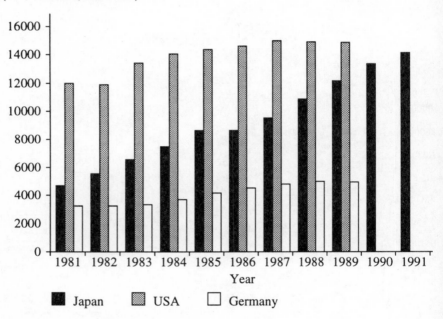

*Source:* OECD, Science and Technology Indicators.

Looking at Figure 10.4 shows that research and development expenditure for new information technologies as forerunners for the actual use of the new machines really indicate a boom in the near future. Moreover Japan again seems to become the major supplier of IT. The inner dynamic between the leading industrial nations,[12] economically and politically, clearly is of utmost importance for the future of this key industry too. Clearly a stronger yen will weaken Japanese exports, but given the overwhelming use of the new technology in almost all sectors of the economy the increase of importance of Japanese producers might not be easy to break.

*Figure 10.5: GDP growth compared: United Kingdom and US (US $ millions; GDP real, base 1987)*

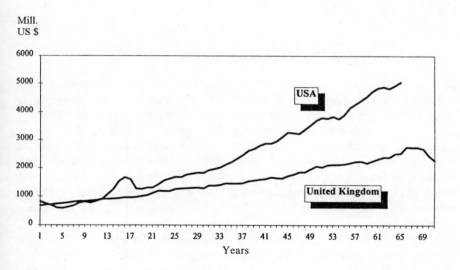

*Note*: for the UK year 1 refers to 1850, for the US to 1929.
*Sources*: US: 'Economic Report to the President 1992' and OECD, National Account Statistics; UK: Mitchell, 1975.

Europe's future importance on the other hand seem to stem from its being the world's largest market-place while the US have to cling to their military dominance.[13] In fact the US economy seems to rely more and more on its demand for military purposes. Part of this source of demand might be hidden by the indirect way in which it is generated, for example for I&C technologies. With a loss of political importance in the world due to the rising new competitors this demand might shrink, if competition goes civilized ways, or increase, if it does not.

Basically the global socio-economic state we have to face is a situation similar to the one before World War I, dangerous but not without hope. Even a rough comparison between the British Empire and US hegemony (as given in *Figure 10.5*) shows that the world economy will probably go through another, though perhaps interrupted, Kondratieff with the US as leading economy. It is this prospect which leads us to the conclusion that socio-economic intervention – that is reformation – is of greatest importance in the current situation. We will come back to this point in Section 3. Before we are ready to do so, some peculiar features of the commodity 'information' have to be discussed, which play a crucial role for the specification of this intervention.

## 2. From Information to Deformation

Let us extrapolate the trend of developments of the information and communication technologies. Besides their well-known multi-functionality, computer-based systems are starting to be multi-medial too. This means that the existing types of information carriers – pictures, sound, text and signals – can be transmitted and processed via the same digital network; the different types of media melt into one stream of digital signals. The terminals where this information stream enters an individual household retranslate it into the original shape. Evidently the functional abilities of these new terminals will be broadened substantially: they combine the traditional technologies such as television, telephone, computer and consumer electronics.[14]

A considerable part of the services consumed by a traditional household through outdoor activities – for example shopping, banking, working, leisure time activities, further education (represented by the various circles and ellipses in the following *Figure 10.6*) – will be satisfied by the use of the multifunctional terminal.

A similar idea was already realised by television: the single household is provided with a certain offer of channels from which the persons can choose. This means that one of the fields of activity, namely the set of leisure time activities, has been codetermined by this technology. To a certain extent further education could be an analogous case if courses come via television. While this technology left space for large fields of activity, in particular the working sphere and most parts of the service sector, to take place outside the private sphere in a narrow sense, it is foreseeable that the new technology will incorporate a centralization of these fields of activity within the private sphere.

But staying within one's private sphere means a decrease of social interaction with others. The big change in the behaviour of household members as compared to the classical situation will be the way they solve their everyday problems. In times when the various life spheres were more separated, locally and perceptually, people were forced to engage actively in interaction with others; this included an active search for relevant information, spontaneous learning within social groups – in short, the accumulation of social experience as personal experience. As a consequence intersections with the activity fields of others will appear frequently (*Figure 10.7* gives a graphical representation).

*Figure 10.6: Household's activity via digital network*

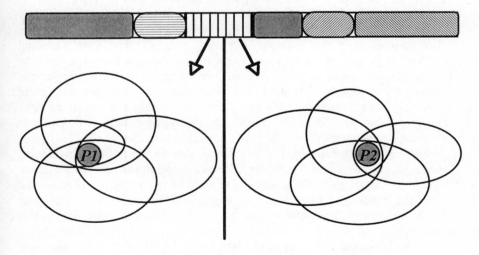

*Figure 10. 7: Common activity spheres without IT*

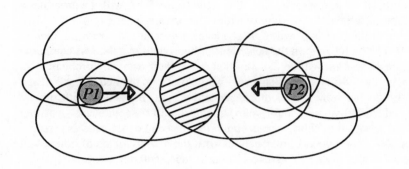

The trends described make it easy to anticipate that in the future active search for relevant information will be replaced, in many cases, by a supply of information via the household terminal. Of course, the crucial question is: who provides the content of the information stream available?

Let us take again the example of television supply. The most important argument of proponents of a privatization of television stations was that the amount of programmes supplied will increase dramatically and will reflect the diversity of consumer demands. The experience of the last decade of privatization falsifies these aspirations: free choice within a set of possibilities chosen by the producer is pseudo-choice. The threat of a similar development in all the fields covered by a household terminal seems to be clear.

What we call 'deformation' is the danger that in many fields of life the households become passive receivers of preselected information. In particular 'information' more and more consists of models, of interpretation schemes, and not of data concerning facts. It is the supplier of information who determines *what* is worth presenting, *which aspects* are highlighted and *how* the information is prepared.

Let us again use the television supply as an example. The first step is to choose the topics promising high participation rates at low production cost. This is why television stations are highly selective concerning their broadcasts. As can currently be observed, the entertainment section is invaded by quizzes and prize–winning games while broadcast times for (expensive) news are continuously shrinking. In Step 2 special features for highlighting are selected: the type of question for a quiz is chosen, the genre of movies is specified, the language for the language course is determined, certain aspects from a political event are sorted out, and so forth. The final step is the most challenging one for the producer: to keep the high level of strong emotions necessary to attract attention, the number of messages transferred has to be speeded up tremendously. High velocity of cut sequences, countless hidden messages aiming at subconscious consumption, all the tricks of 'commodity aesthetics' are applied.

What is observable for television holds for the future multifunctional household terminal, at least in an analogous, though more sophisticated, form. Remember the information suppliers depicted in the information channel in *Figure 10.6*. television stations as well as telephone companies, banks and insurance companies, employers, suppliers of all types of consumer goods, political parties – in brief all types of enterprises are choosing the products or services they present (Step 1). In doing so suppliers define the space of available products and services. note that this is a first *ideological* intervention into household behaviour: In principle persons still could leave their homes and look for alternative possibilities, but they will not do so because they expect gains from this action which will not repay the expected additional cost of search. It is by the force of ideas, of expectations influenced by the information channel, that they behave the way they do – this is what we call ideological intervention.

The highlighted special features of one's product are the topic of the information presented. In other words, in Step 2 a *message* is determined, which is thought to be well received by the consumer. To get messages to work, that is to stimulate consumption, they have to be grounded on real problems of the prospective consumer. Messages usually transform these real-life difficulties into illusory dream worlds, where they seemingly could be resolved by the 'right' choice of product, service or whatever the supplier wants to sell. In general the message does not even reveal the motivating problem but simply displays a shifted, simulated world. Of course this treacherous mirror is no real remedy for the underlying difficulty but only gives temporary satisfaction.[15] The ideological purport of Step 2 is evident: High speed sequences of pictures feed the consumer by use of his emotional reactions. There is no time any more for thinking over the content of a message, for analysing it critically. In this way the view of things in one's mind is influenced without being recognised.[16] Persons start to change their mental *models* of things by using a subconsciously delivered *interpretation schemata*.

To accomplish this, in Step 3 an appropriate way of wrapping up the messages has to be found. The décor has to be designed – certainly quite a challenging task which demands much knowledge about current political and social sentiments and about their symbolic reproduction in a designed solution. Once a design trend is set, it is advantageous to work with the recognition effect of consumers – 'the medium is the message',[17] but it also works the other way round – the message is the medium of the medium. It thus becomes clear why graphic interfaces are booming: The ability of human beings to catch messages from visualized presentations more easily than by reading text or listening to speech, makes visualization into a source of manipulation if the speed of bombarding with pictures is high enough.[18]

An additional aspect of the trend to digital multifunctional and multimedia networks is that more and more areas of life are concerned. While similar problems were already discussed when television was introduced, the new technologies will also cover the working sphere, the education and training sphere and many others. This means that in more and more areas people will get used being bombarded with certain – externally determined – models and interpretation schemata which will not and cannot be criticized anymore, since they satisfy a need, albeit in a perverted way. A horror vision? If there is no counter reaction it would seem to be a rather realistic assessment of the future development. Transferring all the spheres mentioned to the private sphere of households, as the technological trends as well as economic and political trends of 'privatization' clearly indicate, is dangerous in many respects. The problem has been discussed for a long time by feminists in the context of reproduction: Since the reproduction sphere is designated private, all questions related to this sphere are excluded from political discussion. It can easily be anticipated that the more areas go 'private' the less intervention by public regulations is possible – and this will lead to very severe problems. This is so, because the other side of the anarchic privacies of households is the strongly interwoven structure of socio-economic production – and this is where the real difficulties arise.

There will be the strong and rather centralized power in the form of ideological force on the side of information suppliers like firms and (their?) political administrators which will enable them to keep the highly complex and fragile system of world production together. And, as already suggested in Section 1, there will be a boom in world production which is stimulated by the very products – information technologies – needed to control this system. There will be a new type of political regime fostered by these technologies – and at the same time necessary for the dispersion of the new technology. De-socialization breeds deformation and vice versa.

Nevertheless we are only talking about possible future scenarios. There still might be some room for design. In the following section we will evaluate possible sources and opportunities for changing the way information and communication technologies will be used to a more acceptable scenario.

## 3. From Deformation to Reformation

Any change, if it is to have a profound impact on the socio-economic development, needs to be grounded on a contradiction perceived by the involved parties. Therefore the first step to formulate a political programme is to identify the relevant conflicts. This also applies to questions of information politics. So what are the 'battlegrounds' of a social information environment as sketched in Section 2?

Privatization in the information and communication sector led to the same problems as privatization in other sectors: What was a supply of infrastructure made available by the state was transformed into an oligopolistic market for a few private firms – and this implied a basic change of this supply. In many cases the welfare of consumers has decreased. In particular all regulatory measures of the state to enable the socially weak groups to have access to technological goods have ceased to exist. Let us take as an example public transport: while public supply leads to a broad network whose coverage includes rural and marginalized areas, private companies will surely eliminate the latter since they are not profitable.[19] The analogue is true for communication supply: the policy of the big telephone suppliers in the US leads to a price increase for inner city calls, the necessity to have telephone cards, and a confusing variety of telephone companies competing with aggressive advertisements. Note as a contrast that in Austria socially weak persons are exempted from paying the basic fee. Applying these ideas to the above-mentioned network services, it is evident that private supply, being led by profitability considerations, would lead to socially unequal information distribution: expensive information (like news) for financially potent customers, inexpensive information (shoddy entertainment) for the financially weak.

These failures of privatization can be attributed to the fact that firms act according to their profit expectations – and these are at best mid-term. In the long-run this kind of policy will lead to severe damage to the economy caused by inappropriate infrastructure. Long-term goals have to be taken care of by far-sighted intervention by the state.

Another field where personal experiences might clash with the new ideology of privatization has been treated as the contradiction between real and artificial needs. Extending the views held in the well-known discussion in the New Left years ago, we think that even real needs can be artificially satisfied by products by shifting the real needs to artificial needs for products. Let us take an example from commercial advertisements: There is a famous jeans commercial suggesting that the possession of these well-known jeans leads to the feeling of freedom and independence. As a matter of fact many people – and in particular youngsters – are attracted by this advertisement. How does this happen? Obviously living in a certain society means internalizing certain culturally determined values – like for example freedom and independence. Growing up with this positive assessment of these concepts leads to a real need for freedom and independence. Contrary to this 'vision', real-life experiences show that the individual is very dependent on others and a given system of rules. The resulting frustration offers a fertile ground for satisfaction by way of substitution. This is the point where product commercials enter the game. Children suffering from a very strict educational system will try to overcome the frustration by accepting the offered substitutes.

Evidently the real need is not satisfied by these products. Instead the real needs are only repressed temporarily by a certain product. The whole process must be repeated after a while in order to get the artificial satisfaction again. The chance of reformation arises precisely from the persistence of the underlying contradiction.

Along with the argument in the last paragraph goes another marketing strategy, namely 'personal products': computers become personal computers, banking becomes personal banking, all kinds of commonly-used consumer goods become part of the inventory of each household or even of each person in the household. To support this transition, the standardized mass products are marketed as their mere opposite, as reflecting the uniqueness of the buyer. Of course, neither the buyer nor the product is unique. As far as the latter is concerned, at best some features can be customized; in the case of the former, his real need for uniqueness and recognition is the source of his use of artificial satisfaction as discussed above. Mass industry provides both the standardized product and the illusory ideological release from the grey mass of consumers.

Taking this contradiction on the product level to the field of 'personal ideology' proper reveals another contradiction. As personal ideology teaches, each individual is priced like a product – everybody gets what she/he is worth. The individuals at the lower end of the social hierarchy are there because their worth for society is correspondingly low. But since this individualistic view has not reached everybody, and since there still exist individuals whose personal historical experience runs counter to this view, who did experience that solidarity, class action or group action did improve their position more than mere individual action,[20] since therefore different views on the matter co-exist, it should be possible to use this contradictory situation for reformation and institutional design.

Reformation consists of counteracting the observable tendencies described in Section 2. In other words the socio-economic environment of the network presented has to be designed so as to prevent the problems indicated. Basically this means fighting the current tendencies towards privatization. Let us argue this point along the lines of the contradictions listed above.

The threat that society, through the working of privatization in the narrow sense,[21] falls into two parts, an information-rich one and an information-poor one, clearly can only be prevented by state intervention. The state has to provide access to the knowledge produced by the society. In consequence the future network will have to supply various information bases comparable with public libraries. The interactive use of the network might also offer the opportunity to support political decision processes or the establishment of groups. Evidently the latter two objectives call for an institutional environment which executes the outcomes of the information processes.

Concerning the discussion of real versus artificial needs, we would stress that visions should replace utopian personal ideals. A vision is a model which represents a possible future solution of a socially-relevant problem. Though a vision might only sketch the most essential features of a desired future situation, its difference from the current state of affairs is a necessary ingredient for what we call a real need: it motivates and indicates the causal links, the instruments, to reach the desired state. If a vision really grasps the essence of the problem one can call it adequate and a sharp distinction from inadequate personal ideals can be drawn. This latter perverted form of model is systematically distorted to fuel repetitive illusory satisfaction via products. The method to formulate adequate models is thus an important part of a society's knowledge. The network should help to educate all members of society to become model-builders, visionaries, that is conscious political agents.

Take a second look at *Figures 10.6* and *10.7*: in a certain sense what we propose is to reverse the development shown there. Contrary to the tendency to shift more and more life spheres into one's private sphere and to separate individuals and groups from each other, we suggest as development an opening of most life spheres. The underlying idea can be taken from the feminist discussion on the reproduction sphere. By defining it as 'private' it is withdrawn from political treatment.[22] Therefore most fields concerned by the network (for example. labour, education and the like) have to be declared as 'public'. Furthermore the network is to be seen as supplementary to direct group building (between persons P1...Pn) as shown in *Figure 10.8*. Collective experience as foundation for the capacity for political action is to be extended and supported by communication facilities via the network. Joint problem-solving will be preferred to the isolation of individuals. Those groups and individuals which still rely on collective historical experience as described in the third of the above-listed contradictions will profit from such support.

It is clear that designing such a network is part of a political process. As precondition general guidelines for the use of the network have to be formulated and legitimized by a qualified majority of all users. They have the character of constitutional laws and sanctions for disregarding them have to be defined.[23] The prohibition of neo-fascist and sexist propaganda as well as the definition of minority rights falls under this category. There will also exist a body of less basic, dynamically changeable rules, corresponding to ordinary laws, subject to the political will of users as it will be indicated by democratic voting mechanisms.[24] Several approaches to voting theory – coming from logic, from game theory and from a technical perspective – have thrown new light on the matter recently; reformation will have to draw on these results.

As can be seen, it has to be the political context which must provide the framework within which the technical system can be designed. This takes us back to the line of argument expounded in Section 1, the interaction between socio-economic context and technical innovation.

*Figure 10.8: Interaction via the network*

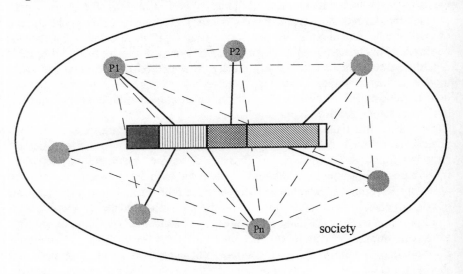

## Conclusion

In Section 1 we suggested that in the early stages of a long-wave upswing it is the socio-economic context which shapes the technological advancements rather than the other way round. In the course of the chapter we came to a position that allowed us to state more clearly what we mean by such a socio-economic reformation. A common, easily derived conclusion is 'beware of privatization'. In a more and more interdependent world 'privatization' is mainly an ideological vehicle for the needs of the politically and economically powerful. Other issues are more difficult to analyse and need further specialized research. Let us name a few:

The first set of research questions are those asking for the '*how*': How have certain institutionalized mechanisms to be designed? For example:

- Which kind of voting mechanisms have to be designed?
- In which way has the time spent by everybody for political decision-making to be balanced with time spent for work, leisure time, education, and so on?
- How has a language for collective decision-making, which is at least partly supported by the network, to look?
- How could a change of the political guidelines, the 'laws' of the network mentioned in the last section, be formulated in order to support reasonable adjustment while preventing distorting manipulations by influential lobbies?
- In which way can democracy be direct democracy involving more knowledge of decision-makers and less intermediate representatives?

The newly defined mechanisms clearly give a new, at least a more precise meaning to some key concepts – they specify *what* they are:

- What is direct democracy?
- What does the concept of privacy really mean? What does it mean that some fields of life are private?
- What happens to the concept of work and its opponent, the concept of leisure time?
- What happens to the function of unions and other bodies representing social groups?
- What is the role of cultural and national units in an international setting?
- What is to be understood as innovation, including not only product and process innovation but also social innovation?[25]

Implicit in the answers to the first two question sets are assignments of entities to the key roles in the mechanisms – *who* has to take the described actions:

- Who will provide new inventions, latent innovations (again including social innovations)?
- Who will construct the models serving as possible building blocks for the interpretation schemes for people's visions?
- Who is going to select relevant information to be included and to discard irrelevant information from the databases? Who produces records of collective experience to be stored?

Finally questions on 'how do we get from here to there', that is questions of transforming the current situation into the new socio-economic context have to be faced. Questions how to *operationalize* the (r)evolutionary reforms envisaged:

- Who should finance the network?
- Where should the time taken for political decision making be taken from?
- Which groups can be considered, or 'won' if one takes the position of classical enlightenment, as carriers to push for the new socio-economic design?
- Can the current situation of increasing international competition (see section 1) be exploited for the purposes of reformation – and if so, how?

It is evident that questions dependent on each other can be grouped to form interdisciplinary research projects. In our view such projects are not only of academic interest, they are urgently needed for policy-making, for setting the frame within which the next Kondratieff will develop.[26] Policy-making in an age of reformation, as we understand it, does only partly consist of supporting certain professional politicians, but as a main goal provides visions – and how to make them come true – for the underprivileged.

## Notes

1. See for example Di Matteo *et al.* (1989).
2. The term is borrowed from Althusser (1970).
3. In particular this applies to the fact that in this paper we concentrate on the developments in industrialized countries and do not give an explicit account of the relation to the developments in their Third World.
4. Compare Kondratieff (1926).

5.   This argument is developed in more detail in Hanappi (1989).
6.   See in particular Schumpeter (1939).
7.   A notable exception to this rule is Gordon (1978, 1980).
8.   An interesting evaluation of the post-war Kondratieff can be found in Kleinknecht (1987 pp. 127–214).
9.   A five-year moving average is necessary to smooth the curve without eliminating Juglars.
10.  Schumpeter calls 'Juglar cycle' what is usually meant by the term 'business cycle': a cycle lasting some four to eight years (Schumpeter 1939). In many empirical studies this type of cycle has been shown to last about ten years, as is the case for the series shown in *Figure 10.1*.
11.  There are different competing explanations for this fact, see for example Lawrence (1993).
12.  Giovanni Arrighi (1993) in a recent contribution presents a view on this dynamic which is similar to the one implicit in our analysis; compare.
13.  In an interesting study Domhoff (1993) shows how military and economic elites in the US melt together.
14.  For further discussion compare Brand (1987).
15.  As a profitable side-effect for the supplier the consumer will be eager to consume again and again at accelerating speed, a phenomenon called 'addiction'.
16.  The manipulation of consumers via media is a widespread phenomenon. In principle there is no difference whether a supplier signals 'environmental protection' via the car promoted, or 'communism is bad' via scandal news. In both cases self-reinforcing interpretation schemata are propagated, which are based on real, though not expressed, problems of the consumer: of course he suffers from several instances of environmental damages as well as from economic crisis.
17.  See McLuhan (1964).
18.  At Step 3 the ideological force of information does not even consist of an 'idea', like a certain argument or interpretation, but of an image, an icon, which hints at a hidden argument. The latter enters behaviour only subconsciously, is nurtured and reinforced by new incoming icons and is rather hard for the individual itself to discover.
    Therefore many countries have state regulations, as for example the Netherlands: 'The advertising that is allowed (it accounts for more than a third of the public broadcasting system's income) is confined to certain times, administered through a public foundation (STER), forbidden on Sundays and subject to strict codes designed to protect consumers.' (McQuail 1992 p. 102).
19.  The possible impact of deficitary public enterprises on the budget deficit, and via that route on consumers' welfare, will, of course, have to be balanced by an appropriate tax policy. The important point is that the state still has means to execute a politically formulated and legitimated goal set.
20.  An interesting phenomenon concerning this trend of 'individualization' are the observable psycho-therapies mushrooming up, which support the idea that everything is individual and personal. This goes so far that conflicts emerging (for

example, in the workplace) are treated as personal conflicts which can be solved only by concentrating on oneself. The result of this ideology can be imagined – there will be no political agitation, but only individual pseudo-problem solving.

21.  Privatization in the narrow sense means a transformation of public enterprises into private firms.

22.  For more detailed discussion see Firestone (1970) and Millet (1970).

23.  Clearly the question of 'cultural identity' will arise since networks are international (Schlesinger 1991). We consider this to be an interesting field of research.

24.  A lot of speculation on 'teledemocracy' has already been made in literature (compare Barber (1984), Hollander (1985), Williams (1982)).

25.  An interesting distinction between the public and the private side of innovation can be found in Nelson (1987 pp. 73–92).

26.  As Hodgson rightly points out this idea is what recently has been labelled 'path-dependency':

Such matters relate to the notion of path-dependency, ... In the historical context this suggests that events occurring during a crucial and formative period of change may greatly influence later socio-economic outcomes. (Hodgson 1991 p. 162)

## References

Althusser, L. (1970), 'Idéologie et appareils idéologiques d'Etat', *La Pensée*, n. 151, 3–38.

Arrighi, G. (1993), 'The Three Hegemonies of Historical Capitalism' in S. Gill (ed.) (1993) 148–85. Gramsci, *Historical Materialism and International Relations*, Cambridge: Cambridge Univeristy Press.

Barber, B. J. (1984), *Strong Democracy: Participatory Politics for a New Age*, Berkeley: University of California Press.

Brand, S. (1987), *The Media Lab, Inventing the Future at MIT*, New York: Viking Penguin.

Coombs, R., P. Saviotti and V. Walsh (eds) (1992), *Technological Change and Company Strategies*, London: Academic Press.

Davidow, W.H. (1986), *Marketing High Technology*, London: Macmillan.

Di Matteo, M., R. Goodwin and A. Vercelli, (eds) (1989), *Technological and Social Factors in Long Term Fluctuations*, Heidelberg: Springer.

Domhoff, G.W. (1993), 'The American Power Structure' in Olsen and Marger (1993) *Power in Modern Socities*, Oxford: Westview Press, 170–82.

Firestone, S. (1970), *The Dialectic of Sex: The Case for Feminist Revolution*, New York: William Morrow.

Gordon, D. (1978), 'Up and Down the Long Roller Coaster', in (*Union for Radical Political Economics* 1978 22–34)

Gordon, D. (1980), 'Stages of Accumulation and Long Economic Cycles', in I. Wallerstein (ed.) (1980), *The Modern World System*, New York: Academic Press.

Hanappi, G. (1989), *Die Entwicklung des Kapitalismus*, Bern: Peter Lang Verlag.

Hodgson, G. (1991), 'Socio-political Disruption and Economic Development', in G. Hodgson and E. Screpanti (eds) (1991), *Rethinking Economics*, London: Edward Elgar, 153–71.

Hollander, R. (1985), *Video Democracy: The Vote-from-home Revolution*, Mount Airy, MD: Lomond.

Kleinknecht, A. (1987), *Innovation Patterns in Crisis and Prosperity*, London: Macmillan Press.

Kondratieff, N. (1926), 'Die langen Wellen der Konjunktur', Tübingen: *Archiv für Sozialwissenschaft und Sozialpolitik*, **56**, 573–609.

Lawrence, R.Z. (1993), 'Japanese Growth Reconsidered', *Journal for Economic Perspectives*, September.

McLuhan, M. (1964), *Understanding Media*, New York: Penguin Books.

McQuail, D. (1992), 'The Netherlands: Freedom and Diversity under Multichannel Conditions', in J. G. Blumler (ed.) (1992*), Television and the Public Interest*, London: Sage Publications.

Millet, K. (1970), *Sexual Politics*, New York: Doubleday.

Mitchell, B.R. (1975), *European Historical Statistics 1750–1970*, London: Macmillan Press.

Nelson, R. (1987), *Understanding Technical Change as an Evolutionary Process*, Amsterdam: North-Holland.

Schlesinger, P. (1991), *Media, State and Nation*, London: Sage Publications.

Schumpeter, J. (1939), *Business Cycles*, New York: McGraw Hill.

Union for Radical Political Economics (eds) (1978), *US Capitalism in Crisis*, New York: Economics Education Project.

Williams, F. (1982), *The Communications Revolution*, New York: New American Library.

# 11. Developments and Alternatives: Hopes for Post-Fordism

**Alain Lipietz**

## Introduction

What unites the supporters of an evolutionary political economy, is not only the idea that the forms of economic organization have evolved since capitalism began and will continue to do so. It is also the idea that the range of possible developments is not strictly delimited by some exogenous factor like the evolution of productive forces or technological revolution, and so on. Evolution takes place through human invention, trials and errors, struggles and compromises, through utopias and constraints. To be evolutionary is not only to set out a realistic programme to understand how the world changes, but also to think that *we* can change the world a little.

This is particularly true as regards one of the central relations of our economies: labour relations – the manner in which labour is negotiated, paid and used.

In Section 1, I explain first the respective role of 'models' and 'constraints' in evolution. Then I set out the 'models' competing for the exit from the crisis of advanced capitalisms, restricting myself to capital – labour relations. In Section 3 I study the constraints on the selection of these developments. Finally, I venture to propose an alternative to the development which is currently dominant.

## 1. Methodological Introduction

To forecast the future of capital–labour relationships is not easy. A broad spectrum of industrial relations exists even within advanced capitalist countries - and the divergences there are actually increasing, in contrast to the 1950s and 1960s where a rather unified model prevailed: Fordism. It is perhaps a transitory situation: the crisis of the formal world, the old world, leads to a period of search for new 'industrial paradigms', new rules of the game in the organization of paid work. A new paradigmatic order may emerge. But it is also conceivable that the march of Fordism towards hegemony was no more than a single 'success story' in the history of capitalism. In future perhaps several types of capital–labour relationships may coexist, even within one country: a *configuration* of complementary models of industrial relations.

However, there are good reasons for believing that social relations tend to adapt themselves to typical forms. The best argument is that all the agents involved are pursuing similar goals: optimization of efficiency, or at least 'satisficing' to survive in competition. In this process, they tend to copy the experiments of others, read management books, business newspapers and journals, follow fashions. People learn. In analysing the future we must ask whether these learning processes may converge.

But we should not expect a single solution to this process of formation of social relationships. In industrial relations, this idea is often connected to the hypothesis of an objective progress of productive forces to which social relationships must adapt themselves through the process of trial and error. This idea, common to old Marxist doctrine and to many current writings on the 'demands of the information technology revolution', is refuted by empirical observation. In fact, between technological development and the stabilization of typical industrial relations, there stretches the vast field of social conflicts influenced by the traditions of previous agreements, national and local. An industrial paradigm is a social *compromise* accepted willingly or unwillingly by managers and by workers. Moreover, this paradigm contributes to form and guide technological development itself.

We have known, since 1989, that the dawn of the 21st century will be capitalist – based on firms producing goods and organized by managers hiring the labour force. *But what capitalism?* That remains the question. The future of the former socialist countries is far from being defined. Their process of learning and imitation may tend to converge on the British model, the Swedish model, or some original type of social compromise. Moreover with the collapse of the 'oriental way to socialism' all the 'national ways to socialism' in the Third

World from India to Algeria have lost their attraction. There the capital–labour relations present an incredible mixture of forms stretching from degenerate small-scale production to semi-Japanese salariats. But will the main developments lead to a 'Brazilian type' or a 'Korean type'? And must one expect a new world hierarchy according to nations' choices of type of industrial relations?

Once again the future seems very uncertain. However, limits still exist. Industrial relations must be *coherent*. First, they must be coherent in themselves, that is to say among their different aspects: pay contracts, organization of work, social reproduction of a suitably skilled labour force. Next, they must cohere, be compatible, with the broader pattern of social life: with general objectives, with the accepted rules of life in society. Third, they must be coherent with the macroeconomy of whatever regime of accumulation exists, nationally and internationally. Last and not least, the world ecological situation now imposes strong constraints on the generalization of most of the models, which will have to be accepted sooner or later, and the sooner the better.

We can draw certain conclusions at this point:

- Technology offers possibilities, without determining the future.
- Social actors are trying to escape from a situation where the old agreements are in crisis. In doing so they jostle, searching for new compromises, in directions influenced by the crisis of the old compromises. As yet, only the questions are known. The answers offered in any country depend on its traditions and local experience. Thus promising answers have more chance of emerging in some countries than others; then some of them can become hegemonic at the world level via imitation of the most successful experiments.
- But partial answers cannot be chosen 'à la carte'. There are only some 'menus' which are coherent; and not all are mutually compatible.

## 2. Two Directions of Exit from Fordism

Since the Second World War, two models of development have been offered to developing countries: the Western model and the 'socialist' model. The latter has now been seen to have totally failed. During this time capitalism in the north-west of the world experienced its golden age. The model of development of this golden age (which we call 'Fordism') experienced a major crisis during the 1970s and 1980s, but nobody thought that it was a question of the 'final crisis of capitalism'. On the contrary, several reforms, which all showed promise at the end of the 1980s, were proposed for this model.

## The success and the failure of the Golden Age[1]

Let us first briefly recall what Fordism was. Like any model of development, one can analyse it on three levels.

- In terms of general principles of the organization of work (or 'industrial paradigm'), Fordism is Taylorism plus mechanisation. Taylorism means: a strict separation between the conception of the production process – which is the task of the organization and methods (O&M) office – and the execution of standardized tasks formally prescribed, at workshop level. Mechanization is the incorporation of the collective expertise of the O & M office in the material apparatus (hardware as well as software). Worker involvement is not required.
- In terms of macroeconomic structure, Fordism involves productivity gains resulting from its principles of organization, matching both the growth of investments financed by profits, and the growth of workers' purchasing power. In consequence the overall share of pay in value added and the coefficient of capital in that value, remained roughly constant, so that the rate of profit was approximately stable and the demand for production and consumption goods rose parallel to productivity.
- In terms of rules of the game (or *mode of regulation*) Fordism involved a long-term contractualization of pay relationships, with strict limits to sackings, and a programmed growth of pay, indexed to prices and to general productivity. Moreover, a vast socialization of income through the welfare state guaranteed workers a permanent income. In return for this the trade unions accepted managerial prerogatives. In this way, the principles of work organization, as well as the macroeconomic structure, were respected.[2]

The Golden Age model thus depended on the contribution of pay to demand in the domestic market of each advanced capitalist country, taken separately. The external constraint was limited by the synchronization of growth in these countries, by the limited importance of the growth of international trade relative to the growth of domestic markets, and by the hegemony of the US economy.

At the end of the 1960s, the stability of the growth path of the Golden Age was called into question. The most obvious reason appeared from the 'demand side'. Competitiveness evened out between the US, Europe and Japan. The search for economies of scale led to internationalization of production and markets. The rise in price of raw materials imported from the South (oil in particular) stoked up competition for exports in the early 1970s. The maintenance of internal demand was now jeopardised by the need to balance external trade.

In the face of this crisis on the 'demand side', the initial reaction of international elites was Keynesian. The main idea, accepted by all, was to co-ordinate the maintenance of world demand. In fact, the growth of real pay slowed down spectacularly, more and more firms shifted their plants to non-unionized areas or subcontracted in Third World countries, but the basic structures of the previous mode of regulation were maintained in the advanced capitalist countries. However, at the end of the 1970s, attitudes changed. The management of the crisis by the demand side had certainly avoided a great depression. But a major limit appeared: the fall of profitability. This was due to a number of causes on the 'supply side': deceleration of productivity, growth of total labour costs (including indirect pay via the welfare state), growth of the capital–product coefficient, growth of the relative price of primary products. In these conditions, Keynesian recipes such as rises in real wages (limited as they were) and monetary laxity, could only lead to inflation and erosion of the value of monetary reserves, in particular of the international currency: the dollar. Thus the turn towards 'supply side policies', that is to say towards 'industrial relations'.

The 'profit squeeze' analysis had become the official explanation by 1980. Profits were too low because workers (and primary product exporters) were too strong, which was because the rules of the game were too 'rigid'. That obstructed the restructuring of the productive apparatus, with the risk of missing the chances offered by the technological revolution. Thus the 1980 Summit of the Seven in Venice, after the second oil shock, proclaimed that the 'first priority' was to combat inflation (rather than unemployment), through the commitment to raise productivity and to redistribute capital from sectors in decline to growth sectors, from the public to the private sector, from consumption to investment. There was a commitment to 'avoid measures protecting particular interests from the severity of the adjustment'. In other words, 'rigid' social compromises must be torn up.

This policy of 'liberal flexibility' was implemented by the governments of the United Kingdom, then the United States, finally in most OECD countries, even socialist/communist-ruled France. The repudiation of old compromises reached different degrees on different fronts: from the rules of pay increase 'inflation plus productivity' to the extent and depth of social protection; from the liberalization of  redundancy procedures to the proliferation of precarious employment. This process was pursued in an authoritarian manner - governments and management taking advantage of union defeats or the political success of conservative parties – or through the negotiation of concessions between capital and labour under pressure of rising unemployment.

The experience of the 1980s did not favour the liberals. The recovery after 1983 can more plausibly be credited to a renewal of Keynesian reflation. It was flexibilization's most determined exponents – the US, the UK, France – whose industry shrank and manufacturing trade deficits worsened; the victors of the competition – Japan, West Germany, EFTA – seemed to have a different solution to the supply side crisis. Let us return to the theoretical explanation of the crisis of Fordism on the supply side. A complementary explanation to 'the profit squeeze under full employment' depends on the erosion of the effectiveness of Taylorism. The elimination of all initiative by direct workers in the production process, seems today of doubtful rationality. It is a good way of assuring the management direct control over the intensity of work, but giving direct workers more 'responsible autonomy' can form part of a superior system of organization, above all in implementing new technology or just-in-time methods of management, which fully involves their intelligence and their willing co-operation with management and engineers.[3] Just such was the alternative chosen by numerous large firms in Japan and Germany, and in Scandinavia. There, pressure from the unions and from other organizational traditions, favoured *negotiated involvement* as a solution to the crisis of Fordism (Mahon 1987).

By the end of the 1980s the superiority of this choice was more and more recognized not only in this second group of countries, but also by the managers and pundits of the first group. Certainly the success of the second group in international competition weighs heavily in this development, but the difficulties of implementing new technologies in a flexible, liberal context, have also encouraged the transformation in management methods. But can liberal flexibility and negotiated involvement be combined 'à la carte'? How far are they mutually coherent?

*After Fordism, What?*[4]

To sum up our survey of recent economic history:

- Management of demand was first given great attention and then dropped, either because internationalization had made it impossible, or because the late 1980s boom had made it unnecessary.

- Two 'supply side' doctrines were developed: liberal flexibility and negotiated involvement.

For the moment we shall restrict ourselves to the supply side. Our only ambition is to shed light on the paradigms competing on the ruins of Fordism. The two doctrines do indeed represent different paradigms, 'menus', even if it seems *a priori* possible to mix them in an eclectic manner. In fact the two doctrines of exit from the crisis can be considered as two axes of escape with respect to the two characteristics of Fordist industrial relations: Taylorism as a form of direct control by management over work, and the rigidity of the work contract (see *Figure 11.1*). The first doctrine proposes a movement from rigidity to flexibility in the wage contract; the second doctrine, a movement from direct control to responsible autonomy. To put it another way; the first axis concerns the 'external labour market', the link between firms and labour seeking earnings from employment; the second axis concerns the 'internal labour market', the forms of organization and of co-operation/hierarchy within firms (Doeringer and Piore 1971). On the first axis (external) there are several dimensions of rigidity and flexibility, as already noted. The 'rules of the game' can include the rules of formation of the direct wage, the rules of hiring and firing, the rules of allocation of the indirect wage: the external market is a more-or-less organized market. This axis is thus a synthetic one. Further, the rules can be established at the level of individuals, firms, sectors, and the whole society.

On the second axis, the internal axis, there are also several dimensions: involvement can mean skill training, horizontal co-operation, participation in definition and control of tasks, and so on.[5] Here again, we are talking about a synthetic axis, but this time as we shall see it is important to take into account the level of the negotiation of worker involvement.

- Involvement can be negotiated *individually* and rewarded by bonuses, promotion, or otherwise. This option is limited by the collective character of the involvement required in the majority of co-operative production processes. But individually-negotiated involvement (I in *Figure 11.1*) can be extended to a team or a department. This does not take us too far away from the incentive practices and it remains compatible with a flexible labour contract.

*Figure 11.1: Developments of Post-Fordism : the advanced capitalist countries*

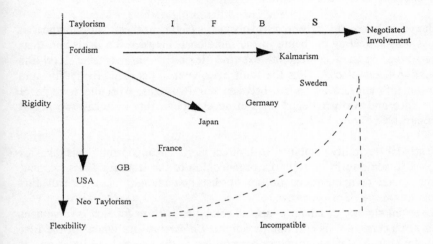

Involvement may be negotiated *firm by firm* between management and unions (F in *Figure 11.1*). Here firm and labour force share the dividends of the specific skills accumulated in the collective learning process. This implies an external rigidity of the wage contract, that is the limits of the right to fire workers already in the firm, but this agreement obviously does not include people outside it.

- Involvement may be negotiated at *sector* level (B in *Figure 11.1*), which limits the risk of competition through 'social dumping' and encourages firms to share training institutions, and so on In consequence the 'external labour market' is likely to be itself more organized: either generally more rigid, or with more socialization of incomes from work.
- Involvement can be negotiated at the level of *the whole society* (S in *Figure 11.1*), unions and employers associations negotiating, at regional or national

- level[6], the distribution of income and the whole direction of the society, on the understanding that the unions will see to it that 'their people' do their best at shopfloor or office level.  Here, the external labour market is likely to be at least as well organized as in the most 'corporative' or social democratic forms of Fordism.

On the other hand, the collective involvement of the workers cannot appear if there is not the feeling of 'being in the same boat' between the firms and their workers, that is in a context of 'external flexibility', at whatever level the negotiation takes place.  Thus the limit of coherence between 'flexibility' and 'involvement' appears as an arc between our two axes, with the triangle of incoherence and two privileged lines of development, that is to say two actual paradigms (see *Figure 11.1*):

- External flexibility combined with direct hierarchical control.  This takes us back to some form of Taylorist organization of the labour process, without the social compensations of the Fordist golden age.  Let us call this paradigm *'neo-Taylorism'*.
- External rigidity of labour contracts combined with negotiated involvement of producers.  Let us call this paradigm *'Kalmarism'* in honour of the first motor works (Volvo) reorganized according to the principle of involvement in a social democratic country, Sweden.

The OECD countries seem currently to be arranged along the arc, with the US and Great Britain emphasizing flexibility and neglecting involvement, certain countries introducing individually negotiated involvement (France), Japan practising negotiated involvement at the level of big firms, Germany practising it at the sector level and Sweden nearest to the Kalmarist axis.  What is then the pull of the axes? The experience of the United States shows that it is difficult to negotiate involvement at the firm level in a flexible, liberal context; still, individually negotiated involvement can perhaps be developed.  On the other hand West Germany seems a socially less-advanced form of the Kalmarist paradigm.  Japan seems to occupy an intermediate situation which we could perhaps call 'Toyotism' with a strong duality (rigid/flexible) of its external labour market.

## 3. Problems of Coherence of Post-Fordism

Industrial relations only define a part of conceivable development models. Capital–labour relations are subject to other constraints than those which develop there. Macroeconomists currently recognize the existence of a demand constraint and of an international constraint. Political scientists emphasize the need for legitimation of the social order. More recently ecological constraints have arisen, of the highest importance. Let us begin with these.

### *The Dangers of Productivism*

Capitalist development has not only 'degraded work' up to its Taylorist paroxysm (Braverman 1974). We can now see how far, following the prophecy of Marx, it has also exhausted nature (as has the state capitalism of the East). In fact the deals between capital and labour have been made hitherto at the expense of nature, and thus of future generations. The ozone hole and the greenhouse effect arose from the great industrial boom of the Golden Age. The economic recovery of the 1980s increased the frequency of industrial disasters, while aggravating the global ecological crisis. Now the limits of any productivist model are fully perceived, at local or global level, and the need for future models of development to be 'sustainable', ecologically coherent, is becoming more widely recognized[7].

Still, the force of this perception varies, which is why ecological limits are not equally perceived as real limits for future models. Local dangers are certainly better and better perceived and rejected, even by workers whose jobs are their cause. The aggregation effects of anti-ecological individual practices are perceived and rejected when they are concentrated in a defined territory such as Los Angeles, Holland and even in a newly-industrialized country like Taiwan. But global effects (for example the greenhouse effect) resulting from a model of consumption inherited from the Fordist compromises, can be ignored for a time. Ecological limits are thus at the same time absolute and vague. Humanity can choose unsustainable models until the first third of the 21st century. The local or regional concentration of environmental damage will encourage the development of social movements opposed to these models ... but in many such cases the local victims will be criticised by the inhabitants of more culpable regions![8]

If we suppose the development of ecological movements in the entire world (and that is the case in the West and in the East, though less clearly in the South) sustainability will become a factor of legitimation for future capital–labour compromises. This will favour the more socialized forms of the Kalmarist compromise, which will be prepared to give the rewards from productivity gains more in the form of leisure time, and the socialized forms of public service, than in purchasing power.[9] In Northern countries where individualist ideologies are too strong, the dominant classes attached to neo-Taylorism will prefer a less radical and less effective solution: repair environmental damage, through ecological industries, at the expense of the poorer strata of society. If the much more immediate constraint of debt weighs heavily on the East and the South they may ignore ecological sustainability altogether.

## *The Problem of Social Cohesion*

Obviously the development models based on Kalmarist industrial relations imply that expertise, education and culture are shared by all, implying a more or less egalitarian distribution of income and power, with the public service well organized and trained in the areas of education and health (Lipietz 1989). By contrast, neo-Taylorist industrial relations imply the polarization of skills, incomes, property and access to health and education. Development models based on such industrial relations are thus more conflictual than the former type. At the heart of the liberal democratic order there appear in these latter models, serious problems with cohesion.

In fact, the neo-Taylorist paradigm has more chance of developing where individualist ideologies prevail and where the employed population is divided. This conclusion is still valid when the involvement of workers is negotiated firm by firm. It is what Aoki (1987) has called 'the dilemma of salaried democracy'. In this case the productivity gains are specific to the firm. Negotiated compensation (higher pay, reduced work time, or securer employment) are limited by the quasi-rent, itself dependent on whatever competitive advantage it can maintain. In these conditions the employees and the management participating in the compromise are allies against newcomers and competitors. This tends to consolidate a 'labour aristocracy' or a 'yeoman democracy' in Piore and Sabel's (1984) version, at the summit of a meritocratic hierarchy generalised to the whole society which can be inherent in the national culture. This hierarchy develops in a completely dualist structure (negotiated involvement/neo-Taylorism) especially when sexual differences come into play as in Japan or Korea, or ethnic differences as in West Germany (see Walraff 1986).

The Kalmarist paradigm can win when the labour movement is strong, reflects the interests of the whole employed population, accepts involvement in the dialectic of struggle and agreement with the management, including the domain of organization and production, and when feminist consciousness is strong. When the salariat is divided by aristocratic traditions, sexual or ethnic discrimination, and when management and unions have a long tradition of antagonism (as in France, in the United States and in the United Kingdom) neo-Taylorism or some kind of dualist configuration has more chance of developing.

## Macroeconomic Constraints

Macroeconomic constraints are well known to economists.    Moreover they represent the more logical aspect of prospective analysis.  We can thus be very brief.    Any model of capital–labour relations must be (1) profitable, (2) competitive and (3) induce equality of demand and supply.  From (1) it follows that when much of the surplus is required for debt service there is little room to negotiate involvement because pay will have to be as low as possible. A debt constraint thus tends to encourage neo-Taylorism.  From (2), the countries which are already engaged in neo-Taylorism and therefore less productive than the 'involvement' countries are also handicapped in the search for a better capital–labour compromise.  As a result in our array the USA, UK and France will have a lot of difficulty in evolving towards Kalmarist paradigms.  It can be expected that Scandinavia, West Germany, Japan and Korea will begin the 21st century in a better position. As to (3), the Kalmarist paradigm is superior. Neo-Taylorism will be associated with a cycle of periods of overheating (with gains to profits and higher earners) and depression (due to over-investment or policies of deflation). The business cycle returns after the much more regular path of Fordism.

The great open question is the possibility of a combination of the two models in the same area of free trade such as the European Union.  Presumably, in the labour-intensive sectors neo-Taylorism can outclass negotiated involvement when pay is sufficiently low.   Thus, transposing the Ricardo theorem on comparative advantage, nations or regions all tend to specialize in the sectors where they are comparatively best 'endowed' either in flexibility (and in low pay) or in negotiated involvement.  The most credible scenario is *the formation of a new hierarchised world economy*.  In place of an industrial Fordist core facing a periphery producing primary products, there will be a new *de facto* international division of industrial employment.   The core economies will be those which will have adopted the Kalmarist compromise for the majority of their production with a possibility of internal dualism (Kalmarism/neo-

Taylorism), for example by gender. These countries will dedicate themselves to high technology and to production less intensive in low-skilled labour. The periphery will be composed of economies organized according to the neo-Taylorist paradigm and dedicated to routinised and labour-intensive activities.

In this case the aggregate level of demand will be limited by the competition of wages due to the coexistence of regions with low salaries and low involvement and of regions with high salaries and high involvement. The greater the possibility of practising 'social dumping' in the neo-Taylorist regions, the smaller will be the islands of 'salaried democracy'.[10] Of course a very simple means of limiting 'social dumping' by competitors is protectionism, either through a low exchange rate or through explicit or implicit barriers to imports. Japan and Korea have been using these two recipes for decades. The EU is not completely open to the competition of the NICs. The USA is less and less open to it. Once it is admitted that it is unjust to be protectionist against a group of countries and at the same time to insist they pay their debts, a reasonable protectionism appears as a means of opening the field to better social compromises than pure free trade. But it only opens the field!

## 4. The Alternative

We have just seen what the recent development of capitalism can teach us. The future seems more open than is sometimes said. I will end by suggesting an alternative route (Lipietz 1989), in the spirit of the social movements which arose from the end of the 1960s, from the French May of 1968 to the German Greens. The key is not to reject technical progress, but to refuse to take this progress as an end in itself. Three themes define the yardstick by which to gauge all 'progress' and each policy: the autonomy of individuals and groups; solidarity among individuals and groups; ecology as a principle of relations between society, the products of its activities, and its environment.

To the crisis of the Fordist paradigm, the alternative thus opposes:

- the transformation of relations among people in work towards a greater mastery of producers over their activity;
- a reduction in (paid) working hours and in consequence a reduction in market relationships in consumption and in leisure, to the advantage of free creation;
- the systematic choice of the most ecological technologies – least despoiling of natural resources;

- the transformation of social relations outside paid employment in the sense of reduction of hierarchy, and respect for equality in difference;
- the transformation of forms of solidarity within national collectivities, from a purely monetary redistribution to help by self-organized activities directed to negotiated social ends;
- evolution towards more organic and less delegated forms of basic democracy;
- a movement from unequal relationships among different national collectivities towards mutually advantageous relations among self-centred communities.

The social base of the alternative will have to bring together the oppressed and the exploited in revolt against alienating social relationships: women, workers who suffered restructuring or devaluing technologies, the unemployed and precarious workers, multicultural youth of the conurbations, peasants excluded from rural society. It is thus a 'new left' democratic successor of all the emancipatory movements. What could be the economic basis of such a democratic alternative: what technological paradigm, what regime of accumulation, what mode of regulation?

*For a new salary compromise on productivity*

As argued above, one real paradigm, 'Kalmarism', seems compatible with the alternative project. Bluntly, the workers' movement and all the democratic movements must take up the challenge and occupy the terrain of an anti-Taylorist revolution; not only as a 'compromise' but as the first step towards historic goals – a society which is more democratic, more self-managed, a step towards the humanization of humanity. But that will also be a compromise. Of course any boss would be delighted to have employees working with enthusiasm with all their intellectual capacities for the greater glory of the enterprise! If Taylorism has chosen to renounce such possibilities, it is for political reasons, reasons of micropolitics, of control of the workplace, but also for macropolitical reasons: reasons of state. A group of workers which is highly trained and proud of being so, by taking the initiative, can contest management control over the intensity of its work, the sharing of productivity, the utility of the products. And a working class conscious of its managerial capacity can aspire to share in political and social direction. If it wants to reunite what Taylor divided, which is what management may propose, what can the employees demand in exchange? First, obviously, greater stability of employment. No employee will be cooperative in seeking productivity gains which would lead to his own redundancy! The problem is that a firm cannot guarantee in the medium term assured employment for the same type of work. The guarantee of employment must thus be a dynamic guarantee with both aspects internal to the firm, and social aspects. This raises the question of 'mobility' and of 'restructuring'. Most employees are rightly unwilling to accept mobility between types of work and between regions. Work is only one aspect of individual and social life. Affective and family relationships are the main condition of self-fulfilment and happiness and they require material conditions: stability of communities linked to territories. The compromise cannot relate simply to the 'right to work' but to the 'right to live and work in a place'. This implies a collective involvement of unions in the local dynamic of creation of new employment at the same rate as employment which has become useless disappears. The involvement of employees in 'how to produce' leads on then to concern with 'what to produce'.

The restructuring of the productive apparatus must throughout be guided by two imperatives. First, *the conservation and enrichment of expertise.* It is both irrational and humiliating to neglect the acquired expertise of workers. That is why employees must be involved in decisions concerning restructuring. They contribute their expertise and can demand complementary retraining. This right to retraining and to control over the objectives of restructuring must be a part of the compromise on dynamic restructuring. Second, *the democratic definition of the social needs to be satisfied.* A temptation for the trade unions is to defend their members' present employment. However, these jobs can be dangerous for the community (nuclear power) or of doubtful value (old mines, weapons industries). That is why the control over 'what to produce' concerns not only present workers, but the whole society. New forms of democratic planning must be invented – probably at the regional level, at the level of local employment areas – which take precedence over the 'judgement of the market'.

## The sharing of the gains

Supposing that the implementation of new industrial relations allied to the information technology revolution leads to a return of high productivity increases, who ought to benefit? Employees, certainly, as much as firms; otherwise demand stagnating while productivity rose would lead to over-production and increasing unemployment. This can be avoided either by a rise in purchasing power per employee (in direct salary or via the welfare state) or by an extension of leisure time per employee. The latter is much to be preferred: principally, because a massive reduction of working time is the most effective way to reduce unemployment rapidly. Further, in advanced capitalist countries (unlike the Third World) most of the population have material living standards such that the pursuit of happiness is limited more by 'lack of being' than by 'lack of having'. Even before the economic crisis, by 1968, the mass consumption model was showing its existential weaknesses. People need time to live with what they have; they need to experiment with new social relations, with autonomous creative activities. Even the new goods produced by the electronic revolution (hi-fi, video, home computers) use time while the typical Fordist goods (car, washing machine) were designed to save it. And in the long term, employees who involve themselves actively during their working time will tend also to be active democratic citizens with leisure for cultural activity and education. Finally, a model of development where full employment is based largely on the extension of leisure time and non-market relations is less subject to economic fluctuations arising from international competition. The 'consumption of leisure time' does not lead to imports and there is absolutely no need for protectionism to make music or drama, read novels or make love. 'To accumulate in the happiness of living' allows more balanced growth and more capacity for democratic regulation of national economies. Of course such a model implies other compromises on the part of employees. As some are currently far below their society's norm of 'acceptable' purchasing power, the counterpart in pay of the reduction in working time must be unequal: the inequality of earnings must be reduced. A new compromise is a compromise *within the salariat* as well as between those at the top and those at the bottom, between managers and workers. This raises the problem of solidarity which in the Fordist model is represented by the Welfare State.

## To resolve the crisis of the Welfare State

As it emerged from the century of union struggles with the victories of social democracy in Europe, with the taking into account by conservative or Christian Democrat governments of macroeconomic and social demands, the Welfare State appeared as a very powerful but very particular form of solidarity. Essentially it is a form of compromise between capital and labour in the form of a compromise between citizens. One part of the distributed income is directly subtracted from the purchasing power of individuals and directed into a pool. This pool provides money income to those who for 'legitimate' reasons cannot 'earn their living normally' by working. This norm has schizophrenic, even Kafkaesque, consequences as much for those in work as those out of it.

Those in work, employers as well as employees, pay taxes and charges to the Welfare State to feed the 'pool'. When this precept becomes too heavy, those in work begin to protest. They are paying for 'idlers', people who do not work. In fact these people would very much like to work, but they are not able to do so for pay and they do not have the right to do so as long as they receive benefits. And they pay the psychological price of this illogicality. If they have no activity they feel socially rejected; they feel like dependent children. If they have an activity (neighbourly assistance, black work) while they are receiving benefits, they are considered as cheats. They can be prosecuted and deprived of their benefits ...

There is a way of avoiding the double schizophrenia of the Fordist Welfare State: the creation of a new employment sector of limited extent (of the order of 10% of the working population, like present unemployment). Its workers, or rather the organizations which would have to pay them ('intermediate agencies for socially useful work') would continue to receive from the Welfare State subsidies equivalent to unemployment benefit (perhaps reinforced by a true citizen's income). They would not, any more than the unemployed, have to pay social charges: the operation would therefore be 'neutral' for the Welfare State. The employees of the sector would receive from the organizations a normal wage with normal social legislation. Their activity, thus subsidized, would be devoted to socially useful tasks: those which are currently provided at high cost (not being subsidized) by certain sectors of the Welfare State itself (care for the sick, help for convalescents); those which are currently provided by the unpaid labour of women; and those which, being too expensive, are not done at all (improving the environment, particularly of poor areas, and so on) In fact since this 'social utility' sector would be subsidized and free of taxes, its services would be less costly and new activities could be opened up. They would not compete with those of other sectors (the private sector, the state) since these sectors take on few if any of these activities, not finding effective demand or not daring to raise enough taxes to finance them. Basically they would only enter into competition with women's unpaid work and black work: excellent! And they would not weigh more heavily on the Welfare State than the unemployment which they would contribute to reabsorb – so long, obviously, as this third sector does not exceed the order of magnitude of current unemployment.

It can be seen that the development of this third 'social utility' sector eliminates most of the faults of the Fordist welfare state. The 'schizophrenia' problem disappears. The tax-paying workers of the first two sectors know what they are paying for: socially useful work. The workers of the third sector have socially better-recognized employment, better for their self-esteem than black work or precarious temporary employment. The microeconomy is respected by the development of jobs which cost the paying agencies little but ensure a stable income to the workers in them, without bringing them into competition with others.

But there is more. In this new economic sector new democratic social relations could be tried out. First, within the sector it could organize itself in little self-managing cooperatives which could combine training and work with the help of psycho-sociologists and instructors. Next, in its connections with the users it could innovate in the search for new contractual links (neither market-based nor patriarchal nor administrative) for service provision, with permanent control by the beneficiaries (local councils, environmental protection agencies, health services, and so on) over the social usefulness of these activities. Thus this new alternative sector could be a school of self-management, of equality of the sexes and of democracy in the definition of tasks. Although immersed in the market, in pay relationships (but protected by its connection with the welfare state) it could be a new step towards the democratization of economic relationships.

## Notes

1. The subsection which follows is a resumé of Glyn *et al.* (1990) and Lipietz (1985, 1989).
2. We see here that Fordism was a 'menu'. The coexistence of Taylorism and pre-Fordist rules of the game in pay determination led to the depression of the 1930s.
3. A long time ago Andrew Friedman (1977) had already contrasted 'responsible autonomy' and 'direct control' as two tendencies in permanent conflict in the capitalist organization of work. We note here the relative independence of industrial relations not only *vis-à-vis* the technology but also *vis-à-vis* other aspects of the internal management of the firm and of industrial organization. This independence remains relative. My view is that new technologies underline the superiority of responsible autonomy (without all the same determining it à la Piore and Sabel (1984)). Moreover responsible autonomy can fit particularly well with the sophisticated forms of industrial organization (JIT, 'network firms' and so on). This goes beyond the field of the present text. On the 'coherent menus' linking industrial relations and industrial organization with their spatial consequences see Leborgne and Lipietz (1987, 1989).
4. What follows summarizes Lipietz (1995) and Mahon (1987).
5. The negotiation of involvement (and involvement itself) can involve aspects external to a firm such as professional training, trade union participation in steering committees at the inter-professional or sectoral levels (as in corporatist states like Austria, Sweden) and so on
6. If it is not at the international level! The problem of the geographical field adequate for social paradigms is difficult and little explored (see Lipietz 1985, Leborgne and Lipietz 1989). We will bring out this point again later.

7. 'Sustainable' is the term adopted for 'ecologically coherent in the long term' in the report to the United Nations Committee on the Environment, coordinated by Mrs. Brundtland (1987).
8. The pundits of the North have recently criticised the Brazilians for burning Amazonia. However the annual contribution of France (40% of the Brazilian population) to the world greenhouse effect is 20% greater than the total Brazilian contribution.
9. When strong trade unions (like the German IG Metall) take account of the 'newcomers' they include the reduction of working time in their objectives in order to combat unemployment and improve the quality of life.
10. It is a new consequence of the Aoki paradox. On the example of the European Union, see Leborgne and Lipietz (1989).

## References

Aoki M. (1986), 'Horizontal vs Vertical Structures of the Firm', *American Economic Review*, December, 971-983.

Braverman H. (1974), 'Labor and Monopoly Capital. The Degradation of Work in the XXth Century', *Monthly Review Press*, New York.

Doeringer P.B. and M. J. Piore (1971), *International Labour Markets and Manpower Analysis*, Sharpe, New York (revised edition 1985).

Friedman A. (1977), *Industry and Labour*, London: Macmillan.

Glyn A, A. Hughes, A. Lipietz and A. Singh (1992), 'The Rise and Fall of The Golden Age of Capitalism: Lessons for the 1990s', in Marglin & Schor (eds) (1990), 344, Oxford: Oxford University Press, for UNU/WIDER, 1990.

Leborgne D. and A. Lipietz (1987), 'New Technologies, New Modes of Regulation: Some Spatial Implications', International Seminar Changing Labour Processes and New Forms of Urbanization, Samos, September, published in *Society and Space*, **6**, (3), 1988.

Leborgne D. and A. Lipietz (1989), 'Avoiding Two-Tiers Europe', paper presented at the European Association of Labor Economist First Congress, Torino, September 1989, published in *Labour and Society*, **15** (2), 1990.

Lipietz A. (1985*), Mirages et miracles, Problèmes de l'industrialization dans le Tiers-Monde*. In English: *Miracles and Miracles. Crises of World Fordism (*1987) London: Verso.

Lipietz A. (1989), *Choisir l'Audace. Une alternative pour le XXIème siècle*, Paris: La Découverte. In English: *Towards a New Economic Order: Ecology, Post-Fordism, Democracy*, (1992, Cambridge, Polity Press.

Lipietz A. (1995), 'Capital-labour relations at the dawn of XXIst Century', in J. Schor and J. I. You (eds), *Capital, the State and Labour: A Global Perspective*, Cheltenham: Edward Elgar.

Mahon R. (1987), 'From Fordism to ? New Technologies, Labor Market and Unions', *Economic and Industrial Democracy*, **8**, 5–60.

Piore, M. J. and C. F. Sabel (1984), *The Second Industrial Divide: Possibilities for Prosperity*, New York: Basic Books.

Walraff G. (1986), *Ganz Unten*, Köln: Kiepenhauser & Witsch.

# 12. Ecology, Technology and the Next Long Wave Upswing

**Andrew Tylecote**

## Introduction

The three preceding chapters in this Part, by Freeman, Hanappi and Egger, and Lipietz, have a great deal in common. With varying terminology, they implicitly or explicitly accept Kondratieff's view of a long wave in economic growth over a period of 50 to 60 years, and Perez's view of each long upswing as requiring harmony between a new technological style and the socio-institutional framework within which it diffuses. (They differ somewhat in the degree of activity or passivity which 'style' and 'framework' have in reaching this harmony.) All three see the current crisis of the world economy as arising, first, from the exhaustion of 'Fordism' and the failure, so far, to make the institutional changes needed to generate a new 'post-Fordist' (or 'ICT' or 'information age') upswing. In discussing those changes, Lipietz focuses on industrial relations, Hanappi and Egger on culture (both terms very broadly understood); Freeman tends to emphasize changes in the organization of firms and the role of government in the economy.

This chapter takes these contributions as an agreed point of departure, and seeks to go further in three directions. First, it relates the current crisis to other cycles besides the Kondratieff. Second, it broadens the focus from the advanced countries to the whole world economy. Third, it discusses the interrelation between the economic crisis and the ecological crisis, and the way in which a 'post-Fordism' may be developed which will finally meet the challenge to sustainable development: to allow some acceleration of income growth and a great acceleration of growth in employment while diminishing the threat to the ecology of the planet. By doing so it seeks to bring together the main themes of Parts 1 and 2 with that of this concluding Part.

## 1. Long Cycles and Long Swings

The long cycle in international relations consists of the establishment of one state as 'world power' or 'global hegemon' (at least as regards trade) in the course of a 'global war' which lasts about one generation; then its progressive decline over a further three generations until the next 'global war' breaks out (Wallerstein 1983; Modelski 1987). The main economic impact of this cycle is through the depressive effect of the 'global war'. (The last two such were the Revolutionary/Napoleonic Wars 1792–1815 and the 1914–45 period.)

The depressive effect arises not from the wars as such, which have mixed effects, but from the lack of any stable structure of international economic relations or sense of global responsibility on the part of the strongest economic power(s); this is well illustrated by the 1930s and the behaviour of the US during that period (Tylecote 1992 Chapter 10).) Arguably, the resolution of the 'global war' provides an excellent opportunity for all kinds of needed reforms: thus the socio-institutional reforms of the 1940s, particularly those at the international level, can be credited to this as well as to the long wave depression which roughly coincided with the 'global war' period. There is no such fluidity in national or institutional institutions now as then; and the US, though its hegemony continues after a fashion, has by no means the power it had in the late 1940s. Reform is therefore likely to be a more protracted and messy process, with the one advantage that the disappearance of the Soviet bloc opens the way in principle to a new dispensation for the whole planet.

The long (or Kuznets) swing, of some 15–25 years, is an essentially economic phenomenon, whose main dynamic seems to involve under- and over-shooting of building activity and land prices. Solomou (1987) and others have identified Kuznets swings in the late 19th century in the US and Western Europe, but at that period the national swings tended to offset each other. In the 1920s on the other hand a long swing at the world level appears. In the Second World War and the immediate post-war period there is no clear evidence of Kuznets swings – which is consistent with the view that they depend on land speculation, an activity which is suppressed in a highly-regulated capitalist economy. Since the mid–1970s the experience of the US, UK and Japan (latterly the least regulated of the major capitalist economies) suggests that something of a Kuznets swing may have reappeared there, with a downswing *circa* 1974–82 and an upswing *circa* 1982–90 (Tylecote 1994). If that is true, they, and perhaps other countries, are now in a double downswing – Kuznets superimposed on Kondratieff – for most or all of the decade. This would imply acute recession, which describes the early 1990s well enough, but not the middle of the decade. To understand the reflationary forces now at work, and their fragility, we have to have a better understanding of the dynamics of the Kondratieff.

## 2. Long Wave Downswings and Inequalities in the World Economy

Tylecote (1992, 1994) argues that the most important determinant of long wave downswings in general, and the current long wave downswing in particular, is intra-national and international *inequality*. Inequality at both levels increases

(a)     with a lag, in response to the long wave upswing, whose long-run consequences favour the political right and reliance on market forces;

(b)     in response to the arrival of the new technological style, of which the better-educated nationally and internationally are better able to take advantage;

(c)     in direct response to the downswing itself: the weaker partners in national and international economic relationships having been persuaded by the upswing to trust themselves more and more to supply and demand, that fickle pair turn against them. The relative price of low-skilled labour, and what it can produce, falls sharply – as instanced by what has happened since the mid-1970s to the terms of trade of the South (World Bank 1991), and the relative wages of the Northern poor (Wood, 1994).

The main 'weaker partners' internationally – the Less Developed Countries, or 'South' – at first refuse to believe that the trend against them is any more than a brief 'blip', and borrow to tide themselves over it: the South borrowed heavily in the late 1970s, as it had in the late 1920s. As a result they find themselves before long – as they did in the early 1980s and the early 1930s – in a debt trap in which, out of their diminished export earnings, they have to pay heavy interest bills before they can buy imports (Tylecote 1992).

   In turn rising inequality depresses economic growth rates, working through supply and demand: on the supply side poverty reduces investment of all kinds in poor people and poor countries. It also reduces demand in familiar Keynesian ways, if the marginal propensity of the poor to consume is higher than that of the rich.[1] Certainly if the balance of payments constraints of poor countries were relaxed they would spend more – particularly on imports – and thus contribute to aggregate demand in rich countries. (On the effect of the balance of payments constraint, see Thirlwall 1979 and McCombie 1993.)

*Figure 12.1   Real GDP per head in world 'regions'*

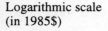

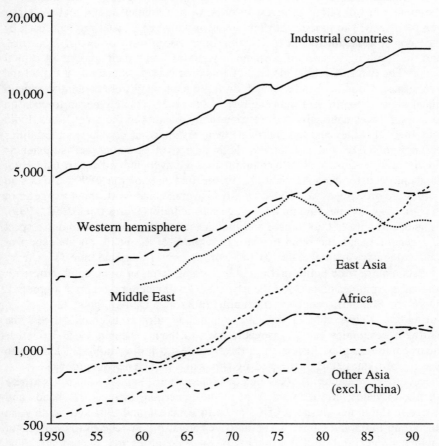

*Source:* Wolf (1994).

All this implies that the South, or Less Developed Countries (LDCs), will suffer more in the long downswing than the North; and most of the LDCs do (see *Figure 12.1*, Real GDP per head). However, in one respect they have an advantage over the North. In the North, Fordism as a vehicle for technological and economic advance is pretty well played out. In the LDCs this is nowhere near true, indeed many of them are far from fully exploiting the possibilities of the *previous* technological style. In principle they have the opportunity to follow in the footsteps of late developing countries like Japan, Taiwan and South Korea, in a virtuous circle in which the more you grow, mainly through manufacturing, the more you can afford to invest in physical and human capital and the faster you then grow... In practice during the downswing most LDCs are held back by the poor demand for their exports: this limits the growth of export industries, and the resulting balance of payments constraint limits their imports of capital goods. The two LDCs least affected by this problem are as one might expect the two largest, China and India, which during the upswing were content to remain much more self-sufficient than the rest.[2] When they belatedly began to open up to market forces nationally and internationally – China in the early 1980s, India only in 1991 – they had the enormous twin advantage of very low net liabilities per unit of GDP and a relatively high degree of economic self-sufficiency: Fordist and pre-Fordist growth could proceed relatively unhindered by balance of payments constraints.[3] Accordingly, in the first half of the 1990s China and India were growing at well above the world average, and (with about a quarter of the South's GDP) pushing up its average substantially (World Bank 1993, 1995).

The opening up of the Chinese and Indian economies conformed in one respect to a general trend: the rapid increase in reliance of the South on the export of labour-intensive manufactures to the North. In its traditional role as primary product exporter the South had found worsening terms of trade combining with stagnating volumes of sales; in the new role of manufactures exporter a group of important Southern countries (including India and China) found themselves, during the 1980s, able to increase volumes rapidly at tolerable prices, the Northern economies being reasonably open to them. Then in 1992–3 another factor came into play. Recession in the North, with falling inflation, had led to low interest rates (to be expected by this stage in a long wave downswing – Tylecote 1992 Chapter 4). This induced international capital to look elsewhere for higher yields, and it found them in the 'emerging markets' for bonds and shares in the more advanced LDCs of Latin America, and East and South Asia (including India and China).[4] The massive capital inflow relaxed the balance of payments constraint, and the imports of these countries rose accordingly. The Northern recession lifted, largely in consequence. The success of the GATT Uruguay Round in getting agreement on further liberalization of world trade helped to induce optimism like that of the World Bank (1995), which looks forward to a period of sustained rapid growth in the world economy in which the demographically ageing North's excess of saving over investment (and current account surpluses) are soaked up by the young South's excess of investment over saving (and current account deficits); the fast growth of Southern economies allowing them to keep their debts to the North roughly constant in proportion to their national income and even falling in proportion to their export earnings.

This new dynamic balance in the world economy had, however, certain fundamental flaws which made it unlikely to last long. One was the effect on the North. Opening Northern economies to imports from the South was always bound to reduce demand for the labour of various low-skilled groups in the North. When the goods concerned were primary products the losses were, at least, shared by the (mostly wealthy) owners of land and other natural resources. Even when the goods were labour-intensive manufactures produced by independent Southern firms, the Northern losers included Northern firms, their owners and managers. However the shift of low-skilled manufacturing operations to the South is now mostly being conducted *within* or at least *by* Northern multinationals – without whom the political momentum for liberalization could scarcely be maintained. In consequence, as Wood (1994) shows, the Northern losers are overwhelmingly the *workers* in those operations. They are added to the heap of low-skilled labour competing for a pool of jobs which is being reduced by other factors, notably the change of technological style. Inequality increases accordingly; although Wood's estimates of how much, are controversial (Lawrence and Slaughter 1993).

Second, many LDCs continue to find that their most obvious comparative advantage arises from their natural resources. At present only a small fraction of the South is involved in the new manufacturing boom, as is indicated by the high concentration of investment by Northern multinationals, who control most of this, like other trade.[5] Third, the Northern market for low-tech. manufactures is limited. The number of potential Northern consumers, whose overall demand for low-tech. manufactures is not very elastic, is increasing much more slowly than that of potential Southern producers. The more Southerners join in supplying the market, the lower the price will fall.

The solution to the demand problem is for the South collectively to consume a rising fraction of its own output of manufactures, and to supply a rising fraction of its own requirements of higher-technology goods and services. It could then continue to act as the 'locomotive' of the world economy. Such a reduction in the polarity of the world economy between North and South would be a new development in world economic history. If it takes place (which seems doubtful) it will largely solve one problem, of world demand, but (as we shall see) drastically exacerbate another, of world ecology.

## 3. The Gathering Ecological Crisis

As earlier contributions to this volume have made clear, the growth of world industrial output must inevitably, at some point, put pressure on the *sources* of material inputs for production, and the *sinks* for its products and by-products. Where sources or sinks are *renewable*, the problem arises only as and when the demand upon them exceeds their renewal capacity; where they are *exhaustible*, the train is so to speak heading towards the buffers as soon as it leaves the station. (We shall use 'exhaustion' as a shorthand term to refer to the overuse of all sources and sinks including renewable ones.) With world population increasing, and output per head increasing, the movement towards exhaustion of sources and sinks must not simply continue but accelerate unless and until the rate of *decrease* in the source/sink use, per unit of output, exceeds the product of these two rates of *increase*. Exhaustible sources – notably, of energy – were the focus of warnings in the 1970s, which proved to be premature. In fact they should be of least concern, for they generally have clearly-assigned property rights. This means that, as they become more scarce, in fact as soon as increasing scarcity is anticipated, their price will rise and there will be increasing incentive for exploration, and substitution through existing and new technology. This is roughly what happened with oil during the 1970s; together with new trends to energy-saving, and the general downswing, it led to a return to low prices in the mid-1980s. (But note that it is much easier to substitute away from one material – coal for oil, say, or aluminium for copper – than to do so from a whole range: for example from exhaustible energy sources as a whole. And as Hinterberger and Seifert point out in Chapter 5 above, a wide range of materials is heading towards exhaustion – or at least much higher extraction costs – in a matter of decades.) Property rights for renewable sources – forests, soil, water, fish stocks, and so on – are mostly not clearly assigned, and not surprisingly current concern over them is greater. Least clearly assigned – and assignable – are property rights over sinks for pollution, and accordingly it is hopeless to count on the price mechanism to help automatically to control their overuse (though governments may usefully mimic it through charges). Another reason for concern over sinks is that in many cases it is not at all clear how they function, what their maximum capacity is, and what is the consequence of overload - *vide* the ozone hole and the greenhouse effect. (See for example Martinez Alier, and Dietz and van der Straaten – Chapters 1 and 7 above.)

Where global sources and sinks are concerned, historically and even currently the North is the greater depleter and polluter by far (see Hinterberger and Seifert above). However the share of LDCs in world energy and other resource use has risen greatly over the last 20 years, and most of them, as pointed out above, are now in an essentially Fordist phase of development. This means unfortunately that their fastest growing sector (manufacturing) is the most resource-using one, and that their style of technology, there and elsewhere, tends to be resource-using. Their share of world energy consumption, for example, is expected to rise from 27% in 1994 to 40% in 2010 (Economist 1994). At the same time their use of local and global sinks, though less easy to measure, is clearly a rising share of the total - partly through the migration of 'dirty' industries from the North. (For example their $CO_2$ emissions by 2010 are expected to reach those of the whole world in 1970 (*Economist* 1994)). Thus the focus of the developing ecological crisis is rapidly moving to the South.[6]

The movement towards exhaustion has different economic effects, as conventionally measured, depending on the category. Increasing scarcity of an exhaustible source like oil with assigned property rights will raise its price and thus lead to redistribution of income from users to owners. (It will tend, through anticipation, to do this early. The resulting economies, increased exploration, and so on, may then lead to a fall in price for a time, as with oil from the mid-1980s.) It will increase inflation and reduce measured output. Increasing scarcity of a renewable resource without assigned property rights, like fish stocks, will raise its price later and more suddenly, and again lead to redistribution from users to those with continuing access to it or a substitute. Again inflation rises and measured output falls. The effects of sink depletion are less clear. Where the burden falls on *consumers* – for example if air pollution gives children asthma – there is currently no measured 'economic' effect since neither their misery nor the expense of treating them reduces Ropke's dinosaur, GDP. Where it hits producers, the effect is not hidden: it raises inflation, and lowers output as with source depletion. (A recent example is the 1990 estimate that the West German timber and agricultural industries lost a total of more than £1 billion per annum through acid rain (Jacobs 1994).) It may also lead to the same result where government steps in to limit further depletion, by charges or otherwise, and forces a shift to more expensive production methods.[7]

The economic effects of the developing eco-crisis can be summed up as twofold. First, at some stage source and sink exhaustion will be reflected by rising prices, eco-taxes or other restriction of access to what were previously free or cheap sources and sinks. This will oblige producers (and consumers) to turn to what were previously regarded as more expensive ways of achieving the same object. In itself that will tend to reduce GNP per head. However, with the availability of huge increases in productivity through the application of ICT (and older technological styles in the South) this need not necessarily lead to an actual reduction in GNP per head or even a deceleration in its growth: the crucial questions would be how sharp a rise in price (and so on) took place in how important a range of factors, and what was the degree of technological flexibility of the country affected. (For example in most of the South severe depletion of per capita soil and water resources could be expected to be very damaging.)

The second effect is quite different, through *uncertainty*. Driver and Moreton (1992) have shown how uncertainty due to macroeconomic volatility depressed investment and thus growth in the UK during the 1980s. Such uncertainty, and demand deficiency partly resulting from it, is characteristic of a long wave downswing. It must be compounded by the present 'eco-uncertainty': on the one hand, any reasonably well–informed business must expect, in the medium term, action by government to make pollution a great deal more expensive, and (with rather less confidence) a similar rise in energy and materials prices due either to government action or increasing scarcity. Thus resource or pollution-*intensive* investments are extremely risky in the medium term, particularly in the advanced countries where firms are likely to be exposed to competition from countries where prices and charges are lower. On the other hand, in the short term the relevant prices and charges are not yet high enough to justify such heavy investment in resource- and pollution-*saving* as would be optimal under the 'most likely medium term regime'. The tendency therefore is to do little of either. The ideal situation for investment, by contrast, would be where governments, in cooperation, imposed substantial charges on all relevant sources and sinks, with a clear commitment to progressive increases.[8]

## 4. A Rock and A Hard Place ...

For the next decade at least, we must expect the uncertainty effect to depress investment in the advanced countries: as Lindegaard has shown (Chapter 8, above), many delays are inevitable before the necessary tax and liability regime is in place, and more before markets have adjusted to it. This makes any world recovery all the more dependent on the new Southern 'locomotives' referred to above. Unfortunately these countries are extremely vulnerable to the effects of source and sink exhaustion, being in general heavily populated and committed to high-input growth. As *The Economist* (1994) showed, if their growth continues at anywhere near its recent rates sharp rises in oil prices are almost unavoidable within a decade.[9] Since the shortages will have been caused by these countries becoming massive importers (China being a net exporter till late 1993; Indonesia expected to begin net imports in 2000), the effects on their balance of trade will be very serious. The prognosis for grain is even more alarming. On the one hand the renewable resource and sink depletion referred to above limits scope for further increases in grain production. On the other hand, Southern demand is increasing, if only because of population growth. Industrialization exacerbates the situation dramatically: fertile valley and coastal land is lost for buildings, roads and dams, and diets shift towards grain-hungry meat. The outlook for Chinese grain imports (it was a substantial exporter until 1992) is already causing grave concern, in China and elsewhere (Brown 1995).

Suddenly the dash for manufactures-led growth looks like a charge up a cul-de-sac, which will end in an impossible balance of payments position.[10] The Southern 'locomotives' will be derailed; the world 'recovery', should it last so long, will halt; the Kondratieff downswing will deepen into world depression – unless drastic changes in course are made soon. What those might be, we discuss below.

## 5. The Post-Fordist Technological Style and the Ecological Crisis

In Chapter 9 in this volume Chris Freeman has outlined certain key characteristics of what he describes as the new 'ICT' (information and communication technology) 'techno-economic paradigm' which he regards as already determined (see in particular his *Table 9.2*). Hanappi and Egger in Chapter 10 insist that key issues as to the direction of technological development remain to be determined by socio-political forces. I agree with both sides, and propose to show how both can be right, with particular respect to the ecological dimension.

Freeman's *Table 9.2* counterposes the information-intensity of ICT with the energy-intensity of Fordism. Clearly, as Perez (1983) and Tylecote (1992) have shown, Fordism in its pattern of production and consumption responded to the low energy prices (and extended network of distribution) which accompanied its birth, while ICT clearly revolves around the dramatic cheapening of 'machine intelligence' and the transmission of information. All kinds of developments are possible (some of which have already begun) which would in effect allow ICT to substitute machine intelligence for energy (and materials, and pollution). Sophisticated control systems of various kinds are the most obvious example. At the same time, it is possible for ICT to continue the main thrust of Fordism, which was to economize on the use of labour. There is a range of possibilities, from massive economy in energy and so on, with some increase in labour input, to massive economy in labour, with some increase in energy and so on. At the moment the incentive is clear for economy in labour input, because (in the advanced countries which dominate technological innovation) the price of labour is high and rising; the incentive for economy in energy and so on is, as we have pointed out, much less clear. This disparity is exacerbated by taxation, of which about 50%, directly and indirectly, falls on labour, while only about 10% falls on use of the natural environment (Jacobs 1994). Here, clearly, 'socio-political forces' need to take a hand – not by following the New Right prescription of greater poverty for the poor, but by switching the burden of taxation and social charges sharply away from labour, to energy, raw materials and pollution.

To quote Freeman quoting Perez, such political intervention would give us a further 'change in the dynamics of the relative cost structure of all possible inputs into production'. As long as it was reasonably clear that 'eco-prices and charges' would continue to rise, it would make profitable a new wave of investment into first the development and then the embodiment of new 'eco-saving' technology. It is not certain, though it seems likely, that the consequent change in relative prices would steer technological change towards (relatively) labour-using technologies. Even if this did not happen in manufacturing, it could be expected in the primary sector (for example with a shift from large thermal power stations to small windmills; from chemical to organic farming) and through a change in the assortment of consumption – labour-intensive goods and services becoming relatively cheaper and thus more popular.[11] So far as the North is concerned, such a shift, while convenient, is not necessary: increased employment could be achieved through increased aggregate demand, and that could come through an increase in investment. As argued above, an eco-tax reform would stimulate that by reducing uncertainty. The South is another matter; we return to this below.

Something more is required, however, than a redirection of the thrust of the ICT techno-economic paradigm. Freeman treats ICT as the basis of 'post-Fordism' because ICT alone is (or is becoming) a 'pervasive technology', *now*. But as Tylecote (1992) has argued, there is another set of technologies which has the potential to be almost as pervasive as ICT, and more quickly than most analysts suppose: *biotechnology*. This arose from the development, in the early 1970s, of 'techniques for the manipulation, alteration and synthesis of the genetic material in cells in such a way that the functioning of the cell is modified'.[12] Genetic engineering joined with more gradual advances in cell chemistry, microbiological techniques for dealing with cells and micro-organisms, techniques for the culture of plant cells and tissues, and the development of relevant chemical engineering techniques. The potential of biotechnology – for example in the development of new strains of crop plant which would be drought-, salt-, and pest-resistant, and even fix nitrogen like the leguminosae – was clearly spectacular, and was soon oversold. Recent developments in plant-breeding have shown the 'sailing ship effect', whereby the apparently-outdated technology (in this case hybridization without genetic engineering) progresses faster than before, and maintains its dominance for a time; though on close inspection the old technology (like sailing ships) is making some borrowings from the new (in this case, for example, genetic 'tagging' of new strains). At the same time public opinion, led by the 'green movement', has been extremely suspicious of the potential for ecological havoc through the release of genetically-engineered organisms. Thus the diffusion of biotechnology as a new 'pervasive technology' is currently obstructed by its own immaturity and by the lack of an established, appropriate regulatory framework. Both of these obstructions can however be removed quite quickly, the first by continuing and increased investment in the industry, the second by government action.

How quickly biotechnology will mature, with a given rate of investment, is a matter of judgment.[13] What I wish to emphasize here is its potential contribution to the world economy and how this will be affected by the 'eco-regime' in place. It is potentially a pervasive technology:

• In *services*, in health and waste/pollution management – both fast-growing sectors, and the first already large in the North. A wide range of medical therapies become possible which would be impossible without it.
• In *manufacturing*, in chemicals, pharmaceuticals and food processing (the last being where 'old biotechnology' began). The main use in the early stages is to produce existing products more cheaply and with higher quality; the greatest input savings being in energy and raw materials. In the longer term there is great scope for developing new materials, for example semiconductor 'chips' and photovoltaics, through biotechnology.
• In the *primary sector*, in agriculture and fisheries, particularly through new strains of plants, animals and micro-organisms.

This is a formidable list, particularly when one considers the continuing dominance of the primary sector in most of the South. It can also make a highly positive contribution to world economic growth. Thus the direction of development for Southern agriculture could and should be to produce seeds and so on which would permit higher output with higher labour input; and higher output would induce more employment in downstream, processing industries. Any quickening of product innovation – such as mentioned in health – must tend to increase employment: consider how much the old of the North will be willing and able to pay for new therapies for their degenerative diseases![14] Likewise, if ecological havoc is avoided, great benefits are possible to both sources and sinks. However – and here we return to the Hanappi–Egger theme – political action is required not only to stimulate but to steer the acceleration of biotechnology. To return to the example of plant breeding, what the world, and particularly the South, most requires are new strains which are drought-, salt- and pest-resistant, and so on, and require less fertilizer: but such developments, under the existing cost and price regime, are not necessarily of most interest to Northern farmers, and certainly not to the chemicals firms which control most of the plant-breeding companies. For them the ideal new strain is *fertilizer-* and *pesticide-tolerant*. A change such as proposed above to the general  eco-cost and price regime will do much to rectify this distortion of effort, but more specific measures may be required, because what is ideally required is the development of new strains which will be in effect the property of the farmers who use them rather than of their developers. One such measure might be for a firm which had developed a new strain to be paid a royalty not by farmers – Southern ones at least – but by national or international aid organizations according to the rate of use, as monitored by impartial observers.[15]

## 6. Post-Fordist Institutions and the Ecological Crisis

In the last section we argued that – without denying any element of Freeman's characterization of the ICT techno-economic paradigm – socio-political forces needed not simply to accommodate themselves to it, but to steer it, and bring forward the contribution of biotechnology as a supplement and complement to it. We now look at the role of economic, social and political institutions in 'rebalancing' economy and ecology. Again, we can find more agreement in the previous three chapters than may have met the eye. Freeman's 'optimistic scenario' in his *Table 9.3* mentions a 'new flexible management style, with 'greater participation of the work-force at all levels of decision-making'; Lipietz (Chapter 11) looks forward to 'Kalmarism', which is much the same thing. Freeman sees 'myriads of small networking firms at local level' (albeit 'in symbiosis with world wide oligopolies'). Lipietz looks to a lively 'Third Sector', innovating in relationships within (and no doubt also among) firms. In other words both have a vision of *workers* at all levels taking more initiative – more bottom-up, less top-down – and more emphasis on horizontal relationships rather than vertical ones. Hanappi and Egger have essentially the same vision of the behaviour of people as *consumers* and *voters* – although they do suggest in Chapter 10 that the current separation among the roles of worker, consumer and voter may not remain unaltered. This section seeks to draw those threads out further, and bring them together.

It is, as Lipietz indicates, important that government activities in support of the poor – designed to release their capacity as producers and consumers, and thus *inter alia* stimulate economic growth – should not interfere with market mechanisms. This can be best achieved by directing these activities to benefit (a) the environment (b) the poor themselves, since both categories are largely ignored by the market as matters stand. Ideally one should aim to benefit both at once, as when for example a poor neighbourhood is linked to a Combined Heat and Power system, and the insulation of the houses improved: one thus has poor people who would otherwise be paid, through welfare benefits, for doing nothing, being paid to benefit poor people and the environment, which would otherwise be neglected. (See Tylecote 1993.) Although the direct effects are enough to justify the exercise, they are only the beginning: the more such people are involved in paid work, and the higher their living standards, the more fit they (and their children) will be to engage in the market economy – thus vacating space in the Third Sector for others, or allowing it to shrink.

The one small fault which the Third Sector has as sketched by Lipietz in Chapter 11 is that the direction of its activities appears to be rather top-down: it is government agencies of various kinds which decide what they will pay it to do. Reasonable enough: as it is government – usually central government – which now pays the unemployment and social security benefits which would be diverted into the Third Sector, Lipietz is simply starting from where we are. However, there are ways in which one could go further, alongside the Third Sector, to encourage bottom-up initiatives:

1. *Through interaction with local government.*

One example could be refuse disposal. Let the current cost of refuse disposal in a street or neighbourhood be $x$. Assume that if it were sorted by the local residents into three or four different categories – some of which could be recycled at a profit – and the organic waste composted for local use, the net cost would fall to $y$. Then $x - y$ could be paid to the residents. There would be scope for local, collective initiative in deciding the methods and extent of sorting, achieving maximum participation, and deciding on what to do with the payment – spend it on public goods like a children's playground, or distribute it, with non-participants perhaps excluded. (Clearly the incentive for such schemes increases as eco-taxation raises $x$.) Another example might be pre-school education: the funds allocated to neighbourhoods could be deployed in them, by them, and 'stretched' by their own contributions in kind.

## 2. *Through Local Exchange Trading Systems (LETS). (See Lang 1993.)*

The aim of LETS is to provide a sort of parallel market for labour which would otherwise be unemployed. Services are offered for sale in a local quasi-currency which, once earned, can then be spent on other services. Thus the sort of informal barter which might be expected among friends and neighbours – you dig my garden and I will teach your child the guitar, and so on and so on – can be vastly extended to escape the classic constraint of 'double coincidence of wants'. In principle a LETS can be an entirely grass-roots initiative, but there are various positive and negative roles for government, local and central. Local government may set up a LETS, providing expertise, administration and initial liquidity. It may use this role to regulate both who may participate and what they may sell (it is easy to imagine abuses). Central government has to have some policy on the taxation of LETS: if successful, they can erode the tax base, so they can scarcely be left untaxed indefinitely, but a high rate or insistence on payment in real money would cripple them. The solution is to impose a modest rate of tax (with thresholds which might be integrated with the 'real' tax system) in the quasi-currency. The tax goes not to national but to local government. The gardener is then called upon to work for a certain time on the garden of an old people's home, say; the guitar-teacher will spend an hour or two a week in a local school or youth club; there would be no need to raise the tax rate to that in the 'real' system, since erosion of the 'real' tax base would be offset by new quasi-revenue from output which would otherwise not take place – or take place in the black economy.

Three observations may be made about such 'bottom-up' or 'interactive' initiatives. First, the extra activity they would promote would impose little or no net extra eco-burden, since extra activity is almost entirely in services rather than manufacturing, and a considerable fraction of the services could easily be steered by local government into 'eco-saving'. Second, they illustrate the need on which Hanappi and Egger insist, for universal participation (in the North) in broad band telecommunications networks. This would greatly facilitate both types of initiative: for example, individuals who would not stir from their screens to attend a neighbourhood meeting on a recycling scheme, might happily participate in the decision-making *via* those screens. Local electronic mail networks would be ideal for LETS. Third, without the telecommunications, they are, like eco-saving technology, well suited to the South. It is to more specific solutions to the problems of the South that we now turn.

## 7. Technological and Institutional Exits from the Southern Impasse

It is in the South that the current economic crisis is most acute – if not in terms of income growth, then in terms of employment;[16] it is in the South that the ecological crisis is of most concern – if not (*yet*) in terms of global sources and sinks, then in terms of local soil erosion, salination, deforestation, falling water tables, and so on. Mainstream doctrine, as preached by academic economists, Northern politicians and international institutions like the IMF and World Bank, proposes market solutions to the economic problems: reduce government intervention in the economy internally and externally. If it seems unreasonable for Southern countries to reduce their trade barriers while the North blocks their exports, then (they argue) GATT should promote freer trade all round. This will allow the South better to exploit its comparative advantage – principally in low-technology manufactures with a high content of low-skilled labour – and that will help to soak up its surplus labour, and by reducing poverty reduce the pressure on its environment.

The mainstream prescription is totally inadequate because the diagnosis is hopelessly superficial. The fundamental Southern problem is not government interference, damaging though this usually is, but the unequal relationship with the North (Tylecote 1989 and 1992 Chapter 7). There is no need to accuse the North of deliberate or overt exploitation at this stage: the damage to the South arises mainly because

1. Unrepresentative elites are able to dominate the society and distort its development through their privileged access to Northern technology. In the cruder cases – such as Nigeria, currently[17] – the technology concerned is weaponry and the distortion takes the rather obvious form of looting on a grand scale. In other cases the dominance is through control of the economy and mass media, and consequent political power: here the distortion is more subtle, to be better understood in the context of point 2.

2. Northern technology is fundamentally inappropriate for the South, because it is designed to suit a 'factor endowment' which is (increasingly) rich in physical and human capital and technological know-how, relative to low-skilled labour. (It has also of course been highly polluting and resource-using,

which is now inappropriate everywhere.) Unfortunately this does not prevent it being attractive to the South, for a variety of reasons explored in Galvao (1995): glamour; various sorts of learning (or indoctrination) processes affecting consumers and producers; and the self-interest of dominant groups with privileged access to the technology or the skills required to use it. Thus the Latin American type of 'import-substituting industrialization' – tariff protection and other state intervention which aims to free a Southern country from its dependence on primary product exports – was exploited by well-connected businessmen to import Northern capital goods cheaply and thereby dominate the national market. With the import-substituting industrialization model discredited and the emphasis now on exports and imports, the same businessmen, and their well-educated friends and relations, are able to exploit their links to Northern multinationals and internal sources of finance, to get privileged access to whatever Northern technology is now relevant.

What the South needs, therefore, are technologies which require little human or physical capital and much low-skilled labour, and are natural resource-saving – *appropriate* technologies (Carr 1985; Ranis 1979). Such technologies, once developed and diffused, will provide work and cheap goods for the poor, but will scarcely suit the elite. There will have to be, then, a profound change in the distribution of power in the South before they receive strong support internally; and such a change is more likely to follow than to precede their diffusion. There is a rather better chance of the impetus coming from the North, for it has not only the resources required, but a strong incentive. Only the development and diffusion of such technologies can soak up the huge overhang of surplus labour which threatens to flood from South to North; that alone can save the South from depleting not only local but global sources and sinks. By drawing on what the South can produce itself, rather than what it must import from the North, it will relieve the balance of payments constraint upon Southern countries and (in the end) raise the price of their labour on global markets – which will help to reduce inequality not only globally but within the North.

## Conclusion

The conclusion to this chapter may serve, I hope, as a conclusion to this volume. We have seen, in Part One, that the ecological prospects for the world, without a major change of economic, social and technological direction, are grave. We have shown, mainly in Part Two, that various kinds of institutional reform are possible which would greatly help in bringing about such a change in direction. We have shown in Part Three that the world, particularly the North, is undergoing a profound technological change, from 'Fordism' to a 'post-Fordism' which is not yet clearly defined. That change is largely responsible for the crisis in the world economy which began in the mid-1970s and continues, while changing its form. The change and the crisis are causing major changes in institutions; further changes will be required to bring the crisis to an end. But it is not at all a question of adapting institutions passively to suit a given post-Fordist technological style. The new style is not yet set hard, by any means: it can be moulded and remoulded by and for new institutions. What is, and is not yet, decided is exemplified by the prices and social costs of key factors of production: we know that the price, and social cost, of 'machine intelligence' has fallen dramatically over the last two or three decades and will fall as much over the next two or three. That is a given in the new regime, which arises from technological change and must greatly affect its future direction. On the other hand we know that the price of skilled labour is high and needs to be brought down by improved education and training (and the raising up of the poor) in order to encourage labour-using technological change. Likewise the price of low-skilled labour needs to be reduced in whatever way does not impoverish its providers. Finally the price of natural resources – of sources and sinks – is far below their social costs and needs to be sharply increased. These three sets of price change are not a given arising from technological change but a challenge to our institutions, which will, when effected, go far to redirect that change. Not that we can simply leave this redirection to the price regime: more direct intervention will also be necessary. This applies particularly to the 'appropriate' technologies desperately needed by the South: Northern governments and charities must develop and promote them vigorously without waiting for the price regime to change in the South.

These changes will mould the post-Fordist technological style and chart a sustainable path for its future development and diffusion: sustainable, that is, in terms of long-run ecological impact, and also in terms of a path of economic growth which will be self-reinforcing, giving more encouragement to innovation and investment the more it is followed. They will, to refer to our subtitle, meet the challenge to sustainable development.

**Notes**

1. *If* the MPC of the poor exceeds that of the rich; this assumption is theoretically obvious, since the rich have large assets which they can freely increase or decrease to smooth out their consumption, while the poor have either no liquid assets or need to keep them against real emergency. However, I know of no empirical work which tends to prove – or disprove – this point.
2. China's autarky arose from Stalinism compounded by the late-1950s breach with Moscow; India's for less obvious reasons (see *Economist,* 1995)
3. By net liabilities I mean net debt plus foreign ownership of domestic assets. In the mid- to late-1980s Chinese and Indian net external debt was insignificant by Southern standards (World Bank 1991, *Table 6.2*); and given their long-standing policies, foreign ownership would have been too. Economic self-sufficiency reflected itself in a relatively low import content in capital goods required for expansion and consumer goods sucked in by it. Moreover the domestic market was so large that Fordist industries could get up to or near optimum scale for their more basic products even without exporting.
4. While net transfers to developing countries had been negative in the second half of the 1980s (World Bank, 1991 *Figure 6.5*), they were decidedly positive in the early 1990s. Direct investment rose from $13.9 billion per annum 1986–9 to $37.1 billion. per annum in 1990–3; net external borrowing rose from $39.7 billion to $72.4 billion (Wolf 1994). $435 billion flowed into the emerging markets in the three years 1992–4 (World Bank 1994–1995 World Debt Tables; see also figure on p. 92 of *The Economist*, January 28, 1995).
5. As Grahame Thompson (1994) has shown, 66% of total foreign direct investment flows to developing countries in 1980–91 went to just 10 of them: 'between 57% and 72% of the world population is in receipt of only 8.5% of global FDI' (foreign direct investment; in 1981–91; p. 22). He finds a similar inequality in trade shares.
6. The South makes another less obvious contribution to the crisis, through migration. While natural growth of population in the North is now very low, immigration from the South is substantial; and given the disparities in living standards each extra Southerner in the North makes a greater demand on sources and sinks than an extra Southerner in the South.
7. As Jacobs points out, the new methods may turn out to be cheaper; but we can only expect to be able to exploit such 'win-win' options near the margin. The really big eco-improvements are likely to be, on balance, expensive.
8. See Jacobs (1994) for various estimates of the resulting increases in investment.
9. As *The Economist* (1994) shows, the problem will be not shortage of reserves, but shortage of capacity, since with current low oil prices the necessary investments in capacity are not being made. Since reserves are ample at least for several decades, the shortage and high prices are likely to last no longer than after 1973; but that is long enough!

10. Of course the oil and grain exporters will gain – but which are they? A few Southern countries, mostly in the Middle East, are major oil exporters; fewer still – like Argentina – are grain exporters. Some Eastern European countries will gain from higher grain prices; the former Soviet Union may gain on oil (and gas); but the major gainers on grain will be in the North. Some Northern countries may however lose heavily. The gas-guzzling US (with two-and-a-half times the energy consumption per head of Japan) is extremely vulnerable to an oil price increase. Although currently a large grain exporter, its grain consumption is also very high and rising, and recent estimates of climatic impacts of global warming suggest that rainfall will decline in the US grain belt. These wages of ecological sin would be added to an already-large external deficit and debt, to produce a severe balance of payments constraint.

11. As Amsalem (1982) has shown, labour-intensive technologies are generally only competitive where scale is relatively small. Small-scale manufacturing (and other) operations are favoured by high transport costs and recycling from consumers. To that extent an eco-tax regime will favour labour-intensity.

12. Sharp (1983, p. 163), quoted in Tylecote (1992, p. 61).

13. For a recent progress report see *The Economist*, 'Survey: Biotechnology and Genetics', after p. 78, Feb. 25 1995.

14. The increase in employment comes first, and foremost, through the increase in investment in order to make and create capacity to produce the innovations. If there is a shift from saving to consumption in response to the appearance of the new product, so much the better.

15. The long-awaited eco-friendly breakthroughs do now seem to be beginning to come through; see Anderson (1995) on the development of pest-resistant cotton in Australia.

16. 1994 UN estimates put the proportion not 'productively employed' there at 30% (Taylor 1995).

17. See for example 'This is how we do it in Nigeria', *The Economist*, 22 July 1995, p. 54.

# References

Amsalem, Michel (1982), *Technology choice in developing countries - the textile and paper and pulp industries*, Cambridge, MA: MIT Press.

Anderson, Ian (1995), 'Killer cotton stalks pests', *New Scientist*, 7 October, p. 9.

Brown, Lester R. (1995), *Who Will Feed China? Wake-Up Call for a Small Planet*, Washington DC: World Watch Institute.

Carr, Marilyn (1985), *The AT Reader. Theory and Practice in Appropriate Technology*, London: Intermediate Technology Publications.

Driver, Ciaran and David Moreton (1992), *Investment, Expectations and Uncertainty*, Oxford: Blackwell.

*Economist* (1994), 'Power to the People: A Survey of Energy', *The Economist*, June 18, 80ff.

*Economist* (1995), 'Survey of India', *The Economist*, Jan. 21.

Galvao, Claudia (1995), 'Choice of Technology in the Brazilian Food Industry: Can apppropriate technology solve the employment problem'? Sheffield: unpublished PhD thesis of the University of Sheffield.

Jacobs, Michael (1994), *Green Jobs? The Employment Implications of Environmental Policy. A Report for WWF*. London: World Wild Life Fund.

Lang, Peter (1994), *LETS Work*, London: Grover Books.

Lawrence, R. and M. Slaughter (1993), 'Trade and US Wages: Giant Sucking Sound or Small Hiccup?', *Brookings Papers on Economic Activity: Microeconomics*, Washington DC: National Bureau for Economic Research.

McCombie, J. (1993), 'Economic growth, trade interlinkages and the balance of payments constraint', *Journal of Post Keynesian Economics* **15**, 471–505.

Modelski, George (1987), 'The Study of Long Cycles', in G. Modelski (ed.) *Exploring Long Cycles*, London: Frances Pinter, 1–16.

Perez, Carlota (1983), 'Microelectronics, Long Waves and World Structural Change: New Perspectives for Developing Countries', *World Development* **13** (3) 441–63.

Ranis, Gustav (1979), 'Appropriate technology: obstacles and opportunities', in Samuel M. Rosenblat, (ed), *Technology and Economic Development: a Realistic Perspective*, Boulder, CO: Westview Press.

Sharp, Margaret (1983), *Europe and the New Technologies*, London: Frances Pinter.

Solomou, Solomos (1987), *Phases of Economic Growth 1850–1973: Kondratieff Waves and Kuznets Swings*, Cambridge: Cambridge University Press.

Taylor, Robert (1995), 'FT Guide to Global Unemployment', *Financial Times*, 27 February.

Thirlwall, A.P. (1979), 'The balance of payments constraint as an explanation of international growth rate differences', *Banca Nazionale del Lavoro Quarterly Review*, **128**, 45–53.

Thompson, Grahame (1994), 'Foreign Direct Investment, Globalization and International Economic Governance', *Open University Faculty of Social Sciences Discussion Papers in Economics*, No. 4, May.

Tylecote, Andrew (1989), 'The South in the Long Wave: Technological Dependence and the Dynamics of World Economic Growth', in Richard Goodwin *et al*, (eds) *Technological and Social Factors in Long Wave Fluctuations*, Berlin: Springer, 206–24.

Tylecote, Andrew (1992), *The long wave in the world economy: the present crisis in historical perspective*, London: Routledge.

Tylecote, Andrew (1993), 'Riding the Long Wave', *Employment Policy Institute Economic Report*, **7** (4), November.

Tylecote, Andrew (1994), 'Long waves, long cycles and long swings', *Journal of Economic Issues*, June, 477–87.

Wade, Robert (1990), *Governing the Market: Economic Theory and the Role of Government in East Asian Industrialization* Princeton, NJ: Princeton University Press.

Wallerstein, Immanuel (1983), 'The Three Instances of Hegemony in the History of the Capitalist World Economy', *International Journal of Comparative Sociology* **24** (1–2), 100–108.

Wolf, Martin (1994), 'Bretton Twins at an Awkward Age', *Financial Times*, Oct. 7, 19.

Wood, Adrian (1994), *North–South Trade, Employment and Income Inequality: Changing Fortunes in a Skill-Driven World*, Oxford: Clarendon Press.

World Bank (1991), *World Development Report 1991*, Washington: World Bank.

World Bank (1992), *World Development Report 1992*, Washington: World Bank.

World Bank (1993), *World Development Report 1993*, Washington: World Bank.

World Bank (1995), *World Development Report 1995*, Washington: World Bank.

# Index